ENDORSEMENTS

Recovering Quantoid hits the "sweet spot" in filling a huge and previously ignored need: helping engineers, accountants, craft people, and other quantitatively skilled professionals become good bosses. This is a mini-MBA for both "quantoids" and "normals," alike.

—Joseph Grenny,
co author of NYT Best Sellers
Crucial Conversations and *Influencer.*

Recovering Quantoid has made a major contribution in helping both quantoids and the rest of us become better leaders in business or whatever avenue we pursue. A fun read, too, and not a single vampire!

—Bill Child—Chairman of the Board,
RC Willey Home Furnishings (retired CEO) and subject of
the book *How to Build a Business Warren Buffett Would Buy.*

Recovering Quantoid meets an unmet need. In it, Bob puts in writing what he has practiced and taught very successfully for many years. I wish all the people who worked in my areas had this two decades ago. Frankly, I wish I had it three decades ago.

—Ron Seidel,
Senior VP Fossil Generation (retired) for the former TXU,
a major electric utility, former President of Texas Independent
Energy and Director of Principal Solar, Inc.

BOB "The Biz Bucks Guy" LLEWELLYN

LEADERSHIP
FOR THE RECOVERING
QUANTOID

Boss-hood for Engineers, Accountants, Analysts, and Others with Severe Quantoidal Tendencies

TATE PUBLISHING
AND ENTERPRISES, LLC

Published by Tate Publishing & Enterprises, LLC
127 E. Trade Center Terrace | Mustang, Oklahoma 73064 USA
1.888.361.9473 | www.tatepublishing.com

Tate Publishing is committed to excellence in the publishing industry. The company reflects the philosophy established by the founders, based on Psalm 68:11,
"The Lord gave the word and great was the company of those who published it."

Book design copyright © 2013 by Tate Publishing, LLC. All rights reserved.
Cover design by Rodrigo Adolfo
Interior design by Jomar Ouano

Published in the United States of America

ISBN: 978-1-62510-202-7
1. Business & Economics / Business Communication / General
2. Business & Economics / Leadership
13.02.26

DEDICATION

To Marilyn and my CHARMS and mini-CHARMS.

ACKNOWLEDGMENTS

I owe much to many.

Marilyn, my eternal pal and partner.

Our six CHARMS and, at present, fifteen mini-CHARMS

The countless leaders, teachers, professors, and writers who have shaped my life's experience.

The many frontline employees and bosses who reported to me throughout my "boss-hood." They must surely have wondered if I would ever be good at it. May their memories of my many failings be short-lived. My overriding goal was always to help them develop and reach their full potential.

The fine people at Tate Publishing.

My loving God and his Son, Jesus Christ, for blessings immeasurable.

Robert N. Llewellyn, Sr.
Phoenix, Arizona, 2013
www.BizBucksGuy.com

CONTENTS

LIST OF FIGURES

LIST OF TECHNICAL ANALOGS ON LIFE AND LEADERSHIP

—Chapter—	——Analog——	————-Principle————-
1	Net Positive Suction Head	Each leader needs the eight qualities of leadership rightness.
2	The Hysteresis Curve	It is difficult to go back to your preleadership position.
3	Planes and Patience	New leaders should not force change too quickly or too slowly.
4	The Redwoods	Core values make an organization strong.
5	Old Dogs and Neuroplasticity	Everyone can change, even the *rain cloud* people.
6	Top-Down Designs	Use strategy to design organizations.
7	Gibb's Equation	Our effectiveness depends on our organizational abilities.
8	Thevenin-Norton Equations	Simplicity is the ultimate sophistication.
9	Fresnel Lenses	Middle management focus strategy on customers.
10	Interstices	Good bosses use informal coaching moments to improve performance.
11	The Project Process	Use the same steps to develop people.
12	Circuit Analysis	Don't jump to conclusions.
13	The VLSI Clock	Everyone must get the message.
14	Control Theory	The three cycles of competence.
15	Synchronous Generators	Don't judge people's performance without seeing the results.

Disclaimer: The companies or individuals referenced herein do not necessarily make any commercial representation of this book.

FOREWORD

Together with my late husband, Dr. Michael Driver of USC, we have been in the career counseling field for nearly forty years. I continue to spend much of my time in private practice counseling people on some of their most important life decisions—including choosing and navigating a career. Mike was the quintessential academic researcher in this field. His theoretical framework, Career Concepts, has helped countless people understand themselves, their motives, and their career paths. Mike, in fact, started the Careers Division of The Academy of Management, the international academic society of some seven thousand management professors. In addition, over the last six years of his life, he amassed with the help of several others, some six hundred thousand inputs into his Careers research database.

Among others, he counseled the participants in USC's Executive MBA program for a decade and a half before his passing. One of Mike's students in the Executive MBA program was Bob Llewellyn, an experienced leader-manager and former engineer in the electric-utility industry.

After his graduation, Bob left his employer and ventured into private practice in management consulting. He asked Mike to present his Career Concepts framework to two companies along the way. The last, a large project in Dallas that I had the pleasure to work with Bob and Mike on, involved training and certifying several people to administer and counsel some six hundred people in Career Concepts.

In our exit interview with Bob, Mike inquired about Bob's next career move. As will be explained in chapter three, Bob is a typical spiral, needing to grow and be creative and then give back the vast experience that a spiral accumulates. After brainstorming some possible avenues, Mike felt none were right for Bob. That is when Bob mentioned the idea of writing a book to help quantitatively-skilled people transition into leadership. Mike was excited—He knew there was a tremendous need for such a book. Mike left happy, knowing Bob had a plan for his next career step. And I left happy, having met Bob and feeling good about his future writing plans.

Unfortunately, I next met with Bob at the 2005 Academy of Management's Career Division Memorial Session honoring Mike. I had asked Bob to speak at this session, held in conjunction with the Academy's Hawaii conference. Bob shared how Mike's Career Concepts framework had helped him and others. Bob shared that after teaching a small group of engineering managers about the four career concepts one came up and passionately shook his hand, saying with depth of emotion, "Thank you. I did not expect a career-changing event today!" You will read many more accounts like this in this volume.

As the book began to take shape, Bob asked if I could help him edit chapter three on Career Concepts. Liking what I read, I went on to read the entire manuscript of the book.

Leadership for the Recovering Quantoid is a must for people transitioning from numbers work into management. I plan to introduce Recovering Quantoid to clients in my career counseling practice who are going through such a transition.

In addition, Bob's treatment of Career Concepts is thorough and a testament to its power—not only for recovering quantoids, but for all of us!

—Dianne Sundby, Ph.D is a Psychologist and Director of Career Counseling and Assessment Associates in Los Angeles.

PREFACE

What's a Quantoid?

Since 1996, I have taught business acumen to over 4,000 participants in corporate educational courses. I recognize a portion of each class enters with some trepidation. For some, a course in financial decision-making means they are returning to the days of math anxiety they struggled with in high school or college. To put them at ease, I tell them there are two types of people in this class. The first are quantoids. "A quantoid," I jokingly say, "is someone who gets up the morning, looking for that very first equation of the day to solve."

Continuing, I ask, "So if you are not a quantoid, what are you?" I get a variety of answers and then divulge, "If you are not a quantoid, then you must be a *normal*." I then make it clear that the course is for the *normal* people, not just those with high quantitative skills. Much anxiety is alleviated. Then, the course begins with some degree of humor.

For the purposes of this book, a quantoid is someone who has a depth of experience or education in a quantitative field, such as engineering, technology, plant operations, maintenance crafts, accounting, programming, statistics, or finance. Quantoids are skilled in difficult concepts of analysis, problem solving, and advanced mathematical operations. Quantoids are good friends with such esoteric activities as constructing statements of cash flows, converting Laplace transforms, calculating nonlinear regression, identifying subsynchronous resonance, and solving partial differential equations (although many have not actually used these skills since walking out of the ivy halls of their alma mater).

Conversely, unless acquired through other life experiences, quantoids may be only superficially introduced to leadership and management principles of involvement, rewards, motives, dealing with ambiguity, processes, projects, people development, visioning, implementation, communication, strategic planning, financial design making, handling uncertainty, delegation, team building, markets, scarcity, organizational structures, organizational change, communication, and many more principles of business acumen, leadership, and management discussed in this volume.

WHO IS THIS BOOK FOR?

Primarily, this book is written for those quantoids who are currently considering a career path into management. It will also be useful to those who are already in management. Normals will also find many valuable principles of leadership within these pages.

Clearly, this division between quantoids and normals is partly for fun. I am well aware that:

> In the township of leadership there are no tract homes.

Each of us is unique, custom-built. Each of us brings a set of values, norms, motives, loves, passions, vices, and habits to the workplace. We would never have it any other way. But many of us with quantoidal tendencies need some specific helps as we attempt the great transition into boss-hood.

WHY THIS BOOK?

In short, this book aims to help assure that *"Dilbert* isn't a documentary" of your organization.

Our quantoid skills are important to our success prior to entering into a management position. However, some might continue to emphasize those skills, crowding out developing the more needed leadership skills.

These quantoid skills can also be a liability for you. Don't let these skills entice you into doing the work of frontline employees. Your role is to use your creative and innovative skills to solve problems in the workplace.

In this sense, we quantoids must be constantly in recovery to be successful in our leadership duties.

It has been my observation and personal experience that quantoids in frontline positions often are not experienced in the people side of business or organizations. Having been promoted into management, some quantoids, to their credit, become quite adept at that most important side of their responsibility. Some bring people tools gained from other walks of life from leadership positions in school, church, charity, or community service. But others slide along for years with minimal people tools, perhaps getting results, but creating misery among their subordinates and peers. Some are miserable themselves, being in the wrong position altogether.

The purpose of this book is to help quantoids see the big picture of leadership and management and to provide a keen understanding of related practical principles. It is my hope that this book will inspire a lifetime of learning leadership principles. With this knowledge and the wisdom to apply it, leaders can help improve organizational results and the workplace.

WHY THE TERM *BOSS*?

Throughout much of business literature, authors tend to bifurcate the principles and skills of this book into those of leadership versus those of management. Both skill sets are distinct, and both are necessary (chapter 1 will discuss this in detail). However, there is no single English word that conveniently captures both concepts. It is sometimes amusing to read the works of great leadership thinkers as they bounce back and forth using the two words interchangeably when they defined them differently in a previous paragraph.

For the purposes of this book and in my training courses, I define a secret code word for the combination of *both* leadership and management skills. It is a simple single-syllable word: *boss*. Yes, outside of this book, that word can have a negative connotation. But get over it! This is far superior to using "leader-manager" or some other concocted phrase throughout this text, and it is a lot more fun. Thus, the subtitle of the book reads, "Boss-hood for Engineers, Accountants, Analysts, and Others with Severe Quantoidal Tendencies" and that implies both leadership and management skills.

Someone who is not a boss will be termed a *frontline employee*.

STRUCTURE AND STYLE OF THE BOOK

After chapter 1, which defines real leadership, the book is divided into four parts:

Part I – Should I Become a Boss?
Part II – What Do Good Bosses Know? (Six Skills)
Part III – What Do Good Bosses Do? (Six Skills)
Part IV – Will I last?

Each chapter includes a *Questions for Current Leaders* section near the end. These questions will help existing leaders apply principles and fine-tune skills.

I have attempted to include in each chapter—through anecdotes and even a few outright jokes—a little lightheartedness. If we can't take some time in the work place to enjoy the moment and laugh—particularly at ourselves—we ought to fold up our tent and move on, letting more well-adjusted people take our place.

TECHNICAL ANALOGS FOR LIFE AND LEADERSHIP

At the end of each chapter, I have included a *Technical Analog for Life and Leadership*. Each analog is a principle from physical science, life science, medicine, engineering, or mathematics that has application to the soft science of people. There are many insightful parallels between these two worlds if we only look for them.

My college English professor was biased against engineering students. He had transferred from (read "flunked out of") an engineering curriculum himself. He told us with a reprehensive tone, "You will learn nothing about life from engineering. You should all transfer to English or art majors." All the engineering students got C-minuses at the end of the semester. I took umbrage at both the grade and his attitude about learning life's principles. Ever since, I have tried to identify the subtle parallels between the technical world and our people world. Most of these analogs are merely small capsules of intuition, but a few are mighty castles of insight. I have left the most profound one for last and, because of its length, included it as Appendix E.

These analogs are provided to spur your thinking, from left brain analysis to more right brain intuition and creativity. They also should help you understand the interweaving of nature and our human actions. These analogs may also be useful in your next speech or staff meeting.

WHO AM I?

For the record, I am a card-carrying quantoid. I am a registered engineer who made the transition into management in 1978 after a handful of years as a frontline employee. I know of the difficult transition. My formal education and ongoing training were woefully inadequate for what I was about to experience.

Professionally, I am an independent management consultant. I am not an expert in any one field but an unapologetic, unrepentant generalist. I know a little about a lot as opposed to knowing a lot about a single field. As the reader will discover in chapter 3, I am a quintessential spiral, dedicated to combining personal growth and creativity to make a difference in the world.

My professional mission statement is:

> I am not here to make a world-class fortune.
> I am here to make a world-class difference.

My professional background includes forty years in three organizations: a large multi-national company in technical marketing; a large electric energy company in a variety of technical and leadership positions; and finally for the past fifteen years, my sole proprietorship, Llewellyn Consulting.

I developed a mini-MBA course for energy company professionals. Many people have said it is the best training in their career. I know that is not because I am the best trainer on the planet. It is because people are thirsty for that big picture knowledge that comes from an MBA-like experience.

In recent years, I have also done management systems development for a special client, including their capital projects process and their power plant management-of-change process.

My business acumen courses typically are titled, "Biz, Bucks, and [Something]," depending on the audience. For example, for electric utility professionals, it is "Biz, Bucks, and Bucket Trucks."

With the completion of this volume, I will develop a leadership training course for new leaders in organizations. It is called The Biz, Bucks Leadership Academy. I am also planning an online version of my Biz Bucks training material, called BizBasicsOnline.com.

Consequently, I have become known as The Biz Bucks Guy. I refer to myself in these pages in the third person, using that title.

My corporate leadership experience started with management of a large technical project with a dozen matrixed employees. From there, I led various functions including capital budgeting, the controller functions for the nation's largest nuclear plant, and large-scale organizational change. Prior to my corporate life, I gained much insight into leadership while I lived in Great Britain for two years, serving a church mission.

I have an electrical engineering degree from Arizona State University. I completed an MBA from the Executive Program at USC in Los Angeles for which I flew eighty-two weekend trips to LA while working full time in Phoenix. I hold academic keys in Tau Beta Pi (engineering), Eta Kappa Nu (electrical engineering), and Beta Gamma Sigma (business).

I have had four papers published, two of which were selected by the periodical to go into its "Best Papers of the Decade" anthology.[1]

This is my first book. I am beginning a novel, a geopolitical thriller highlighting some of the principles herein.

I am happily married for forty years and we have been blessed with six children and fifteen grandchildren. I have spent my non-working time with the Boy Scouts of America and church service. My leisure passion (and primary vice in life) is golf in which I maintain a single-digit handicap.

CHAPTER 1

WHAT REALLY IS LEADERSHIP?

Like the ancient near-eastern poetic form, Chiasmus, the most important concept for this chapter is in the middle, *The Four Skills of Leadership*. However, there are some foundational issues to discuss first in support of these four integrated skills. Let's begin with the problem of business jargon.

THE BUSINESS WORD SWAMP

It is foreign to us quantoids to have a discipline of learning in which major concepts are based on words that are ill-defined. How would it be if capacitance and inductance (two largely opposite electrical phenomena) were the same word? Engineers would be lost, trying to communicate circuit designs. What if *debit* and *credit* were the same word in accounting or if there was only one word for *acid* and *base* in chemistry or, for that matter, *multiply* and *divide* were the same term in basic math? Communication would be nearly impossible. The nature of the physical and mathematical world supports terms that can be easily developed and defined, and communication is thereby enhanced.

But in the softer sciences and particularly business, the words are not crisply defined. For example, the common word *capital* has so many meanings and nuances in business that context is the only way to know the intended meaning of the author or speaker. Another is *commodity* that has a street English definition and a precise economics definition. Many business terms have multiple synonyms (like, *profit, gain, margin,* and *earnings*). Some are homonyms (with a same pronunciation but different meaning, like, *warrantee* and *warranty*). Others are complicated acronyms like EBITDA and NAIRU.

The words of leadership and business are seemingly in a word swamp! Many important terms lie in its dark, dank depths, covered with moss—slimy, unrecognizable from many other words in the swamp. They are soggy with imprecise use so much as to render real communication difficult.

As The Biz Bucks Guy says to his Biz Bucks course participants, "If the words of business are difficult and frustrating for you, please realize it is not *you*. It's the words themselves!"

So absent a taxonomy of terms for business, we must define some key words immediately. Let's start with two.

LEADERSHIP VERSUS MANAGEMENT

Leadership and *management* themselves are fuzzy terms. This book takes the tack that leadership is different from management and that both skills sets are necessary to be a good boss.

For many years in American business, literature for bosses focused on management only, not leadership. Management is often defined as the ability to get things done through others. As definitions go, it's okay but not too insightful and certainly not too motivating. One might say it also sounds a lot like a good definition of leadership. Are they the same thing?

Not in The Biz Bucks Guy's book—literally and figuratively, nor in the books of many well known scholars.[2]

Management

Management consists of skills that are largely left-brain oriented. Leadership skills are largely right brained. Psychologists concluded decades ago that the brain has two hemispheres. The left side controls the activities of analysis, logic, speaking words, counting, and rational thought. On the right side are the softer skills of intuition, creativity, forming thoughts before being sent to the left side to be converted into words. By the way, the sides are reversed for left-handed people.

Consider this partial list of management processes:

- work planning and budgeting
- financial analysis and justification for projects
- organizing and staffing
- controlling
- evaluating performance (particularly in easily measurable jobs)
- determining rewards

Each of these management processes is heavy on analysis and logic. The left brain is fully in gear. Guess what? This is the same side our quantoid heads have been using for years while we diagnosed problems, wrote code, calculated partial differential equations, or reviewed blood workups against established clinical norms.

These left brain management functions seem to feel good to the ardent quantoid.

For many quantoids who received a promotion into boss-hood, we were rewarded because we were good at this left brain stuff. It makes perfect sense for quantoids to think that is how they will be successful in boss-hood as well.

Leadership

However, nothing could be further from the truth. A quantoid-turned-boss must also be able to use the other softer skills to be successful. One might even argue that the soft stuff is the hard stuff.

Consider now this partial list of leadership processes:

- Motivating workers
- Envisioning the future
- Developing creative alternatives to problems
- Using your intuition to balance both financial and intangible considerations in decision-making
- Changing an organization to align with a new strategy
- Discovering hidden organizational misfits (more on this in chapter 7)

Each of these leadership processes requires a large measure of right-brain thinking—creating options, inferring implications, discovering motives, balancing competing good approaches, and knowing your subordinates' skills. The Biz Bucks Guy would argue that if you had to accept being good at only one of the two bulleted lists, the leadership skills are more important. You can always find a fellow quantoid to help you with many left brain management skills.

Leaving Taylor

Throughout most of the twentieth century, in typical large organizations within American business, there has been an overemphasis on management skills, particularly for first-level supervision and a lack of training of true leadership skills. Engineers and other quantoids became supervisors and managers, not leaders. They went to training and became good at budgets, policies, and performance metrics. They used physical metaphors, comparing their people to cogs on a wheel, their department to well-oiled gears, and their company to a finely crafted watch.

They espoused the tenants of Fredrick Winslow Taylor, the first management consultant who convinced a nation in his 1911 work, *The Principles of Scientific Management*, that the laborers labored and the managers did the thinking.[3]

They hired more engineers and taught them good management principles. The whole system bred more left brain thinkers.

Finally, in the early 1990s, American business began to wake up to the difference between leadership and management. Leadership began to be the focus in literature not management. Referring to this awakening, Tom Peters, considered by many to be the first of the rock star business gurus, said,

> Leaders focus on the soft stuff. People. Values. Character. Commitment. A cause. All of the stuff that was supposed to be too goo goo to count in business. Yet it's the stuff that real leaders take care of first. And forever. That's why leadership is an art not a science.[4]

Leaders tend to use more organic metaphors, such as "We are becoming a soaring eagle," "Our enthusiasm could melt a glacier," and "We all are connected at the brain!"

Let's consider a few aphorisms regarding these two skill sets:

> Managers manage numbers, leaders lead people (Which have you been hired or promoted to do?).

> A manager is someone you would follow into a budget meeting. A leader is someone you would follow into war (Isn't business a lot like winning a war in a market?).

> Leadership is the engine that drives change[5] (Isn't change necessary for progress?).

The goal of management processes is to produce order and predictability. The goal of leadership processes is to produce change[6] (Aren't both perspectives needed in differing situations?).

Measure to manage, build relationships to lead.

Managers become managers because someone assigned them to become a manager. Leaders become leaders because people choose to follow them[7].

Management is efficiency in climbing the ladder of success; leadership determines whether the ladder is leaning against the right wall.[8]

THE DIFFICULT LEADERSHIP BALANCE

There are many fine lists related to leadership and management: lists of skills, lists of traits, lists of virtues, list of styles, lists of processes, and the soon-to-be-divulged four skills of leadership. Many overlap. Many are not very actionable. Regardless of which list one uses, quantoids should realize that being a boss requires balance across the entire list. Being outstanding in one aspect at the expense of other important skills can render the leader ineffective. Maintaining this balance is both imperative and, for many, daunting.

The need for leadership balance has been understood for centuries. Sun Tzu, the famous ancient Chinese warrior and author, captured this need for balance with his list of five virtues of leadership in his book *The Art of War*:

> Leadership is a matter of intelligence, trustworthiness, humaneness, courage, and discipline…Reliance on intelligence alone results in rebelliousness. Exercise of

humaneness alone results in weakness. Fixation on trust results in folly. Dependence on the strength of courage results in violence. Excessive discipline and sternness in command results in cruelty. When one has all five virtues together, each appropriate to its function, then one can be a leader.[9]

THE *BIZ BUCKS* FOUR SKILLS OF LEADERSHIP

As noted, no consensus surrounds the definition of leadership. Many definitions are lists themselves. To be an effective boss, this quantoid needs a broad but actionable definition. Absent such, The Biz Bucks Guy was left to create his own. The *Biz Bucks* Four Skills of Leadership has been synthesized from life experiences with bosses, corporate training courses, business literature, academic study, personal observations, and common sense.

These skills are actionable, meaning one can put this framework to use immediately to practice the art of leadership. That is because these four skills are presented as processes not philosophical ideas (see chapter 8 for more details on processes).

These four skills provide a necessary framework for discussion throughout this book.

As summarized in figure 1, leadership is the art of

1. creating and being passionate about a vision of the future,
2. building and maintaining a small team who is also passionate about the vision,
3. communicating the vision to the larger group, and finally,
4. implementing the vision through power, skills and appropriate tools.

Let's take a closer look at each of these aspects of leadership.

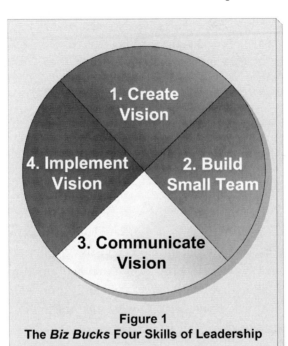

Figure 1
The *Biz Bucks* Four Skills of Leadership

1. Creating Your Vision of the Future

You can choose to be a boss with or without vision. Be aware that bosses without vision are *very* boring to work for.

So let's quickly reject the boring option. Vision is simply knowing where you are going. Obviously, a leader needs to shinny up the organizational palm tree and see the way to go for his department, work unit, division, or company. The Old Testament proverb, while actually referring to prophetic vision, also fits this context,

Where there is no vision, the people perish.[10]

Without a direction, the organization itself perishes.

Chapter 4 discusses how to create a vision and how it fits into a strategic plan.

2. Building a Small Team

The skill to build and lead a team is a key competence of leadership. This skill is sometimes overlooked. Consider the following:

> A freshman in high school wanted to go to a prestigious military academy after high school graduation. He decided his ticket to get accepted would be his academic prowess. He gave up many social, extracurricular, and athletic endeavors in favor of studying. At the end of his high school experience, he was the valedictorian of his large high school, a tremendous accomplishment. Unfortunately, he was not accepted to the academy. After the rejection, he was told by a recruiter, "Valedictorians are a dime a dozen. We want to know if you were captain of the football team." They were looking for proven leaders.

As the small team buys into the vision with the same passion as the boss, they then help the leader communicate and implement the vision to the larger population.

See chapters 7 and 14 for more details on teams.

3. Communicating the Vision

As important as visioning and team building are, communication is the grand competence. In the context of this third step of leadership, one point is mandatory: we should strive to over-communicate!

John Kotter, of the Harvard Business School, warns us that we often under-communicate the vision by a factor of ten or more.[11] He simply means that communication is difficult. So think about how much communication is necessary regarding sharing your vision. Then, multiply that by ten, and you will be closer to what is really needed. This will be known in chapter 13 as the Communicate × 10 principle.

4. Implementing the Vision

With the vision set, a small team behind you, and world-class communications to all stakeholders regarding your direction, the fourth step in leadership is usually the most difficult: the ability to implement the plan and reach results that bring the vision to reality. Implementation has received an increased amount of ink in the past decade or more. And no wonder.

One study[12] lists the intangibles that Wall Street uses to add (or subtract) value from stock prices once a base price is set from its projected cash flows. The most important of all these intangibles is the ability to implement a strategy not the ability to produce a strategy (which was listed as third).

Much of this book is about implementation and results, particularly chapters 8, 9, and 16.

LEADERSHIP AND MANAGEMENT STYLES

As with the definition of leadership itself, there is no agreed upon list of styles for leadership or management. Scholars differ in their assessments and nomenclature. An online search provides various lists from three to six and beyond.[13] Given this lack of consensus, Kurt Lewin's time-tested list[14] of three provides a useful framework for understanding various leadership styles. They are:

1. Authoritarian—The boss is, well, the boss! Decisions are his. He may elicit input, but he chooses to be the one who directs everything. Some synonyms are dictatorial, autocratic, heroic, and Taylorized.

Stereotypical example: Surgeon in operating room
Illustrative positive phrases: "Wow, he knows his stuff!" and
"We don't mess around getting to the bottom line in our staff meetings."
Illustrative negative phrases: "Just tell me what to do, and I will do it, boss," and "Shhh, here comes John Wayne."

2. Participative—The boss involves the team. The decisions are theirs and hers. She encourages the individuals to contribute and grow. Synonyms are democratic, consensus builder, and Japanese.

Stereotypical example: Total quality program manager
Illustrative positive phrases: "I'm in." "We did it!"
Illustrative negative phrases: "Can someone just make a decision around here?" "This is too touchy feely for me."

3. Delegative—The boss sets the overall direction but delegates decisions to the team or selected members. The decisions are theirs, not his. He may be too busy to act otherwise. He has regular reporting meetings to keep in the loop. Synonyms are free reign, laissez-faire, and hands off.

Stereotypical Example: Mayor of large city
Illustrative positive phrases: "Okay, let's vote." "Hey, she really trusts us."
Illustrative negative phrases: "Where is she when we need her?" "We don't have enough direction."

Good leaders should use all three styles. It is situational. Most leaders have an official style that they use when things are going well and there is no big crisis or significant emotional event.

However, when things get rough, some leaders default to a backup style; often this is authoritarian. Simply put, they become a dictator.

Some may say the style should always be authoritarian (dictatorial) in high stress situations. You typically don't have a team meeting to discuss the fire in the building. However, consider the following example.

> Many years ago, a commercial plane in Hawaii lost its back door in midflight. While some people immediately lost their lives by being sucked out of the fuselage, most were okay after the rapid decompression and altitude adjustment. The plane was difficult to handle. Everyone was still in grave danger. The pilot had been well trained in participative management. He literally called a meeting of the crew and asked for their input to solve several problems. A few minutes of brainstorming resulted in a set of creative ideas and an implementation plan. The pilot and the crew, using the ideas, got the plane down safely, and no one else was hurt. He credited his airline's training to having the meeting instead of landing without the crew's input.
>
> A few months later, a similar event took place over South America. The onboard tape recorder showed the pilot became a dictator. The plane crashed. All were lost.[15]

Yes, being dictator may be a necessary thing at times, but be careful to know when.

THE FRONTLINE LEADER

Throughout this book, leadership is used in the context of an organizational hierarchy. A leader, herein, is someone who has others reporting to her. They are, as noted earlier, the boss.

Of course in some contexts, leadership is broader than that. If a quantoid determines that being a boss is not the right career move, that quantoid can still become known as a leader, a maven, an influencer, and a people developer. Leaders step out and influence behavior. It is not required to have a perch on the company organization chart to do so. Frontline employees are often the ones who start initiatives, speak out for change, embolden others, motivate up, and thus, make a big difference.

A powerful example for frontline leadership and a delegative management style comes from D-day, the June 6, 1944, turning point for World War II in Western Europe. The allied forces, under the direction of General Dwight D. Eisenhower, were trained to think for themselves in combat. At Omaha Beach, after the initial waves were decimated by Nazi fire, AD hoc and self-directed teams were formed by remaining troops and led by gallant (frontline) leaders. They continued toward reaching the objective.

To the contrary, the Nazi forces could not make decisions in the field in the same manner. They had to call Berlin for permission to make tactical changes. Just before the battle ensued, Hitler had taken sleeping pills and asked not to be disturbed. Rommel was away in Paris. Abundant Nazi forces were not able to be redeployed without top leader approval. The bravery of both forces is well known. Some historians have concluded the reason the allies won the battle was the ability to decide tactics in the field.[16]

This is the way frontline experts make a difference by exhibiting leadership based on the power of their abilities and expertise.

Additional Thoughts on Real Leadership

Time Commitment: Leadership is hard! It may not be worth it to many. The hours of unpaid overtime can add up. When The Biz Bucks Guy went back to MBA school, he calculated he had donated about three full years of unpaid overtime to his company.

Communication Style: The difference between coaching and micromanaging is a matter of communication style. Everyone wants to be coached in the workplace. Most do not want to be micromanaged.

Leadership Training: Many quantoids may initially think that training is a key to becoming an effective leader in an organization. While such training has its place, experience is the best teacher. As Sir Anthony Jay, the British author and producer, once said, "The only real training for leadership is leadership."[17]

Your Friends: Once you become a boss, you aren't the same person to your friends. Some will admire you. Some will think you have gone over to the dark side. Some will be jealous. Get used to it. However, leaders should attempt to maintain these relationships. You will probably need them someday.

Leaders and Courage: A leader will need courage to implement change. Change is always risky. The Biz Bucks Guy knows this well. "Leaders are visionaries with a poorly developed sense of fear and no concept of the odds against them," Dr. Robert Jarvik, the developer of an early artificial heart, said.[18]

The Servant-Leader: Many espouse the concept of a servant-leader. This is a noble framework based often on one's view of religion or philosophy. Using a term popularized in the last two decades, an enabler seems to be the closest thing to this servant-leader concept in business literature. Consider one leader's assessment of being a servant. "The first responsibility of a leader is to define reality. The last is to say 'thank you.' In between, the leader is a servant," Max DePree, the former CEO of Herman Miller Furniture, said.[19]

DOES LEADERSHIP MATTER?

In national and world affairs, it is easy to see the effects of a George Washington, a Martin Luther King, a Lincoln, a Churchill, a Roosevelt, or a Reagan, as well as a Lenin, a Stalin, a Hitler, or a Mao Zedong. Where would the world have been if Roosevelt and Churchill had each died in separate near-fatal events in the early thirties, Roosevelt in an assassination attempt and Churchill in a car-pedestrian accident?[20]

Leadership certainly matters on the world stage.

But regarding more modest environments as in a large business, academics have struggled to measure and draw conclusions about the effect of leaders. Many studies differ as scholars wrestle with the difficulty of measuring the soft stuff.

We quantoids are left to our own observations about how much leadership matters to organizations. A widely held axiom of human resource management is: People join companies. People quit bosses.

On that alone, it should be clear that leadership matters.

Furthermore, the Hay Group, a global management consultancy, found that trust in top leadership was the single most reliable predictor of employee satisfaction in an organization.[21] Clearly, leadership matters.

Bad leadership poisons an organization. Good leadership invigorates it. Bad leaders are victims of the uncertain environment. Good leaders courageously navigate through uncertainty. Bad leaders are in it for themselves. Good leaders are in it for the team, including themselves. Bad leaders are arrogant and above the crowd. Good leaders treat the little guy with respect.

Given the chance at leadership, you can make a difference, too. For many quantoids, it may require a formidable change. For insights into this transition, let's do a deep dive into Part 1 of *Leadership for the Recovering Quantoid* which answers the question, "Should I become a boss?"

QUESTIONS FOR CURRENT LEADERS

1. As a newly anointed boss, did you monkey with the organizational chart early in that experience? That is largely a left brain activity for most, and that might have felt

good as you considered your new role from the perspective of a recent frontline quantoid. Perhaps you might have spent your time assessing the work environment and then formulating a vision for your department. Both are more right brain dominant activities, perhaps foreign to your earlier workplace experience.

2. Have you developed a small team to help you communicate your vision?

3. In developing your leadership style, have you come to realize that leadership style is situational? Often, you need to be participative, and sometimes, delegative, and occasionally even authoritarian.

TECHNICAL ANALOG FOR LIFE AND LEADERSHIP: NPSH AND LEADERSHIP RIGHTNESS

Net positive suction head (NPSH) is a concept concerning liquid pumps. A pump must have a certain minimum pressure at its inlet for the pump to operate properly. Without this minimum head, the pump will lose efficiency, may cavitate (causing voids in the fluid), and severely damage itself. Each pump has its own characteristics. Engineers and designers must be careful to have the available NPSH exceed the required NPSH at all times.

Likewise, leaders should have a minimum set of qualities as they enter into and perform their boss duties. As noted in the next chapter, without the eight qualities of leadership rightness, leaders will not be efficient, will cause voids to appear in leading their department, and may seriously damage the effectiveness of their department. Such qualities are not merely for the beginning of leadership. They must be maintained, reinforced, and even strengthened over time.

PART I

SHOULD I
BECOME A BOSS?

CHAPTER 2

IS LEADERSHIP FOR ME?

MY DOG, ENGINEER

A travelling salesman was driving through a rural farming community and noticed the last farmhouse at the end of town was immaculate. The fence was magnificently painted bright white. The front lawn was manicured. There were no signs of trash or debris. He was so impressed that he stopped and knocked on the front door to congratulate the owner. When an old farmer came to the door and heard the compliment, he was humbled and thanked the traveler for his kindness but admitted, "I can't take the credit. It's all about my dog, Engineer."

"Huh?" said the visitor. "You have a dog named Engineer?"

"Yep, and all I have to do is take the top of the paint can off, and Engineer grabs the paint brush and repaints the fence."

"Come on, you don't expect me to believe that, do you?" said the salesman as Engineer came out wagging his tail wanting to be petted by his owner.

"Not only that," continued the farmer, "but he regularly chews on the grass and makes it a consistent perfect height. He also runs the moment he sees the wind blowing some trash onto the property. He picks it up, dashes behind the barn, and jumps up, letting the trash fall into that big trash barrel."

Leaving the front porch, the salesman said, "Wow that's amazing, sir. Nonetheless, I congratulate both you and Engineer on your fine work."

Two years passed, and the salesman was once again driving through the same town. He was excited to see the beautiful home once again. However, this time things were different. The fence needed painting. The lawn wasn't mowed. Trash was everywhere. He was afraid something had happened to ol' Engineer. He stopped and inquired. The farmer was embarrassed.

"It's all my fault," said the farmer. "I decided to give Engineer a promotion for doing such a great job for me all these years. So I changed his name to Supervisor, and now all he does is sit on the porch and bark!"

Unknowingly, the story of ol' Engineer is relived over and over in organizations. Rewarding outstanding frontline performance with promotions to boss-hood, particularly performance of technical people, can be appropriate. It can also be strikingly stupid. If the person is not (1) right nor (2) ready for a leadership assignment, the organization is shooting itself in the foot, not once but twice! Once, because a new boss is in the wrong job, which creates a multitude of problems for herself and the organization. Twice, because the organization has lost a top-performing engineer, analyst, control room operator, assembly room tech, or accountant.

One more barking boss is never needed. And the fence will constantly need painting.

So how does one know if they are right and ready? This chapter provides some insights into that question and a self-assessment tool to assist those considering a career path into supervision.

BEING RIGHT FOR LEADERSHIP

Being right for boss-hood relates to one's development, the acquisition of certain attributes, traits, and attitudes. These are discussed below as the eight qualities of leadership rightness. Without a good measure of these attributes, an outstanding employee may not be right for the job *at this point* in her career.

This should not imply that she will never be right. People grow. People change. A decade of experience can add many facets to our already deliciously complex temperaments. Someone who may not have certain qualities for leadership today may develop into an outstanding candidate for leadership down the road. However, this metamorphosis to rightness probably takes several years.

There is nothing ignoble or shameful about not having developed a measure of these leadership qualities. Quantoids tend to be highly educated, dedicated, and valued people in large organizations. Some simply develop qualities in other areas, such as technical judgment, creativity, and systems thinking. For many quantoids and normals alike, being the boss is a distasteful proposition.

Consider the talented professor who was promoted to assistant dean. After a year, he asked to return to his prior professorial role, saying, "I realized I had become part of the problem instead of the solution." Leadership was just not his thing. He returned to being a fantastic and revered teacher of quantoidal concepts to budding MBA candidates.

GETTING READY FOR LEADERSHIP

Getting ready for boss-hood relates to learnable or trainable skills. Once upper management deems someone right, they should help that person get ready for the transition. Nonetheless, a person who desires leadership opportunities is responsible for acquiring as many of these skills as they can, regardless of corporate support. These are listed later in the twelve skills of leadership readiness.

These skills can be learned through formal training. When properly planned, this preparation will take several months. For many newly minted bosses, these skills are learned on the job. As noted in chapter 1, in the end, the only real training for leadership is leadership. It is an art.

SOME GIVENS

Not included in the qualities of rightness or the skills of readiness are certain givens. Anyone interested in leadership should have developed in her frontline career the following prerequisite attributes. These are not unique to leadership but needed by everyone throughout an organization.

1. Honesty – This is the fundamental virtue on most lists of virtues. Without it, a person is unable to be effective.
2. Results Oriented – In your current frontline position, you must have demonstrated a yearning and the ability to get things done. This is partly a matter of personal ambition to succeed but mostly the drive to make a difference.
3. Ability to Organize, Prioritize, and Manage Your Time – Time management skills are now automated. These tools are useless unless we systematically use them. The first boss position is not the place to learn these skills. They only become more crucial and more difficult in leadership.
4. Desire to Innovate – Innovation is the seed of improvement and competitive advantage. In your frontline career, you should have enjoyed a measure of creativity and gained the ability to use it to make changes.
5. Functional or Technical Skills – You have a measure of those skills necessary to succeed in your current frontline position. However, you need not be the department expert to become the boss.

6. Problem Analysis – Problem solving has two components: analysis and decision-making. Almost all quantoids have become adept at analyzing situations and determining the root cause of problems. Analysis is the precursor of decision-making. Depending on the environment, decision-making skill is not a given for a frontline employee; therefore, it is listed as an important skill of leadership readiness below.

7. Loyalty to the Organization – If you have been cynical about the purpose, mission, and vision of your business, division, or department, you may not be a good candidate for leadership. As boss, you need to be emotionally connected with the direction of the company and you willingly give a bit extra to make things work.

8. IQ Horsepower – In any organization, frontline employees match wits with people. We all need a nominal level of intellectual ability to be effective in argumentation, to maintain coolness under fire, and to field complaints. Leaders also need such horsepower to coach, to balance priorities, or to confront bad performance.

9. Balanced Strength in Four Areas – Leaders should strive to become balanced in physical, mental, emotional, and spiritual facets of life. The culture of the twenty-first century does not place an emphasis on the last of these four personal strengths. In fact, many are uncomfortable with discussing spirituality and religion in general. Nonetheless, many top leaders and successful frontline employees are grounded in an appreciation of deity and faithful living. The reality of a supreme being will be discussed in appendix E and also supports the first of the following eight qualities of leadership—love of people.

EIGHT QUALITIES OF LEADERSHIP RIGHTNESS

The following eight qualities permeate the daily work of leaders. These are summarized in figure 2. No one, from CEO to foremen, is perfect in all of these qualities.

Figure 2 - Eight Qualities of Leadership Rightness

As prerequisites, a candidate for leadership should:
1. Love People
2. Be Able to Deal with Ambiguity
3. Enjoy Coaching
4. Apply Judgment and Take Risk
5. Be Able to Work Long Hours
6. Desire to Make a Bigger Difference
7. Be Willing to Leave Prior Expertise
8. Have Charisma

1. Love People

A true leader has a type of affection for the people that work with him and for him. He earnestly wants to see them succeed. Real leaders enjoy the complexities that come from managing the people's work, mutually setting goals, communicating, assessing their performance, and providing rewards for their home runs.

Within the bounds of propriety, a real leader attempts to invoke change in people so they grow and are better prepared for the many bumps in the road of professional and personal life.

A true leader is only mildly amused by *Dilbert*, knowing that a cynical work environment that *Dilbert* lives in is a lousy way to spend one-third of one's life. A leader knows a positive environment is infectious and wants such an environment for the group.

A true leader respects the diversity of thought, values, motives, customs, and ethnicity.

A good boss has a spiritual strength whether from a religious foundation or personal deduction.

A good boss understands that everyone has a unique set of motives. A good boss lives by the platinum rule as well as the golden rule. Most of us have been taught and lived by the golden rule. A common English rendering is: "Do unto others as you would have them do unto you."[22] However, in leadership, a higher law is better. The platinum rule is a wonderful term coined by Dr. Tony Alessandra. "Do unto others as *they* would have *you* do unto *them*."[23]

Simply put, leaders need to know the motives that drive their people. Until a leader understands that we are not all wired the same and each of us has a different set of drivers, a leader is unable to effectively lead his team.

One might reject this initial quality of leadership of loving people as too touchy feely, particularly if your education and experience is quantoidal. But consider the words of Warren Bennis, widely held as one of the world's greatest minds in leadership thinking. Dr. Bennis said of what he has learned about leadership:

> The process of becoming a leader is similar to the process of becoming a fully integrated human being…and…giving and receiving respect is a basic human need and crucial to strong leadership.[24]

If such considerations are too lovey-dovey for you to buy into, this may be a good barometer that leadership is not right for you at this point.

2. Deal with Ambiguity

A true leader knows that the world doesn't piece together perfectly. She knows not all the puzzle pieces are in the box and that some of the pieces don't fit together. A good boss recognizes there are many shades of gray on almost every issue rather than black or white. A leader understands that anxiety comes from uncertainty but that uncertainty is ubiquitous. Hence, they have an ability to withstand Maalox moments. Ambiguity affects us on a variety of planes. One is known as office politics and is a way of life in organizations. A leader recognizes that not everyone in power in their organization has a firm emotional foundation, and some may act irrationally, vindictively, or in fierce competition.

Abraham Maslow developed a convenient framework for thinking about the emotional needs of people.[25] Viewed through Maslow, it is easy to see that certain people are missing something in their lives. You don't need a PhD in psychology to see it. According to Maslow, we have a hierarchy of needs starting with basic physiological needs such as food, water, sleep, and breathing. The next level is safety, including security of health, employment, and property. The third and fourth are love followed by esteem. Finally, after all of these needs are met, Maslow calls the final need, self-actualization. This is a difficult-to-define state of being. Maslow once taught it is when you do things not simply for the outcome, but because it's the reason you are here on earth.[26] It is a wonderful way of life.

A company, in its most base view, is a community of people who only share a common need for financial remuneration. The need for employment is only at Maslow's second level. The company needs to help its people reach love (particularly a sense of belonging to a successful enterprise) and esteem (respect, achievement, and confidence). When an organization is full of people who largely are not self-actualized, it breeds all sorts of mischief, dysfunction, turmoil, and discontent. Summed up, this yields the darker side of office politics.

Leaders need to navigate around and through these choppy political seas. To do so is great training for eventual larger responsibilities.

3. Enjoy Coaching

A true leader understands the need to encourage the heart, to suggest ideas, to confront and correct unacceptable performance, and to resolve conflicts in a fair manner.

4. Apply Judgment and Take Risks

A true leader has the ability to weigh and balance competing principles, opinions, feelings, and positions and determine the best path. A good boss has a good sense of what risks are acceptable and what risks bet the farm.

5. Work Long Hours

A true leader has the stamina to work long hours on large problems when the situation calls for it. This is usually with no additional renumeration. In case no one has ever told you, initially, a new boss may be overwhelmed with work. Good leaders get on top of this within several months. Organization, time management, and delegation are the key.

6. Desire to Make a Bigger Difference

A frontline employee has been successful in her current role. Her desire then becomes the ability to leverage her skills through increased organizational power to make an even bigger difference. This difference-making stuff can be addictive and encourages many bosses to continually seek increasingly larger responsibilities. Making a bigger difference is a major motive of many bosses.

7. Leave Their Expertise and Learn Skills of Leadership Readiness

Any newly promoted boss has just changed careers, particularly if his prior work was mostly quantoidal. The new boss must leave the prior world of technical expertise and begin a lifelong assent up a steep mountain of learning related to leadership, management, business, workplace psychology, and organizational theory. These are the skills of leadership readiness. Without this willingness, a person should stay in his valued frontline position.

8. Have Charisma

The role of charisma in leadership is much studied and much debated. Needless to say, a leader with little charisma may be successful in some situations. However, referring to the four skills of leadership, one who has the allure of the leader can be better at building teams, communicating vision, and implementing change than one who is charismatically challenged. Unfortunately, there is no charisma pill. As Ricky Ricardo used to say on *I Love Lucy*, "Some of us got it, Lucy, and some of us 'dunt.'" Charisma is not always based on acting within some popular set of social norms defined by central casting. Jack Welsh, the famously effective CEO of General Electric spoke with a distinct stutter. No one doubted his focus, intensity and vision.

The Biz Bucks Guy has known a CEO or two who did not have an abundance of charisma. The organization was well managed, but organizational transformation was slow at best.

TWELVE SKILLS OF LEADERSHIP READINESS

If you judge yourself right for being a boss, there are twelve skills that you need to begin to develop to be ready. No one is deep in every area when he enters his first boss assignment. The skills represent a lifetime of focus, practice, and study.

The twelve skills are summarized in figure 3 and are the organizing framework for parts 2 and 3 of this book. They are largely right brain skills.

Figure 3 - Twelve Skills of Leadership Readiness

Each Leader should strive to master processes, tools, and principles of:	Each leader should strive to master the behavioral skills of:
1. Strategic Planning and Implementation	7. Developing People
2. Customer Focus	8. Decision Making
3. Quantoidal Smarts of Finance, Accounting, and Statistics	9. Communications
4. Organizational Smarts	10. Delegating
5. Managing Work: Processes and Projects	11. Team Building
6. Managing Individual Performance	12. Leading Change

1. Strategy Development and Implementation

Effective leaders, particularly those who rise beyond the first line of leadership in their organizational hierarchy, must know the processes of strategy development and implementation. In chapter 4, a process model for strategy will be presented. Not all levels of the organization will use the full model. This model is fundamentally the four skills of leadership on steroids. It is also a version of the so-called Deming cycle of plan-do-check-act.[27]

2. Customer Focus

Every department, every employee, every boss has at least one customer, whether internal or external. Each boss must learn the needs of each customer and instill that knowledge with her direct reports. Knowing your customer is key to a results-driven department.

3. Quantoidal Business Smarts

Each boss needs to understand the basics of accounting, finance, economics, and statistics whether these relate to the company or a not-for-profit entity. They should have a clear understanding of income statements, balance sheets, cash flow statements, variable and fixed costs, marginal and average costs, relevant and nonrelevant costs, supply and demand, and financial valuation tools such as net present value. Statistics form the foundation for understanding processes and how to improve them.

With this knowledge, the boss will be better able to communicate both up and down the organizational hierarchy regarding setting and obtaining company goals and objectives. Additional training will be necessary. The Biz Bucks Guy attempted to gain this knowledge through organizational osmosis, indeed on the fly without any formal education. He was not successful. He has learned through trial and experience that the financial and accounting competence necessary to function well in leadership is largely gained from a formal college-level classroom experience.[28] Quantoids who have not been introduced to these topics will usually groove on this type of development. It has a familiar feel of their prior left brain education.

4. Organizational Business Smarts

Similar to accounting, finance, economics, and statistics, each leader needs to understand the basics of organizational theory, including organizational structures, organizational fit, performance management, and rewards. Unlike the previous, more quantitative topics, organizational smarts are more easily learned on the job, in corporate classrooms, and by individual study rather than a formal college experience.

5. Managing Work: Processes and Projects

A process is defined as a series of tasks or steps that end in a business objective that *recurs*. A project is a series of tasks or steps that end in a business objective that is *unique* and happens only once. Given these definitions, all work within an organization can be grouped into one of these two broad areas.

To optimize work, a boss must know the tools of both process management and project management. Process management deals with issues of flowcharting, performance metrics, simplification, control, and process ownership.

Project management deals with issues of work breakdown structure, critical path analysis, resources, potential problem analysis, communications, estimating, control, and closeout.

6. Managing Individual Performance

A key to being a successful boss is the ability to manage performance of his direct reports.[29] The processes of performance management include setting a performance plan, coaching throughout the performance period, and evaluating performance at the end of the period.

This is a process that typically is imposed by a one-size-fits-all human resource department as an annual cycle tied to financial results. It would be better to integrate performance management with the work cycle involved for each person or at least each team or department.

7. Developing Your People

The truly great leader is one who is passionate about developing his people. Much good for the leader, the employee, and the company comes from excelling at this skill; however, it is one of the least competent skills in American business.

8. Making Decisions

The day-to-day work of bosses is largely decision-making. The higher the boss climbs on the organizational chart, the larger the decisions become.

Quantoids are usually adept at analysis of problems. This is a great first step. But decision-making is much more. It deals with ambiguity and uncertainty. It deals with emotions and buy-in.

9. Communicating

The most difficult aspect of leadership is communicating with your boss, with peers, with customers and suppliers, and most importantly with your employees, particularly your direct reports. For those familiar with this challenge, no explanation is needed. For those not familiar, no explanation is fully possible. No one hits home runs as the great communicator every day. And when they strike out, the ramifications can be serious.

10. Delegating

In the qualities of leadership rightness, reference was made to long work hours. Often a new boss will charge into his new assignment like a football player, sacrificing his body on every play. As the hours mount, as family commitments are missed, as nerves become frayed, the new boss must find a way to return to the life balance he left as a frontline employee. There are only two clues to do this. First, simplify the work, or second, delegate like a maniac. Delegation is the key to sanity. It is not always easy and takes discipline.

11. Building Teams

A boss who can build a high performance team is valued. There is much garbage in corporate America written about teaming. To be an effective user of teams, a leader must cut through this hype and learn the many types of teams and how to deploy them. In a forthcoming chapter, *The Biz Bucks Guy* will emphasize seven special types of teams that have proven useful.

12. Leading Change

In the final analysis, most leaders have been placed in their roles to effect change. The new boss's boss knows about the history, problems, trials, personalities, and performance that exist in a department. She may have personally selected the new boss because he is the right person to fix these issues. The effective leader knows how to plan and implement change. Like most of the business of being boss, it is an art not science. It is the essence of leadership whether you are leading a department of your former peers or president of our great nation. It relies on many of the principles discussed in prior chapters. Thus, it concludes the list of skills of leadership readiness.

THE RIGHT AND READY SELF-ASSESSMENT TOOL

Each person, particular a quantoid, should do an honest self assessment to determine if he is both right and ready for leadership. To assist, The Biz Bucks Guy has provided a set of questions as Appendix A. It is designed to help you honestly assess your traits, skills, desires, and motives regarding boss-hood.

THE REWARDS OF LEADERSHIP

Some quantoids may have begun to be concerned about all the traits and skills associated with leadership and gotten dismayed or discouraged about their prospects of success. If your honest self-assessment points you to that first boss opportunity, The Biz Bucks Guy encourages you to take the leap. Go for it. Fear is the opposite of hope. Put on your hopeful hat. The rewards can be significant.

The primary reward is the increased leverage of your skills and talents to make a larger difference in your organization and with your people. Examples appear throughout these pages. Making a difference in people's lives, seeing them grow and succeed, sensing the team is strong and performing well, implementing change that helps thousands of shareholders, customers, the community, or the environment make for a wonderful compensation.

Second, leadership positions in large organizations are usually better paid. If you matriculate up the organization chart, the financial rewards can become significant. However, if this is your primary reason for desiring boss-hood, as our New York friends might say, "Fegetaboutit!" The hours, the frustrations, the wear and tear on your psyche, the people problems, the tough decisions, and the potential effect on your personal life, marriage, and children are not worth the new boat, the big vacation, or even getting that mortgage paid off sooner.

Go into boss-hood for a higher reason than pay.

HOW DO I GET PROMOTED?

Most frontline employees, who are considering boss-hood as a career path, want to know how they get their first chance. Here are some practical ideas.

First, the best advice is have other people say good things about you. This means to make sure your work is so outstanding that others willingly speak of your competence. You will need to accept assignments that are highly visible, hit it out of the park, and others will give notoriety to your work.

Beware. This does *not* mean to solicit others to say good things about you. You will be quickly labeled a butter-upping, brown-nosing, social climbing, overly ambitious snob. Even using the overwrought phrase, "If I do bad, tell me. If I do good, tell others," can get you in trouble. It is simply better to let your actions do the talking.

Second, have an active employee development plan with your boss. This plan should be based on developing the skills of leadership readiness. Then, implement the plan. Attend training. Enroll in night school. Ask for tough projects with impossible deadlines.

Third, demonstrate the qualities of leadership rightness as part of your daily work.

Fourth, volunteer to help your boss be boss. Ask if you can help with the department budget (minus the salary information). After your boss recovers from a myocardium infarction, she may take you up on it. Volunteer to organize the department team building session. Suggest you be named the process owner for a key process in your area.

Fifth, be an inwardly happy person. It takes one to be a good boss. If this is not natural for you, seek help from experts such as trusted counselors, church leaders, therapists, or employee assistance programs.

Sixth, ask your boss where you should be working in five years. Ask him if you can discuss your career with the leader of that department.

Finally, get feedback from others. See if others think you are right and ready for leadership.

You may learn something about the degree of Maslow's self-actualization of your current boss. Much of this will require you to have a boss who is a true people developer. There are some bosses who just can't bring themselves to help their direct reports get ahead.

WHAT DRIVES US?

There is one significant area of leadership expertise that must be added to our understanding to be effective in leading others and to do a comprehensive self-assessment. It deals with our individual motives and those of others. We need to answer the question: What are my deeply held motives regarding my career? If a person, quantoid or normal, leader or front line, can come to know their underlying drivers well, life navigation is vastly improved. This topic is of such importance and power that it deserves a separate chapter that follows.

QUESTIONS FOR CURRENT LEADERS

1. Were you missing any of the eight qualities of leadership rightness when you received your first leadership position? If so, has it affected your ability to lead? How did you develop that quality?
2. What do you like most about your leadership opportunity? Is it the money? The opportunity to work with people? The ability to make a difference?
3. Which of the twelve skills of leadership readiness should you work on now? Which have you gained expertise in from your leadership experience?

TECHNICAL ANALOG FOR LIFE AND LEADERSHIP: THE HYSTERESIS CURVE

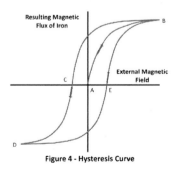

Figure 4 - Hysteresis Curve

In electromagnetism, an interesting phenomenon is observed. From the Greek word meaning "lagging behind," an unusual curve, the hysteresis, is seen when a nonmagnetic piece of iron is magnetized by imposing an external magnetic field on it. The external magnetic field is zero, and the resulting magnetic property (flux) of the iron is zero at point A. When the external magnetic field is increased, the iron becomes magnetized to a maximum level at point B.

One might think, by reversing the field of the external magnetic field, the iron would return to its nonmagnetic state. However, the magnetic property of the iron has a different idea. The iron can never be brought back to its nonmagnetic state. The iron may have its magnetization reversed (moving from point B to point C and ultimately to point D), but it never can return to the zero point (point A). Re-reversing the external magnetic field only changes the iron's magnetism back to its original point B after passing through point E. The iron can't return to normal. The iron seems to have a memory. In fact, this is the scientific basis for memory and data storage on hard drives.

This hysteresis effect is seen in other areas of endeavor, including cell biology, neuroscience, and even economics.

Among other avenues of life, taking a leadership position has a hysteresis effect. It is very difficult to go back to your original frontline view of the organization or your career. You are a changed person. You see things differently. You have experienced the wonderful high that comes from leveraging your talents and making a larger difference. You may have become a great people developer and know that is the best part of being a boss. You have learned to deal with an increased level of ambiguity. The experience of leadership shapes your thinking forever. You can never quite go home after leaving the cocoon of followership.

And for most, that is a good thing.

CHAPTER 3

KNOWING YOURSELF

I SHOT MY CAR

The Biz Bucks Guy's late good friend and business associate, John Dietrich, told the allegedly true tale of an ardent quantoid who was promoted to a managerial position at his company. He was a gifted technical resource. He had been given boss responsibilities to leverage his technical skills across a group of people. It didn't go easy for him. After giving it a decent try, he went into his boss and resigned his position, asking the opportunity to return to his former quantoidal frontline job.

His boss agreed and then asked him, "When did you first realize you were not suited for this position?"

He answered resolutely, with glazed eyes in a distant focus, "When I shot my car!"

He explained the frustrations of leadership, the ambiguity of applying the many requisite softer skills, and the constant pressure to evaluate and motivate others' performance had built up massive unreleased emotions.

That morning was a freezing cold day. He explained when he stepped out of his warm home to get in his car; everything seemed okay. But as he turned the key in the ignition, the engine wouldn't turn over. He had forgotten to connect the engine block heater the night before.

He calmly got out of his car, went inside, pulled his shotgun off the rack on the wall in the living room, loaded the gun on the way out, slowly lifted the hood of his car, and calmly—with premeditation—shot the engine dead!

He realized he had never shot a car before and did a quick self-talk, which caused him to see a "tight correlation" between his new leadership job and his inability to control his rage. To his credit, he realized boss-hood was not for everyone. He once again became the valued quantoid, revered by his colleagues.

How much better it would have been if he had a way to assess his rightness and readiness for boss-hood. This chapter deals with an important way to gain some big clues about yourself.

KNOW YOURSELF

The famous Chinese warrior and general Sun-Tzu wrote, "Know thy self, know thy enemy. A thousand battles, a thousand victories." [30]

This chapter is about an essential framework for understanding not only yourself but others, maybe even a few enemies. The scholar who developed the framework named it Career Concepts. Without hyperbole, The Biz Bucks Guy considers this the most powerful tool on the planet for managing yourself and your people.

DEVELOPMENT OF CAREER CONCEPTS FRAMEWORK

The Biz Bucks Guy was introduced to Career Concepts while in the executive MBA program at the University of Southern California (USC). Dr. Michael Driver was, before his passing, a significant contributor to that MBA experience. A credible argument could be made that Dr. Driver was the dean of careers in academia. He founded the Careers Division of the Academy of Management, the academic society for college professors of management. Dr. Driver was the originator of Career Concepts.

His work spanned several decades.[31] After graduation from USC, The Biz Bucks Guy was honored to have some consulting gigs with Dr. Driver, who certified him to teach the basics of Career Concepts.

While there are many fine tools, theories, instruments, and constructs for assessing and navigating careers, none approached the power of this framework as an organizing theory for understanding yourself and your people in the workplace. The Biz Bucks Guy knows of several examples where this tool has helped people know themselves better. It changed attitudes, improved motivation and productivity, ended manager malaise, and revitalized energy and focus within them. Properly applied, it provides a way to assess organizational structure changes before you pull the trigger and reorganize.

Career Concepts will be referenced in several of the twelve skills of readiness chapters that follow. Thus, it is imperative that a leader, new or seasoned, takes time to absorb, ponder, and ruminate on the principles of this tool. It takes soak time. After reading all the relevant chapters, the power of Career Concepts should be apparent.

THE BASICS OF CAREER CONCEPTS

Here is a summary of the framework in five points:

Point 1: We all carry a personal concept of a successful career. Everyone has a concept of career success that was programmed into our psyche during our childhood or early professional life. Our career concept, whatever it may be, comes from such things as our parents and family, our national culture, our company culture, a mentor, or even our birth order. While we sometimes believe our own concept of career success is shared by everyone else, the opposite is true. The research behind this framework shows there are four distinct concepts and seven hybrids of the four.

Point 2: There are four *career concepts.* As shown in the accompanying table, the framework posits four distinct career concepts. Each is unique, and no single career concept is right for everyone. Of the four, the first two have been intuitively known for some time. The final two are not widely known but highly useful in career counseling and apply to many people in the workplace.

Type	Career Concept	Career Motives
Linear	Upward	Power Achievement
Expert	Stay in one Place	Expertise Security
Spiral	Lateral (5-10 Years)	Growth Creativity
Transitory	Lateral (2-4 Years)	Variety Independence

Figure 5: Career Concepts and Career Motives

The four concepts are:

The Linear: Happiness for a linear only comes from moving up the corporate ladder. This proves to be a difficult concept to yield continued success. Movement up the organizational pyramid provides fewer positions into which to advance. Many who carry the linear concept are frustrated. Many leave positions of influence when they become topped out. The delayering of organizational levels beginning in the nineties left many linears disillusioned. For many, being a linear is an emotionally brutal career concept.

The Expert: Happiness for an expert is being known as the best among his peers. This includes the craftworker who yearns to be the best welder at Good Ol' Amalgamated. It is also the trial lawyer, garnering community recognition for a high profile case, the surgeon with national recognition for an innovative procedure, or the accountant with the most knowledge in the department of GAAP and FASB. Those who carry the expert concept may have been told in their youth to grow up to be good at something. Parents of baby boomers may have been influenced by the Great Depression wherein the ones who kept their jobs were often the ones with the best skills.

The Spiral: Happiness for a spiral is being able to move from one position to a related but often broader position usually every five to ten years. Broadening is the key. A spiral's parents may have taught her to be well-rounded. Each new position is a natural progression based on a prior position. A spiral is the engineer who migrates into project management and then to capital budgeting and eventually to corporate budgeting functions. Spirals amass a vast amount of knowledge and experience. Many spirals in midcareer feel a strong desire to share the wealth of knowledge with others. This leads many spirals to leave large companies to become consultants or teachers.

The Transitory: Happiness for a transitory is being able to change jobs often. Movement is more frequent than spirals, perhaps every two to three years, and the succeeding jobs are often unrelated to past work experiences. A transitory may move from a funeral director to draftsman. These are often people from the extremes of economic backgrounds who don't value security. They either were raised in a poorer economic environment (and know they can survive on very little) or in an upper economic stratum (and presume money will always be there). Transitories can play key roles in companies that are expanding, both geographically and into new markets. They make good startup people. Transitories tend to value work with high people involvement.

Point 3: There are four *corresponding sets of career motives.* Each career concept has a set of underlying motives. These are the things that make us happy at work that energize us. They are our passions—our drivers.

Linears are motivated by power and achievement.

Experts seek expertise and security.

Spirals value growth and creativity.

Transitories are passionate about variety and independence.

Point 4: We should align our career concept and our motives. Unfortunately, many people have a particular concept of career success wired into their belief system but have strong underlying motives that tie to a different concept. Such a misalignment between concept and motives will almost always lead to chronic dysfunctions, like discord, despair, lack of motivation, cynicism, and frustration.

As one common example, consider the well-rounded son of the high profile executive who is truly energized by growth and creativity. He may believe he needs to be successful like Dad and focuses on climbing the corporate ladder but does not have achievement and power as his primary career drivers. This perceived need to climb ever higher and the resultant constant gamesmanship of company politics impedes his stronger desire of continued growth and the opportunity to apply his experiences creatively. This misalignment leads him to, at minimum, frustration and possibly cynicism and even bolting from a valued corporate position.

Point 5: We can more easily change our career concepts than our motives. If an employee has a set of motives that do not fit her concept of career success, she can more easily change her concept of success than the underlying motives. This achieves alignment and mitigates dysfunctional feelings and behaviors about her career. In the prior example of the executive's son, if the son understands creativity and growth motives are most important to him, career plans can be changed to provide logical growth into broader areas dropping the perception that up is the only source of success. Such recognition of misalignments and subsequent actions to achieve alignment can reenergize and refocus employees in a dramatic fashion.

SEVEN CAREER HYBRIDS

A logical pairing of the four concepts yields the possibility of six hybrid pairs. In fact, many of us identify with more than one career concept. These six are:

- linear-expert
- linear-spiral
- linear-transitory
- expert-spiral
- expert-transitory
- spiral-transitory

A seventh hybrid is a person with a combination of three or four of the Career Concepts motive sets. This is known as the good news-bad news hybrid. The title is apropos because someone with so many strong motives can go many directions in their career. However, no one job will meet all their psychological needs. They must supplement their work-life job that supports certain motives with other activities that support the other motives. This could include charity, church, volunteer work, hobbies, or creative talents such as writing or musical composition.

Leadership Fit

People with certain career concepts or hybrids are good candidates for leadership. Obviously, one with purely linear motives is a natural fit for leadership, subject to the qualities of leadership rightness in the previous chapter.

Pure spirals will enjoy a leadership assignment or two on their road to broadening themselves. For them, leadership is viewed more as another opportunity to learn than a quest for power.

A linear-spiral hybrid will typically be happiest progressing toward a general manager slot, that is, one with multiple functional duties where they can learn much about new departments that report to them.

A linear-expert hybrid will typically be happiest as the manager of the department or function he grew up in. These people value being (or becoming) a renowned expert in their chosen field and also grooming others to become like them.

A pure transitory can also view a leadership opportunity as something positive as long as it is a new experience and would not tie her down for more than a few years. The difference between a pure transitory and a linear-transitory hybrid is that the pure transitory is often more ambivalent about future leadership assignments while the hybrid desires to keep a leadership position while moving from a top spot in one company to a top spot in another company. For example, an American company acquired another company with a Paris location. No top manager from the acquiring company wanted to move to France. A woman who was not in top management volunteered. It was a sizable pay increase and a new job. Having strong transitory leanings, she saved the bacon of the acquiring company. She moved later to another location and did the same thing. Those with transitory motives should not be underappreciated by top management.

Those with pure expert motives and the expert-transitory hybrid are probably not especially interested in leadership positions.

The remaining two hybrids (expert-spiral and spiral-transitory) might undertake one first-line leadership position, reflecting their broadening motive. However, their inclinations, skills, and motives concerning future leadership should be re-assessed periodically. This is important because people's motives and, hence, leadership abilities can and do change.

DIFFERENCE MAKING AND DYSFUNCTION

Each of these four motive sets can represent a valid, self-actualized, meaningful career path. In different ways, each can be difference-makers. Obviously, a successful linear will achieve many professional accomplishments because of the power he obtains from his climb up the chain of command.

An expert can make discoveries in medicine, environmental control, or welding techniques. A spiral can amass an incredible knowledge base, providing a balanced view in decision-making, being a source of wisdom and experience, and teaching others an integrated view of the workplace. A transitory can fit into many tough and undesirable spots and save the day, just for the fun of variety of experience.

Conversely, all might represent dysfunctional behavior in a large organization. Linears can be dominating and out of balance. Experts can become disheartened if the organization does not value them. Spirals could be frustrated if the organization does not allow them to grow. Transitories can leave for their next gig just as their ability is needed in a crucial situation. Each needs to be aware of his motives and how he applies them in the workplace.

HOW MANY OF EACH?

The Biz Bucks Guy's experience with about six hundred people in a workshop setting in the USA showed—for career concepts— about a 30-30-30-10 distribution with transitories being the smaller portion. For career motives, however, the distribution was more even, about equal for the four. More people seem to value variety and change *down deep* than they believe themselves to do.

The important point is: There are plenty of each of the four concepts and plenty with the respective motives. We should embrace this reality as we manage, direct, reorganize, and develop our people and departments.

PEOPLE CHANGE

Unlike many other career-related instruments and assessment tools, an underlying principle of Career Concepts is that people change. Someone may be an expert now, in ten years a spiral, and wind up later with a chunk of transitory or even linear in them. This is an unusual notion in the career-concept field. Most other career instruments brand the participant for life and make a big deal about making plaques or paperweights so everyone can know what concoction of letters or colors you are for life. The change can be quite fast. For example, an expert may become a transitory quickly if Aunt Tillie leaves him a nice package of stocks and bonds at her passing.

THREE CASE STUDIES

For illustrative purposes, let's consider the following anecdotes that show the power of the Career Concepts framework. The first concerns a CEO showing these concepts apply at high level. The second shows the immediacy of its use. The third deals with the impact on critical career decision making.

The Misaligned CEO

A pure expert would probably not be right for leadership position. A CEO of a chemical company took the Career Concepts instrument, which divulged he was a pure expert. When the Career Concepts workshop leader interviewed the CEO and told him what his underlying motives were, the CEO broke down in tears. He had internalized for most of his professional life a pent up anxiety about work. He had been such a successful chemist that he was promoted and then promoted again and again, all the time wondering why he really wasn't happy. He was supposed to really like being CEO. He didn't. He just wanted to be the one to make the big breakthrough in the lab. It was a significant emotional event for the CEO.

The Stealth Restructuring

The Biz Bucks Guy was teaching a two-day course for a large company. Two outstanding participants were in the front row. As we began the second day, these two participants were looking like they could sit on a dime and dangle their legs. Something had cut them low!

At the first break, they informed us that at their hotel room the night before, they both got surprise calls from the plant manager. Their jobs that they loved had unexpectedly been eliminated in a plant restructuring. They were lucky. They were not let go. They had been assigned new positions in two different departments, well out of their prior functions. They were emotionally broken. The Biz Bucks Guy dumped the standard course outline and spent valuable time teaching the Career Concept framework. After the next break, both participants were "back," both physically and emotionally. They smiled and pointed to their name tents. Each had written Spiral on his name tent. The Biz Bucks Guy was amazed at the speed at which they internalized the framework and reconciled their lot in a positive way. He kept in touch for a few months. Both seemed to be doing well.

The Long Tall Texan

The Biz Bucks Guy once ran a series of complex, residential, four-day, culture-change simulations for a large company. During the first morning of the last simulation, a tall thin cowboy came in. He was *sportin' a 'tude*. He sat down and was visibly annoyed at being in a hotel for four days away from work. Everyone saw him, and many commented privately about his bad attitude.

The facilitators met that evening and decided—on a split vote—to allow him to spend one more day before tossing him out. He did not improve on day two, but again, we allowed him to stay, and were we glad. On day three and day four, he was great! He was engaged with his team. He contributed in the plenary sessions. Something had happened. It was apparent it happened right after Career Concepts were taught on the afternoon of day two.

At the end of the simulation, the microphone was passed to each of the fifty participants to explain the primary take-away for them. All the facilitators held their breath as the microphone came to our long, tall Texan.

He stood and, in essence, said with some emotion, "You may not have noticed it, but I came in here with a bad attitude.

"I have been miserable at work," he said, "and I made myself a promise that I was quitting the day I got back from here. I hated work. Then I found out I am a transitory. I had been doing the same job at work for fifteen long years. I am one of the best, but I am bored stiff. I called my boss that evening and explained. He understood. He told me on Monday, I could do a new job. He also told me in two years, if I wanted, he would see that I got a different job. I am a new person. Thank you." A fifteen-year employee with family responsibilities was almost driven to do something stupid. The Career Concept framework made a huge difference that day.

THE AMERICAN LINEAR FIXATION

In America, we have a cultural fixation on climbing the corporate ladder. Often people starting careers feel success is only in moving up. Certainly, corporate pay programs and a capitalist society in general grow that norm.

However, each person navigating in the workplace should realize being a bona fide linear is a brutal career path. The higher you go, the fewer the possible positions and the more others shoot at you. The pyramid gets small at the top. Those that make it to high position in organizations (and maintain their perch) usually deserve it. They have developed a certain toughness and have mastered many of the skills of leadership readiness.

To the contrary, some other countries do not have this same norm. In parts of Europe, the expert is the revered career. They value the prized chocolate maker or the fifth generation fine watch craftsman.

The realization of four valid career paths and hybrids is a memorable moment in many people's lives. You get to define what success is for you.

HOW ONE MAY VIEW ANOTHER

Without this framework, people who have various motives do not understand how others are wired between the ears. This can bring out some dysfunctional behavior and attitudes.

A linear may see an expert as one who was not good enough for management.

An expert may see a linear as one who was not able to do the real work, so they fled up the organization chart, following their oversized ego.

A linear or an expert may see a spiral as disloyal to his prior functions.

A linear or an expert may see a transitory as an airhead who can't do a job long.

A transitory or spiral may see an expert as someone in a boring, dead-end job.

Thus, the Career Concepts framework helps us all understand one another better. This is an extension of the platinum rule mentioned in chapter 2.

ALIGNMENT AND THE GOLDEN HANDCUFFS

Getting one's career concept and motives aligned is relatively easy. It only takes a thorough understanding of the framework and modifying one's concept to match one's motives. Once that alignment is accomplished, for some, the tough work begins. Experts are happy to stay in their current line of expertise. However, at worst case, linears, spirals, and transitories may need to leave a company.

This may be difficult if you have much seniority. At some companies, benefit packages are designed to keep you, not allowing you to progress away from the company. Defined-benefit pensions, vacations, and health insurance make it difficult to leave. This is sometimes called the *golden handcuffs*.

Each person will need to weigh her circumstances. If leaving is not advisable financially, those who have a misalignment at work might improve their well-being by pursuing outside avenues after work as a substitute for what is missing at work. For example, a linear-spiral hybrid who is not in a management position at work might become a top leader in a volunteer organization, like, Scouting or a charity.

KNOWING YOUR CAREER CONCEPT AND MOTIVES

Many people can get a flavor of both their career concept and their underlying motives by doing some honest self-talk and also by asking for input from others.

However, an impressive online instrument CareerView formally assesses both your career concept and your motives.[32] [33] It also provides much insight and commentary tailored to the information from the individual. The multi-decade research by Dr. Driver and his colleagues now includes data from over one million people. Statistical validity is assured. [34] [35]

Remember, people change. One would be well served, redoing this instrument periodically.

TWO TOOLS TO SELF-ASSESS

With the leadership Right and Ready Self-Assessment (discussed in chapter 2 and appendix A) and the CareerView instrument introduced in this chapter, a quantoid should be able to have a broad picture of their viability for boss-hood. These two tools will help the prospective leader know himself better. With that important assessment as a foundation, let's delve deeper into the twelve skills of leadership rightness. Each of the twelve follows as a separate chapter.

QUESTIONS FOR CURRENT LEADERS

1. Do you have any concerns about your current career? What are they? Does it help or impede you in reaching Maslow's self-actualization?
2. Do you think your career concept and motives are aligned?
3. What is your next career move, given your understanding of the Career Concepts framework?

TECHNICAL ANALOG FOR LIFE AND LEADERSHIP: PLANES AND PATIENCE

When a jetliner enters turbulent air, the trained pilot seeks to find a balance between speed and comfort. There is an optimum turbulent penetration velocity. Usually that means to slow down a bit. There is an ideal speed for each situation, and a few minutes of delay to smooth out the ride is usually appreciated by the passengers.

Organizations should also seek their *optimum turbulent penetration velocity*. The winds of economic change can surprise a CEO. Particularly for a start-up company, the maniacal focus on growth can be fatal. (Interestingly, the airline industry has many examples of growing too fast.) Unlike a jetliner, which is designed to withstand the worst of turbulent air, a new company typically has a weak balance sheet (too much debt). A little economic wind can quickly lead to bankruptcy. CEOs should apply a little patience as they grow their business, strengthening their financial ability to enter turbulence.

Correspondingly, new bosses should also exhibit a bit of patience as they begin to implement change in a small department. Whether the department is new or has a long history, there is a breaking point at which any department cannot digest more change. New leaders should not force change too quickly or too slowly. The key: listen to your people and find the *optimum change velocity*.

Part II

WHAT DO GOOD BOSSES KNOW?

CHAPTER 4

STRATEGY: THE ULTIMATE TOOL FOR RESULTS

THE STUPID PRODUCTS HALL OF FAME

Many years ago, during the height of the quality movement, a streetlight manufacturer bought into the total-quality-management bandwagon and set a corporate objective to produce a *zero-defect* light. After the organization rose to the occasion, spending enormous amounts of both financial and human capital, the company reached its goal and began to market the *perfect* light fixture. They quickly found out no purchaser of streetlights cared that a light—twenty-five feet in the air—was perfect. No one paid more for the perfect light. The entire idea was a bust. Why? It was not driven by strategy. Strategic direction comes, in large part, from the marketplace.

Much of what was done under the quality banner of the 1990s was half a loaf—powerful but not integrated with the total strategic picture. The quality movement was unfortunately—in many applications—a management fad. The perfect streetlight took its place in the Stupid Products Hall of Fame, next to the concrete life jacket.

This chapter focuses on the most powerful tool known to move an organization to higher ground. Strategy, both the planning of strategy and its implementation, is listed by many CEOs as their most effective tool to improve results.[36] A survey of financial analysts who do valuation studies of company stocks listed the ability to *implement* strategy as the most important intangible competence a company can have to help stock price. The ability to *formulate* a strategy was listed as the third most important competence in their list of ten.[37]

The really amazing thing about strategy, particularly in light of the good ink in business books, studies, and MBA classes, is that the principles are not widely used. Ninety-five percent of employees don't know the corporate strategy. Ninety percent of strategic plans fail. Eighty percent of top executives spent less than one hour per month discussing strategy.[38] So the principles of strategy in this chapter must be classified as *esoteric*, that is, understood only by a few.

Much of this chapter will focus on strategy for large organizations. It will conclude with application to smaller settings, such as a small department of frontline employees headed by a new supervisor.

THE POINT GUARD OF MANAGEMENT TOOLS

Strategy is listed first in the "Skills of Leadership Readiness" because it is the point guard for the other skills. Without an integrated strategy, all other tools, processes, models, and techniques are like a collection of superstars on the basketball court, all with outstanding ability, but no one to pull them together, to coordinate their efforts, to focus their energy and talents. Strategy is that tool. It is all-encompassing. It coordinates all the other possible corporate interventions. It is the source of motivation. It is the basis for communications. Other interventions should be only appendages of a well-oiled, finely crafted strategy.

Nothing should be done in a large organization unless it is part of, correlated with, integrated within, and inculcated throughout the organization's strategic plan. That includes benchmarking, performance management, strategic alliances, culture change interventions, internal customer meetings, and any new corporate fad that may come down the business-school pike. All of these change interventions have noble goals and can be effective. However, without being linked to the entire organization's strategy, they are, as mentioned about a poorly planned quality initiative, half a loaf. Given this point guard role, consider:

Rule 1: Never do anything unless it is part of the strategy.

Rule 1 means that no training program, no software purchase, no equipment upgrade, no hiring freeze, no hiring program, no corporate communication, no reorganization, no creative idea of any kind should be implemented unless it is specifically included in, obviously supportive of, or clearly tied to the organization's strategy.

Beware of the popular word *tactical*. The Biz Bucks Guy does not use *tactical* concerning smaller efforts by an organization. It gives license for smaller groups to do things that are not really tied to strategy. Therefore, work is either *strategic* itself or *strategically driven*. This is an amplification of Rule 1.

STRATEGY AND DIFFERENCE-MAKING

Strategy helps both line and staff functions. If properly developed and implemented, strategy drives dramatic improvement in results for line functions. Strategy also significantly helps staff functions make a difference in their often tough-to-measure settings. Let's consider three examples of staff departments. Line department examples are included in chapter 16.

The Pernicious Pejoratives

The Biz Bucks Guy spent several years in leadership positions in staff groups. A staff group is one that does not engineer, produce, or market the product or service of the company. Among others, staff groups typically include budgeting, human resources, information technology, security, finance, and accounting.

Through much of his years on the staff side, The Biz Bucks Guy had several assignments to implement corporate change initiatives, some of which became known as *Corporate Fad 1993*, *Flavor of the Month*, or (a personal favorite) *Management by Best Seller*. One VP boobird actually said, referring to an important corporate intervention, "I know if I hold my breath long enough, you will be gone eventually." After an enthusiastic launch and much effort to implement, corporate initiatives go on life support when these pejorative phrases begin, first by the *line* leaders and eventually their frontline employees. The staff leaders implementing the initiative begin pushing a rope, meaning frustrations mount, and the effectiveness of the initiative is minimized. The half-life of the intervention is shortened.

However, you dedicated staff initiative leaders, take heart! There is a way out of this cycle.

If the corporate change program is integrated with strategy, the likelihood of the boobirds using such pernicious pejoratives is greatly reduced. After a five-year stint in leading culture change initiatives, which were tied to strategy, The Biz Bucks Guy did not hear such language *once*. Prior to that, they always appeared after a few months after launch. Integrating a change program with the organization's strategy makes a big difference. That is only possible, however, if the organization actually has a strategy.

The Quantum Jump in Acceptance

If you are a leader of a staff group and want to make a difference, corporate strategy is a key. Consider the HR department in a company who measured the internal customer satisfaction for all departments on a regular basis. HR typically had the lowest scores of any department. Only about 42 percent of respondents said HR was good or very good at serving their internal customers.

Then, the company began to manage by using an integrated strategic plan. HR was well represented in the strategic initiatives listed in the plan. The next survey showed the HR department's customer service rating had climbed to over 90 percent! The entire organizations now knew of HR's important role in serving the line departments. The reason for the improvement was two-fold: the line departments understood HR's strategic role, and HR now had a strategy on which to integrate their work. The strategy provided the mode for both the communication and the focus.

Wasting the Covey Ticket

A large company had turned around their performance through the development and implementation of strategy. In the middle of that transformation, one HR guru at the company became enamored with—and eventually certified in using—the corporate training process implementing the *Seven Habits of Highly Successful People* from the late Stephen R. Covey. The Biz Bucks Guy thinks Covey's material is highly useful, but in coaching this HR guru, he suggested the guru wait for several months before launching *Seven Habits*. It was not yet part of the driving force in the company—the strategy. "You only have one ticket to spend with Covey or any other major intervention," said The Biz Bucks Guy. "Let's do it right and propose it for the next revision of the corporate plan. It deserves that powerful support from top management. We will need the next big thing by then, and Covey's stuff would be ideal."

Unfortunately, the HR guru was too impatient. The HR VP passively allowed it to move forward. Much time was spent orchestrating it from the staff side, not the line side of the organization. Only a few people were moved by Covey. Many never attended. The Covey ticket was spent with little overall benefit to the company. Rule 1 was broken. The HR guru had not tied his work to strategy. His efforts had minimal impact.

THE BIZ BUCKS STRATEGY CYCLE

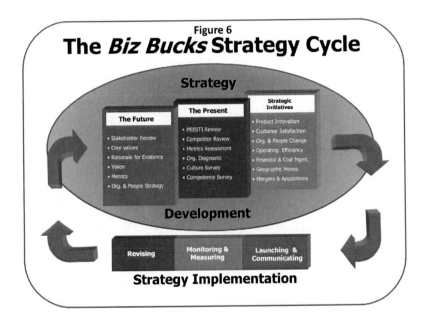

Figure 6
The *Biz Bucks* Strategy Cycle

Based on his MBA education and several consulting experiences, The Biz Bucks Guy has synthesized a model for strategic planning (see figure 6). The cycle is similar to the Deming cycle of plan-do-check-act. The strategy development oval represents *plan*. Strategy implementation represents *do*, *check*, and *act*, respectively.

Much of this chapter is focused on the strategy development. This however is a small percent of the collective effort of an organization using this cycle. Experience, education, and peer discussions support the notion that strategy implementation, not its development, is, many times over, the more difficult of the two phases. Organizations, particularly corporate settings, will want to use this cycle on an annual basis. After the initial cycle, unless there is radical change needed, updating the strategy should be less of an effort. Strategy development is the *heart* of the strategy cycle. Strategy implementation is the *art* of the cycle.

Using the model assumes a planning team has been formed of key people. If this is a corporate use, the CEO is the lead. Her direct reports are included. Perhaps a communication specialist is also added and selected others invited. An experienced facilitator is also needed. Each team member will have substantial homework between team meetings. This eventually means the results of the strategic plan are owned by the team. This is *not* a process where a high-powered consultancy is contracted to produce the plan and give it to the company executive team. That is rarely as successful as determining direction with an internal planning team.

Using the model will take several team meetings. Some steps of the model may require certain financial expenditures.

If you are an executive and believe this commitment of time, energy, and fortune is not possible for you, perhaps a demotion is advisable. Strategic planning and implementation is the essence of any executive role. If you shun strategy work, what part of leadership *do* you want to do?

Forming this planning team relates to the second of the four steps of leadership developed in chapter 1—build a small team.

THE PLANNING HORIZON

The planning team determines the time frame for the plan. The goals of the forthcoming strategy will be realized how quickly? In two years? Three years? Five years?

The planning horizon should be based on several key aspects, not just the aspiration to change. These might include the length of key business processes for the organization such as product development, the level of trouble the organization's market currently is in, and pending events, such as ground-breaking legislation, which might shape the market of the future.

STRATEGY DEVELOPMENT: FUTURE FIRST!

The three tombstones in the oval are sometimes known as gap analysis, but with one substantive change. In standard gap analysis, one determines the present, envisions the future, then closes the gaps between the two by implementing initiatives. By considering the present first, gap analysis usually gleans incremental improvements. Leaders push the organization forward. This is like sweeping up gold dust.

This model reverses the approach, and for good reason. By reversing the order and considering the future first, the future seemingly grabs hold of the organization and pulls it forward. Large step changes, not incremental improvement, are realized. It can be like finding the gold nuggets, even the mother lode.[39] All planning in this model and throughout this book is based on the future first principle.

The goal is to look into the future in three markets: products/services, people, and capital. Then, make a reasoned prediction of what each market will require at the planning horizon for organization to build success. So the strategic plan, its vision and metrics, should be market-driven and based on *future-first thinking*.

SIX STEPS TO DEFINE THE FUTURE

The model identifies six steps to determine the future of the organization.

Stakeholder Review

A stakeholder is anyone who has a stake in the outcome of the strategy. To begin the process, the planning team identifies the key stakeholders. This may include key customers, suppliers, regulators, shareholders, community groups, and politicians. For each stakeholder group, a small subteam should be identified and given the assignment to return at the next meeting, understanding the expectations of the assigned stakeholder.

Core Values

Some years ago, it became popular to determine the values of the organization. Values are the things the collective organization believes deeply in. The team will need to have an open and straightforward discussion. This list should be kept reasonably small. The company executives will be expected to walk the talk. Every list should include something that concerns honesty, such as trustworthiness, integrity, ethical behavior, or truthfulness. Our capitalist society is based on honesty. All lists of virtues include this fundamental trait.

Rationale for Existence

The planning team discusses and determines why this organization should exist at the end of the planning horizon. This is also called the value proposition. This rationale answers the fundamental question: How does this organization create value for the key stakeholders, particularly the shareholders, customers, and employees?

For example, a company might exist in the future because they have developed a mousetrap equal to the current state of the art, but at 50 percent of the current price of mousetraps. They might exist is they have developed a better mousetrap, but with no increased in price. They might exist because they have found a way to use mice to the betterment of humanity, where their elimination is no longer valued. Whatever the rationale, it needs to be clearly and succinctly written so it can be communicated.

Vision (and Mission)

Planning literature does not agree on the definitions of vision and mission. For The Biz Bucks Guy, vision is what you are going to be at the end of the planning horizon. It should be stated in present tense, not future tense, "We are" as opposed to "We will be."

This vision statement can be lengthy, and therefore, a vision summary is advisable. The vision summary should be a motivating, pithy phrase that captures the essence of the vision. It will eventually become a slogan for organizational change. However, it is not a marketing slogan, which implies a statement to get customers to consume your product or service. It is primarily for internal motivation. Yes, secondarily, it could also be used in marketing.

A good example is Ford Motor Company. For many years, Ford used "At Ford, Quality Is Job #1." This was a message to every employee that Ford will not compromise on quality which was the big problem with American automakers during that era. It was actually created by a frontline employee and used to turn around their company's poor quality. It was also used for marketing. The vision summary is what people remember. You can determine if strategic implementation is going well by seeing how many frontline employees know and can passionately explain the vision summary.

A mission is usually an extension of the vision and tends to be a statement of the function or the charter of the organization. Often the difference between vision and mission is slight. There are books for vision and mission statements from various companies. Such compendia show there is no one official definition for these words.

Getting the planning team to agree on the vision statement, the vision summary, and, if needed, the mission is often more work than any other part of the strategy development process. It is crucial. It must be motivating for the entire organization and help create a sense of urgency for change.

Metrics

How will you know if you are successful in implementing the mission and vision? A comprehensive set of metrics, a.k.a. measurements, goals, or objectives, is necessary. Each metric has four parts:

1. A metric area such as safety, financial performance, process effectiveness, employee creativity, or customer satisfaction.
2. A specific metric statement such as "Improve Customer Satisfaction in Product A Customer Deliveries" accomplished by a random survey each quarter of 5 percent of all customer deliveries using a five-step Likert scale[40] of very satisfied, somewhat satisfied, neither satisfied or dissatisfied, somewhat dissatisfied, or very dissatisfied.
3. A numerical goal or target such as "Customer satisfaction… will be 95 percent very or somewhat satisfied." This target must be based on future needs in the marketplace.
4. A timeframe such as "Customer satisfaction…will be 95 percent…by March 31, 2014."

Interim goals and timeframes are also advisable for long planning horizons. "Customer satisfaction…will be 80 percent at YE 2014, 90 percent at YE 2015, and 95 percent by March 31, 2016."

It is important that all key stakeholders be represented with at least one metric. Because of this, the list of specific metric statements may be long. One company successfully managed change with over fifty metrics. The identification of stakeholders drives the vision, mission, and metrics and yields a comprehensive list of metrics. As a check, the planning team should use the balance scorecard framework. This powerful approach forces four metric areas: financial, customer, employee (learning, creativity, growth), and internal processes. Developed by Kaplan and

Norton, studies show over half of global companies use a version of their framework.[41]

As another check, the planning team should assure each metric complies with the age old adage of being SMART. That means *s*pecific, *m*easureable, *a*chievable, *r*esponsibility assigned, and *t*ime bound.

The Biz Bucks Guy adds another important check. Each metric should not be DUMB. They should avoid being *d*ubious, *u*nbelievable, *m*inor, or *b*oring.

Dubious means in doubt or unconvincing. The planning team should set metrics, particularly the numerical targets, which can be justified to the entire organization (This is *not* to say the goals should not be future-market based). The metric must be believable, meaning employees should be able to buy-in. The metric should not be insignificant. We should not make small plans or use minor measures. The goal must be motivating, not boring or unchallenging.

Beware, however, of calling them stretch goals. This term gives the organization an out when they don't meet the goal. The organization should feel the chance of attaining the goal is just about an even bet. Setting metrics is as much an art as developing the vision. The key is to unflinchingly aim at the market needs at the end of the planning horizon. As nineteenth century American poet James Russell Lowell wrote, "Not failure but low aim is crime."

At this point, a short revisit to the business word swamp is in order. This text will use *metrics, objectives,* and *goals* interchangeably. To try to differentiate subtleties between these words is fruitless. They are used throughout business literature and in casual conversation in such broad ways as to render precise definitions impossible.

Goals both for organizations and people can be (1) ongoing, continuous goals that are often repeated each planning cycle (with perhaps a change to the target) or (2) project goals that are unique and timely for a specific period.

Organization and People Strategy (OPS)

The planning team must identify changes in organizational theory and human resources needed to meet the vision. This should include performance management, rewards, culture changes, and employee and leadership competencies that need to be developed. The planning team should develop three lists for cultural behaviors (1) new behaviors to install, (2) old behaviors to abandon, and (3) old behaviors to keep. More details with examples are included in chapter 16.

The strategic planning team—or a subteam—should also recommend an organizational *fit* model that defines the key elements of the organization (see chapter 7 for more details).

SIX STEPS TO ASSESS THE PRESENT

Now that the desired future has been defined, the planning team must assess the current state of the organization. This begins with a broad analysis and ends with specific diagnoses. All of these six activities are done to indentify gaps between the future and the present. This leads to a comprehensive set of strategic initiatives.

PEESTI

Figure 7
PEESTI Analysis

	Internal Perspectives		External Perspectives	
	Strengths	Weaknesses	Opportunities	Threats
Political	1. 2. 3.	1. 2. 3.	1. 2. 3.	1. 2. 3.
Economic	1.	1.	1.	1. ... ...
Environmental				
Social				
Technological				
International				

A PEESTI is a form of SWOT analysis. In strategic planning, SWOT analysis means assessing your internal *strengths* and *weakness* and then assessing your external *opportunities* and *threats*. PEESTI means repeating the SWOT process from six different views, being the *political, economic, environmental, social, technological,* and *international* (or global) perspectives. This results in a table of findings in a format similar to figure 7.

In 1990, two now well-known scholars of business, C. K. Prahalad and Gary Hamel wrote *The Core Competencies of the Corporation.* Ever since their seminal paper, strategists have focused on identifying and improving the core competencies of an organization. The Biz Bucks strategy cycle does not relate directly to this approach. The organization's competencies will be identified in the PEESTI analysis as the *strengths* portion of each individual SWOT analysis. This list of strengths will include a few *super strengths.* These are the core competencies of the organization and should be protected and maintained above all other strategic initiatives.

Competitor Review

The planning team must carefully list each competitor, either current or emerging, over the planning horizon. This is crucial to leave no future competitor off the list. Think outside the box. At one time, the banking industry listed Microsoft as a competitor, meaning that online banking might be done by software people, not traditional banks. Each competitor should be reviewed using SWOT or PEESTI, pretending you are them. Competitive intelligence, legally obtained, may be needed. As Sun Tzu said,

There are no areas in which one does not employ spies![42]

Another tool exists for assessing the competitive business setting. Michael Porter of the Harvard Business School developed a five-point model for assessing the competitive environment of a product, service, or industry.[43] It overlaps the PEESTI and the competitor review and should be included in a full assessment of the present competitive situation. The Porter model asks five cogent questions:

1. How strong is the rivalry among existing competitors?
2. How much power do the suppliers in this industry have?
3. How much power do the customers in this industry have?
4. How strong is the threat of new entrants and the barriers to entry?
5. What is the possibility of substitute products or services?

As a reminder, planning teams should keep in mind that Porter analysis and all six steps of the present assessment are largely done to identify the organization's strategic initiatives.

Metrics Assessment

With a comprehensive set of metrics, the planning team now analyzes each metric for current and, if available, historical performance. Some may think this must have already been done to set the future targets. Not so! Remember, if you set your targets based on the present, you will get incremental improvements, not bold improvements.

Organizational Diagnosis

The planning team determines the major gaps or misfits between the current organization and its strategic goals, division goals, systems, processes, structure, and rewards. The planning team probably will only have time to do a partial review of the organization. A more complete organizational diagnosis may become a recommended strategic initiative itself. Chapter 7 provides a model for a full diagnosis.

Culture Survey

The planning team should design and run a culture survey to get a baseline. The survey will probably be a strategic initiative and rerun frequently, as much as every six months. The questions are based on the three lists of cultural behaviors developed in the organizational and people strategy noted above.

Competence Survey

The planning team should do an assessment of competencies for both front line and leaders. The list of competencies was also developed in the organizational and people strategy, as mentioned above. From this list of competencies, the organization can develop a survey to ask the employees themselves about the current state of the abilities within the organization. Such a survey should be run frequently. The Biz Bucks Guy personally ran such a survey twice a year for five years during a successful corporate culture change initiative and knows how powerful this tool can be.

STRATEGIC INITIATIVES

With the future defined and the present assessed, gaps between the two will jump out. To close the gaps, the organization will identify interventions called strategic initiatives. The planning team may develop more strategic initiatives than can be accomplished immediately. Obviously, prioritization is needed. However, the planning team needs to recognize that delegation is the key. Not all of the initiatives will be corporate-wide. Some divisions may be able to specialize in their own list of initiatives in the strategic plan. This builds momentum for change throughout the organization.

These initiatives may cover a wide gamut of topics: product or service innovation, customer satisfaction, organizational or people change (including performance management, rewards, culture and competence surveys, and related interventions), operating efficiency and effectiveness (process and project management), financial and cost management, geographic moves, and mergers and acquisitions.

The implementation of these strategic initiatives is the challenge and also the fun of strategy. Completing the strategy-development phase will seem like a big effort. But comparatively, the planning team will discover why investment analysts value the ability to implement strategy higher than the ability to develop the strategy itself.

STRATEGY BY THE POUND?

Those using this strategy cycle for the first time may have a notion that the end product is a large three-ring notebook with hundreds of pages. Such may be the case if the strategy is produced by a high-powered consultancy that gets paid by the pound.

For strategies based on a full use of this Biz Bucks strategy cycle, the end product should be less than twenty pages, including all values, metrics, PEESTI analysis, and initiatives, in addition to the vision and mission. This is a key to communicating the strategy throughout the organization.

CASCADING STRATEGIC PLANS

In a large organization of a thousand or more people, the above strategy development process can be repeated at lower levels, once the top of the organization has completed its plan. How many layers of organization should do this process depends on factors of size, trends, locale, and need. In theory, each subgroup all the way down the organization chart to the supervisor with an intact team could use this process but in increasingly simplified ways. This will lead to vertical alignment of goals and strategy.

The strategy cycle can also be adapted for use by temporary teams as they are assigned a new project to perform. The project manager will find no better team building activity.

STRATEGY FOR SMALL ORGANIZATIONS

This description of the strategy cycle obviously assumes a corporate or at least a large division size of the organization. Each boss will need to adopt them to the situation. The planning team for a department, section, or intact team will be able to see those items of the model to jettison or handle superficially. Other parts, particularly the vision development, must be done properly.

The Biz Buck Guy has seen quantoids in boss positions who want to write the vision for the group. Nothing is worse. Sorry, you brilliant quantoid, you just aren't as smart as the total team, no matter how creative, thoughtful, or sincere you are.

Some supervisors justify doing the vision themselves because "We just can't afford to have people doing this soft stuff when there is so much real work to do." Okay. Have it your way. Be a manager, not a leader. Just how much time does it really take? Just how much time *should* you and your team be spending together on sharpening the saw of your work? It usually takes about five meetings of about an hour each to complete a small group visioning exercise. It pays dividends for months, even years. Done once, it will be a regular event periodically as things change and people move and are replaced.

Some supervisors may feel that it is not their job to have a vision for their small department. In response, remember from chapter 1,

> A boss without a vision is a very boring person to work for.

Yes, it is true that your vision may be limited or narrow compared to the total organization. But don't be deceived; narrow does not mean unimportant. If your vision is to automate a new process in two years or develop a rotational program for your frontline people in six months or complete the latest project on time and within budget, such vision is a key to motivating your people and frankly yourself.

In a small group setting, such a strategic plan is sometimes called a charter. It is a mini version of a strategic plan. It is often a single page.

The Biz Bucks Guy once led an internal group of consultants with a mission to help intact teams develop their charters. Over one hundred teams went through that process. Figure 8 is a fictitious example of such a charter. This also includes a list of key processes and process owners, which will be discussed in chapter 8. Note the vision summary, "Boxes Built Best!"

Figure 8 - Department Charter Example

Acme Refinery Complex
Control Panel Fabrication Shop
Department Charter

Our Vision:

Through our constant striving for continuous improvement, we are the most effective and efficient place for individual refinery plants to procure new control panels. We are known for

Boxes Built Best!

Our Mission:

We serve as the central fabrication force for control panels (boxes, wiring, instrumentation, digital displays) for Acme Refinery Complex. We develop and maintain strong relationships with the engineering, operations, maintenance and leadership of each individual refinery concerning the quality, cost, and fabrication performance of our panels.

Our key processes and process owners are:

1. Fabricate panels (Milt Randall, department supervisor)
2. Install and startup panels (Jenny Hernandez, lead fabricator)
3. Maintain panels, if requested by refinery (Jamal Counter, maintenance tech)

We know we are successful if we:

1. Meet fabrication schedules
2. Have no rework
3. Find innovating ways to reduce fabrication costs
4. Are recognized as equipment experts in refinery controls
5. Respond to emergencies beyond our customer's expectations
6. Have a perfect safety record

The major stakeholders of our business are:

1. Refinery engineers
2. Refinery maintenance managers
3. Refinery operations managers
4. Protection and Control Test Teams
5. Instrument, component, and commodity vendors
6. The Director of Refinery Special Services (our boss' boss)

If your group or team does not report to a higher department that already has a strategic plan, you will have to make do and frankly guess what is important. You can still have a motivating vision and metrics and pray for better leadership from upper management.

VISIONING TIPS

Here are some tips to vision development.

1. Form a subteam from your intact team. Ideally, it should be about seven participants. Don't exclude anyone if you have a small intact team of eight or fewer. Have two chairs at each meeting for other members of the group on a rotating basis.

2. Use a facilitator who is objective and understands the process.

3. Discuss the strategic plan of the organization(s) above your group. Focus on aligning your group with their vision and metrics.

4. Pound on the words. Word-smithing takes time and energy and can be exasperating. It is necessary to elicit the ownership and passion from the organization necessary to make real changes.

5. Be careful of "we wanna be best" visions. These are sometimes hollow statements that will have little lasting effects. One well-known national company states that they want to be the best company in the world, bar none. Perhaps that works for them, and perhaps not. Time will tell. The test is: Does it motivate?

6. Make your vision statement nontransferrable to other departments. It is amazing that even large companies sometimes produce elegant visions that say nothing about

their unique contribution. Word for word, it could apply to a bubble gum company or a defense contractor. Platitudes, clichés, and banality are never motivating.

7. Find a pithy vision summary. This may be the toughest step of all this effort. If the team bogs down, see the next item.

8. Do right brain exercises to get creativity flashing. Ask the group to silently consider a question and then have everyone report their favorite answer. The question is: "If this department were an animal (or a car) what type would it be and why?"

This forces some right brain thinking. It may also be appropriate to ask the question twice. "Today what kind of animal are we? In three years, what kind do we need to become?"

When everyone has explained their thinking, go back to the vision summary step and see the creativity explode. Always the ultraquantoid, The Biz Bucks Guy was doubtful about this technique's real effectiveness until he tried it. It has worked each of several times he has used it. Consider the following example.

The Popeye Planning Platoon

The Biz Bucks Guy once facilitated the development of a strategic plan for a large group of managers. This group was both large in number and large in stature. Large in number because the director did not want anyone to miss. They had twenty-five on the team. Large in stature because each was a former lineman for an electric utility. Linemen bend wires, big wires, cables that carry thousands of volts. That makes for huge forearms. It was a collection of dedicated, smart, and very buff dudes. Each could have auditioned for the next Popeye movie.

After the facilitator pounded out the vision statement, they began to tire on the vision summary. Energy was down. Progress was nonexistant. "What kind of an animal does this outfit need to be?" asked The Biz Bucks Guy. After hearing twenty-five responses, he asked them what their vision summary should be. Ideas began to pop. They built small control equipment with electronic batteries of six volts. They also constructed substations and towers with up to 500,000 volts! After only a few minutes of brainstorming, one leader in the back smiled and said with some degree of pride and passion, "From six volts to lightnin', we build the best!"

That was it! The T-shirts and ball caps were ordered. Their motivating strategic plan was complete. The frontline employees thought it was great.

The Biz Bucks Guy learned the technique of having people compare their organization to an animal from a professor in grad school. It is a wonderful way to get people, particularly quantoids, thinking on the right side of their brains. The results were instant and amazing.

ADVICE FOR QUANTOIDS

This overview of the Biz Bucks strategy cycle has emphasized the mechanistic process steps. Clearly, there is a creative, intuitive, motivating component in this planning process. A recovering quantoid will need to marshal that side of his brain to lead his team to produce a motivating vision and metrics. In doing so, the leader will have accomplished the first two steps of the four steps of leadership introduced in chapter 1, creating a vision and forming a small team to help implement it. He is also well on the way to communicating the vision, the third of the four steps.

Whether applied to a small team setting or a large corporate plan, some hesitate awaiting to discover the perfect vision before moving forward. As the old adage goes,

It is better to be vaguely right than absolutely wrong!

Your understanding of the desired future may be hazy, but it is better to forge ahead and modify your vision as necessary than await for some cosmic epiphany of a precise landing point for your organization's voyage for the next three or four years.

The lack of vision and direction means your organization is doomed to a constant life of firefighting, never getting the smoldering timbers cold before the next blaze erupts. So why be good at firefighting when you are paid to design, produce, manufacture, distribute, or service clients with world-class products or services. Leave the firefighting competence to the pros in the big red trucks.

Having deftly avoided any depth about customers in this discussion of strategy, we turn our focus to them in the next chapter.

QUESTIONS FOR CURRENT LEADERS

1. Does your boss have a strategic plan for her area—one on which you can build your department's plan? If not, what can you do about that?
2. Does your group need an energy pill? Has it been waffling along with mediocre results? When was the last time you provided the visionary leadership to motivate the team?
3. Can you adopt a participative management style in team meetings that will allow your planning team to thrive and produce a strategy?

TECHNICAL ANALOG FOR LIFE AND LEADERSHIP: LEARN FROM THE REDWOODS[44]

Many have visited the giant redwoods of California. Stretching from Monterrey, California, north into Oregon, along the Pacific coast, these massive monoliths have presided over centuries of history. Many live as long as two thousand years. They can weigh over five hundred tons, and many stand over 350 feet tall. However, there is a little known fact that can be applied to the study of leadership.

The roots of the redwoods are shallow. Typically, they grow four to six feet in depth and can spread as much as 125 feet radially from the trunk. Often erosion causes the roots to be exposed. Even with the long span, this root system would be insufficient to support a three-hundred-foot, five-hundred-ton tree in a strong wind. Roots have a strong tensile and compression strength but not a strong shear strength. It is relatively easy to snap them off.

Why do the giant redwoods survive? It is because they intertangle their roots with their neighboring redwoods.

Below the surface and out of sight, there is a lattice of roots that form a strong mat as big as the entire grove itself. This lattice can hold up the heaviest of redwoods. Without this, a redwood would blow over before becoming the gracious giant it should be.

Organizations become strong when the individuals agree on a direction, called a strategic plan, and then join with one another through their shared values. When a group of people are motivated at their core with common values, it is like a lattice of roots that will help any organization survive all but the strongest of storms. This is why the Biz Bucks strategy cycle includes the important step of identifying the organization's core values.

CHAPTER 5

KNOWING YOUR CUSTOMER

"WE DON'T HAVE CUSTOMERS..."

When The Biz Bucks Guy left the technical marketing department of a large equipment manufacturer and became, for the first (and only) time, a real engineer in a new company, he was a bit disoriented during the first few days. Fortunately, the supervisor called a staff meeting. Near the end of the meeting, The Biz Bucks Guy asked a question. His phrasing was based on his previous experience in marketing. "Being new, I need to ask something. Who is my customer?"

One senior member of the twenty-engineer team got a look of disdain on his face. He leaned forward, and with a certain rancor in his voice, he pompously responded for the group, "We don't have customers. We're *engineering!*"

The Biz Bucks Guy supposes there was some redeeming social value to his attitude. It is nice that one has pride in one's job. But this senior engineer could not have been more wrong. Everyone has a customer in business. They may be real (external) customers who buy products or services and therefore are the lifeblood for a company. They may be internal customers who use the output of your work as input for theirs to create value within a given business process.

If the senior engineer really believed he had no customer, The Biz Bucks Guy hopes he hid his head as he backed up to the pay window each payday. In business, everyone serves. Everyone is an important supplier of products or services to someone.

FIVE KEY CUSTOMER PROCESSES

This chapter deals with mostly internal customers. While not always the case, most quantoids will gravitate to leadership positions in functions that serve internally. Nonetheless, the principles in this chapter will apply to external customer situations as well.

The processes to know your customer are few but vital:

1. Identify your key customers.
2. Talk to them, and learn what they expect of you.
3. Measure your performance.
4. Exceed their expectations
5. If you fail, recover quickly and strongly.

While simple, these principles are sometimes deceivingly difficult to apply.

1. Indentifying Your Customers

If your group has developed a list of stakeholders for your strategic plan or charter, this step is probably complete. If not, take the time to talk to your frontline employees, to your boss, and to potential key customers to see if they agree whom your key customers are. In a broad sense, all stakeholders are customers. For example, a regulator that your department supports with information may be viewed as such. For the purposes of this chapter, however, we will focus on either internal customers or external customers, not other stakeholders.

2. Talking to Them—The Customer Meeting

Once identified, you and your team should begin developing a lasting relationship with each key customer. There are many ways to do that, both formal and informal.

The primary way to begin, which is a blinding flash of the obvious once understood but not always appreciated initially, is to have at least one formal customer meeting with each key customer. The Biz Bucks Guy led an internal consulting team that facilitated over 250 customer meetings. Here are some suggestions based on those experiences.

a. Make a formal request for a meeting. Explain your objectives and agenda.

b. Prepare your staff. Some may be reticent or flat-out scared. It can be a sweaty proposition for some to meet their customers face-to-face. Admit to them that there are four kinds of customer meetings and only one is desirable:

   o   War – Hostilities could breakout and improvement of relationship would be delayed significantly.

   o   Advertisement – The team makes a presentation about their charter, and there is no real feedback, only passive interest. Everyone leaves wondering why they had to meet.

   o   Love-In – Both your team and the customer representatives express appreciation to each other, and no real improvements get discussed.

   o   A 4F Meeting – The ideal customer meeting where *f*rank *f*riendly *f*orthright *f*eedback is obtained.

c. Determine if an objective facilitator is necessary. You will sense the answer to that while preparing your team.

d. At the meeting do the following:

- o Review your draft charter, as discussed in chapter 4. Tell the customers that you intend to revise the charter based on their input from this customer meeting.
- o After reviewing your draft charter, focus on needs of the customer. Revise those parts of the charter accordingly.
- o Always ask if there is any work you do for them that could be simplified or eliminated.
- o Always ask if another group does similar work for them.
- o Develop ways of measuring your performance and their satisfaction (see process 3 below for more details).
- o Discuss the value of the meeting and the possible need to hold another.
- o Let the meeting naturally flow. Many discoveries are possible.
- o Sincerely thank them for their time.

The vast majority of customer meetings turn out as positive 4F meetings. It is amazing how many frontline employees do not know the people they serve. Just getting to place the face with the voice or the e-mail writer can be a wow for many.

Here are three examples of productive 4F customer meetings:

The Case of the Cocky Customer Service Reps

One team was very *creative* in rebelling against the notion of meeting with their customers. Their customers were real, external, bill-paying customers of the company's services. These team members were customer service reps or CSRs. The CSRs claimed, "We are all so experienced in serving our customers that it would be a waste of time to have a special meeting." They all had twenty-five or more years in the same general position.

In preparing for the meeting, the CSRs wrote a department charter and listed the expectations of their customers, at least as the CSRs understood them. With the *encouragement* of their VP, they reluctantly set up three customer meetings.

In each of the three meetings, the customers were perfectly clear on what their primary expectation was. It was the same item from each customer. Interestingly, that expectation could not be found on the draft charter. More interestingly, the customers maintained the company was not doing a good job of meeting this expectation.

What was it? The customers did not want to call the company and get shoveled around from person to person to get an answer. They wanted someone to advocate for them and help them get the right person quickly and stay with them until this issue was resolved.

The charter was revised. Training proceeded. Performance improved. If you don't take time to communicate with your lifeblood, the real customers, sometimes, you have one year of experience, twenty-five times.

The One Number Report

Near the end of another customer meeting, one member of the team asked if their customer had any comments on the timeliness or completeness of a major monthly report that this person produced for this customer. The report was over an inch thick. It contained operating information for several plants and their sales. It took this analyst three days each month to gather and produce the report. It was a major deadline for the department each month. He was justified in asking if he could do anything better to help the customer. What he learned was shocking.

"Excuse me. Did you say you did this report for me?" asked the customer. "I use *one number* on page 2 each month. Surely you do this huge report for someone else."

"Nope. Just for you," replied the analyst as his and his boss's jaws both dropped open. This *doorstop* report had been assembled for years. Then dismay turned to delight. The analyst got a huge smile as he realized he now had three days each month to do more productive and meaningful work.

The supervisor was a bit embarrassed, but that is okay. Better to have a little egg on his face now in a controlled setting than laying a big one if this was discovered in a more public, uncontrolled setting. Unintended productivity improvements often result from these small customer meetings.

The World's First K&HH Meeting

Some decades ago, before the advent of personal computers, a project engineer had been promoted to budget manager for capital projects in the construction division of a large capital-intensive company. The company spent about $1 million each day on capital. The capital forecasting and budgeting system was broken. The finance department was raising more capital than needed each year. The annual forecasts from the construction division were always high. Real high. Fifty million dollars high. The new capital budget manager was supposed to fix the problem.

The first clue was learning what their customer really wanted. The new quantoid-turned-manager took his entire department on a trip to visit the finance department, several miles away. Not knowing the concept of a customer meeting, he called this a K&HH meeting. K&HH stood for *kiss and hold hands* with your customer.

In the first of three K&HH meetings, the capital budget team learned that the level of accuracy that was really needed was about $500,000 each month, not the $5,000 as presumed by the construction division executives.

To meet the incorrectly perceived needs of the finance department, the construction division had established a very bureaucratic, paper-heavy estimating system. A flurry of paper flew around the project departments. Engineers estimated and reestimated. Managers reviewed, discussed, and returned and rereviewed. There was no difference between a capital expenditure for one thousand dollars and one for a one-billion-dollar decision.

Each project was approved multiple times in its life cycle. This was multiplied by several hundred projects active at one time. It was a burdensome, unresponsive, untimely, and inaccurate approach.

Common sense says the nature of a project engineer is to think both optimistically and myopically about a project. Using their rosy scenario perspective and translating it into a forecast of future cash flows will always yield an unduly high request for funds. When the K&HH meeting divulged the real accuracy needs was less stringent on a monthly basis, the capital team was able to devise a simpler system, and they were eventually allowed to adjust the requests for funds from the project engineers at a summary level. The capital budget became much more accurate. The finance department was elated. The project engineers were also. The forecasting efforts were easier and less frequent.

Why? Because a department talked to its customer. And then got creative.

3. Measuring Customer Satisfaction and Performance

Measuring customer satisfaction is a broad topic. It allows a new quantoid-turned-boss to practice dealing with the ambiguous.

Regarding a small group, you will probably not contract with JD Powers to tell you how your internal customer feels about your services. Some ideas for measuring (or at least sensing) your customer performance are:

a. A Survey. At the initial customer meeting, the customer may agree to complete some sort of a survey. Today this should be web enabled, perhaps using collaboration software, such as MicroSoft's SharePoint. The design of the survey may be the subject of a next customer meeting. The survey might be run more frequently at first and then less frequently thereafter.

While a survey is probably the only valid way to quantoidally measure feelings, it is sometimes not culturally acceptable. If every department is doing a unique survey with each customer, the entire organization will experience *survey fatigue* quickly.

Some large organizations have opted to do an internal customer satisfaction survey (ICSS). A central group runs this effort. Every small group participates at the same time and rates their internal suppliers. Consistent measurements are realized. Consistent objectives can be set. Top management can find out which groups need extra help.

b. Keep statistics on projects and other products or services, such as on-time-ness, adherence to estimates, and scope changes.
c. Have ongoing customer meetings to ask how you are doing.
d. Take their boss to lunch. On a one-on-one basis, you, as leader of your group, should visit regularly with your counterpart of your customers. Learn how your group is doing. Make adjustments and provide feedback, as necessary.

All these, along with your own creativity, help your group avoid the "throw it over the wall" service ethic. They will want to know how they are doing. Your people will naturally rise to the level of expectations made clear in the customer meetings. The two old adages still apply,

> If you can't measure it, you can't manage it.
> People don't do what you expect. They do what you inspect.

4. Exceeding Expectations

Some people call this the art of *underpromising and overperforming*. It is not a bad approach in many cases. For the purposes of this chapter, if there is a consistent lack of performance in the eyes of your customer, you probably have a *process* problem, not a *people* problem.

In any event, your team will generally know how to improve performance. If you use a participative leadership style, you can lead them to exceed their key customer's expectations. This is critical because no organization has the resources to exceed every expectation of every customer.

5. Recovering after Failure

Occasionally, your team will fall short of expectations. Studies indicate that recovery after failure of service can cement relationships between suppliers and customer more than consistently good performance.[45]

WING-TO-WING

One not-well-known customer technique deserves mentioning. Many are familiar with how General Electric used Six Sigma and WorkOut processes to revolutionize its processes under the former CEO, Jack Welch.[46] Before Jack retired, he and Steve Kerr, GE's chief learning officer, implemented a lesser-known tool called wing-to-wing.

GE supplies jet engines. But there may be many things it might do to help an aircraft company in developing a new plane. By looking wing-to-wing, GE can see the big picture through the eyes of their aircraft-building customers. Wing-to-Wing became a metaphor for seeing beyond your normal services when working with customers by seeing all their challenges, regardless of the industry. You may see things outside of your normal products or service and be able to supply your customers with other products or services. All it takes is knowing your customers, learning their challenges, and applying your creativity.

This may seem to have less application for internal customers than external customers. But what if you run a team who is versed in project management techniques and one of your customers has been given a rare but significant project. Your assistance to educate and assist your customer with project planning and control could pay dividends in many ways to them, your group, and the entire company.

NEGOTIATING WITH CUSTOMERS

This chapter rightly focuses on small teams, improving their internal customer relationships. If your customers are external, you will also need to develop skills in negotiating which are largely beyond the scope of this book. One negotiating principle is worthy of mentioning.

Each quantoid-turned-boss should know you can win too much in a negotiation.

Real-life examples abound, but consider these two examples.

Genghis Khan and Jaws

This is an artificial experience at a training course, which in reality was not artificial at all. People's careers and reputations were involved.

Many years ago, The Biz Bucks Guy attended a weeklong negotiating workshop put on by Harvard Business School and sponsored by his large equipment manufacturing employer. Sixty attended, thirty from supply chain and thirty from marketing. The workshop pitted five teams of buyers and five teams of peddlers. On his peddler team was the most aggressive, mean-spirited, overbearing negotiator at the conference. They were put into several negotiations with other teams. Because of one member of their team, their resident Genghis Khan, they won. And they won. And won some more. Each day they were undefeated. No other team could match their performance.

At first, the entire team was enthused. But that soon waned. The ego of Mr. Khan began to grow each time they came back to the plenary sessions. He was ruthless. He was often less than ingenuous. To advance their team's score, he took great glee in breaking promises with alliances with other teams. The sponsoring company was famous for using results of these sessions to promote people. It got very serious.

On the final day with about thirty minutes to go, the other nine teams formed an alliance. None of them cared who won among them. They only wanted Genghis Khan to lose…and lose big. This collusion was successful. Their team was tromped by the nine. They came in dead last! The other teams were thrilled. Most of their team had an inner smile also. Mr. Khan left with his head down. He just faded away after the close. The Harvard professor was spot on when he concluded the week's event by saying, "We have all learned an important lesson, *even Jaws dies at the end of the movie!*"

Long-term relationships and honesty in business count.

A Brazilian Triumph

A business school anecdote concerns a large consumer of cocoa who sent a new buyer to Brazil to negotiate a long-term contract with their cocoa supplier. He returned with the best contract ever seen. There was a glut of cocoa on the market and demand worldwide was down. He negotiated his supplier to his knees. He returned triumphantly.

The president of the company called him in. He told him that this company did not do business like that. He told the buyer to get on a plane, return to Brazil, and renegotiate a higher, more typical contract. He did.

A few years later, the market turned. There was a bad crop of cocoa. This buyer was able to secure all the cocoa they needed at a reasonable price while many other users of cocoa were unable to get any product at any price.

Relationships matter. As the phrase goes,

> You can shear sheep every day,
> but you can skin 'em only once.

YOUR INFINITE AMOUNT OF SPARE TIME

Returning to the small group setting, some may say, "This is all well and good, but we don't have an infinite amount of spare time to meet with customers. Our workload is too stifling. Our customers are in the same boat."

The Biz Bucks Guy suggests you find a way. Think about what percent of time should be spent by your entire team in a "sharpen the saw" mode. In the long run, building customer relations will save your group time.

QUESTIONS FOR CURRENT LEADERS

1. Do you know all the problems of your internal or external customers? Can you apply the wing-to-wing tool? Are there things you might be able to supply to help them?
2. How are you *really* doing with your customers? How do you know if you don't ask them?
3. Do the members of your team have personal relationships with your team's customers like you do? If not, why not? What can you do about that?

TECHNICAL ANALOG FOR LIFE AND LEADERSHIP: OLD DOGS AND NEUROPLASTICITY

For decades, psychologists have told us that the only real opportunity to shape one's brain use (feeling, thinking, basic behavior, or emotional balance) is the early years of life. After that, we are used and broken furniture. Fortunately, that idea has been inducted into the dopey ideas hall of fame. The phrase used by researchers to describe the brain's ability to change is *neuroplasticity*. Academic researcher and author James T. Summerhays writes,

> As it turns out, more recent research into neuroplasticity has firmly established that the adult brain is capable of profound changes even in the later stages of life.[47]

Hurray for us old dogs. We *can* learn new tricks.

More importantly, people whom we lead can learn better attitudes, adopt more broad thinking, adapt to the changes in strategy, and generally be happier and more cooperative at work. The catalyst may be some help from their leadership.

We all know a few "rain cloud" people. These are the people on whom it is constantly raining at work. No matter where they go, it is always raining on them. They allege no one understands them. They are the smart ones, but no one ever listens. The boss is incompetent. If they were boss, everything would fit together, and we would not have so much waste. The one thing a rain cloud person wants is to have you walk under their cloud and get rained on with them. Watercooler conversations make for an ideal place for the rain cloud to grow.

Whether you believe the latest research in neuroplasticity or just your common sense, all leaders should strive to help people see a better, happier, more productive life at work. If you have inherited a rain cloud person, it is part of your leadership duties to help them change. The Biz Bucks Guy knows, from personal experience, that people change. It is a wonderful part of the leadership job.

CHAPTER 6

QUANTOIDAL BUSINESS SMARTS

The quantitative skills of business are covered in four subject areas: statistics, accounting, finance, and economics, or the *SAFE* subjects. In chapter 2, The Biz Bucks Guy suggested that the quantitative skills of business are not easily learned on the job and that a classroom environment is best. Therefore, this chapter assumes that if you are needing development in these subjects, you are going to take coursework soon in each of these four areas.

This chapter presents useful background in each of these four subjects and a few examples to support the need for more education.

Some may have obtained many of these skills outside of formal training. To help a new leader know if he has the requisite quantitative skills, The Biz Bucks Guy has provided Appendix B which has lists of principles for the *SAFE* subjects. By reading these lists, one may know if additional education is necessary.

Each of these four academic fields has spawned an enormous set of jokes. A few of the classics are included in the lists.

STATISTICS

All leaders at every level of an organization should be conversant with several concepts and principles of statistics. Most college-level courses go much deeper into this fascinating subject than necessary for most leaders. The basics are not nearly as difficult. However, without these basics, leaders will be impeded in doing their job.

For example, if you have been given an average score for your department on an attitude survey, your first question should be what is the standard deviation of the data? Standard deviation is the measure of the spread-outed-ness of the data. Did most agree on each question or were there many outliers?

Another important use of statistical competence for most leaders is the skill of improving your business processes. Business process improvement (BPI) is a skill set all leaders should master. This requires a certain depth in statistics.

ACCOUNTING

There are four general types of accounting: financial, tax, regulatory, and managerial. Managerial includes cost accounting, such as activity-based accounting. Governmental regulators of business require businesses to use the first three. Firms do managerial accounting for themselves to help them manage the business. Unfortunately, many budget systems and accounting reports are designed to meet the needs of the first three types, not the managerial needs of the leaders of small groups or departments.

If a leader does not have the basic understanding of income statements, balance sheets, and cash flow statements, they will likely not progress up the chain beyond first-line supervision. Furthermore, budgeting will be a mystery. Why can't I add operating costs with capital costs? What is depreciation? Why is our profit not pure cash, but some convoluted, garbled version of cash? These are representative of a myriad of questions that a non-accounting literate person will have if moved into leadership.

FINANCE

The finance department has three primary roles: (1) to raise capital for the operations of the firm, (2) to forecast long-term capital needs, and (3) to consult with management on financial decisions. A new leader in a non-financial area, such as maintenance, engineering, construction, product development, marketing, or advertising, will interface with finance regularly on issues that arise in the course of business. The more the leader understands this vital support area of the company, the easier it will be to support them and to know what to ask from them. Much of this interface will concern spending decisions.

Spending decisions can be grouped into two types: operating decisions (short-term, relatively smaller dollars) and investment decisions (long-term, typically larger dollars). The ability to make such decisions requires a full understanding of time-value of money principles and the strengths and weaknesses of various valuation techniques.

A simple example is the purchase of a new piece of equipment, such as a new pump. Not all pumps are created equal. For your situation, you may consider an inexpensive pump that has poor operating characteristics and therefore high operating costs. Conversely, you might consider an expensive pump with low operating costs. A recommended selection will largely be based on the future, after tax, relevant cash flows, discounted by a risk-adjusted discount rate. This is an axiom of finance. This classic example will repeat itself in many situations, like a new welding training course, an advertising sign, a design decision on a new product.

Competence in basic financial principles is a basic attribute for upward mobility in most organizations.

ECONOMICS

Economics is the study of scarcity.[48] Its principles play out in almost every aspect of society. Free economies decide prices of all products and services. Non-free economies create shortages.

The two branches of economics are micro- and macroeconomics. Microeconomics deals with the price and quantity for individual products and services. It is all about supply and demand on a individual product basis. There is almost complete unanimity between economists on the fundamentals of microeconomics.

Macroeconomics deals with the ramifications of economic policy on large entities, typically national economies. There is almost no consensus between economists on macroeconomics. Macro is fraught with political opinion. Because of this ideological bent in macroeconomics, little will be discussed in this volume. For more depth in macroecomonics, a leader can refer to The Biz Bucks Blog (www.bizbucksguy.com) which includes several 250-word essays on macroeconomics.

While there are many camps of macroeconomists, they tend to form into two large groups. The Keynesians believe in demand side, government based solutions to economic problems. The Hayekians believe in free markets and supply side solutions.

Each new leader should be familiar with microeconomic principles to navigate well in their organization. Macroeconomics becomes more important if promotions move the leader up the chain of command. Certainly, top management positions need great depth in both micro- and macroeconomics. Street-smart economic intuition is developed largely by learning principles and then reading and pondering about classic case studies in economic situations. Here is a personal case study to help start new students on the road to economic competence.

The Barstow Bargain

A well understood principle of macroeconomics states that all shortages are caused by government intervention into a market. This seems far-fetched to some who have not contemplated such an assertion. Here is an anecdote to help economic newbies understand this principle.

In 1973, The Biz Bucks Guy with Ms. Biz Bucks and Baby Bucks #1, aged 11 months, were travelling from Phoenix, Arizona, to San Jose, California, where The Biz Bucks Guy was working for General Electrics' nuclear energy division. It was January 2.

The Biz Bucks Guy was a bit naive about the roads. His map showed a nice wide road from Barstow to Bakersfield. He did not appreciate that the road went over the southern tip of the Sierra Nevada mountains at the Tehachapi Pass. He also did not know a winter storm was coming from the west. Fortunately, they needed gas in Barstow and stopped west of town. The Biz Bucks Guy was instantly aware of trouble as an eighteen-wheeler pulled into a pump next to him. The truck had about twelve inches of fresh snow on the hood. The Biz Bucks Guy asked the driver about the road ahead. He was told that, without chains, he was going nowhere tonight. The Biz Bucks Guy was only slightly introduced to the concept of chains, having grown up in the desert Southwest. With Ms. Biz Bucks's encouragement, they made an abrupt turn and found a Motel 6 in Barstow for the night.

The Biz Bucks Guy got the weather report. He needed to get home to San Jose that next day. He must be at work on the following day. He began to call around to find out where he could buy a set of chains in Barstow.

His first phone call startled him. The price for a set of chains, which was normally about $8 in those days, was suddenly $15! "That's a rip off," he told the store clerk. He called another number. The price was now $17! He was very perturbed. "How can this be? Taking advantage of a young couple with a small baby like that...the thought of it. It's just not right!"

So he made another call—$20! At that point, The Biz Bucks Guy got the message. Buy now! He got in the car and found a gas station. He happily bought a set of chains for $24. The owner said he housed about two hundred sets in a locker out back. Every ten years, he sells out in one day. Today was the day! He was going to order another two hundreds sets soon.

At breakfast the next morning, The Biz Bucks Guy compared notes with several other travelers in the same predicament. For one person, the price that morning was $64!

"That's gouging!" the economically challenged Biz Bucks Guy said to the person.

Speaking across forty years of experience, The Biz Bucks Guy now would say to his younger self, "Wait a minute, young Biz Bucks Guy, the old Biz Bucks Guy chooses to differ. Gouging is not a term of economics; it is a term of politics."

Any time there is a change in supply and demand, the market adjusts, often rather quickly. A new market clearing price is determined so fast that a politician hardly has time to get in front of a camera to tell everyone they will fix everything for all you poor souls who have to live in a free-market society.

In reality, if a politician had the time to impose a cap on the price of chains that day, here's what would have happened. There were only so many chains in Barstow. A few entrepreneurs had taken a business risk and inventoried a stockpile of chains, some apparently for ten years. Nonetheless, there was only a finite amount of chains. When the snowstorm hit, the demand for chains rose immediately. The entrepreneurs knew this was their time to receive a return for their risk. The price began to rise. Each entrepreneur began sensing the prices buyers were willing to pay. These are price signals. If the phone kept ringing, the sellers would raise prices. If the calls slowed down, prices might drop. Apparently, the phones kept ringing right into the morning.

Demanders represented various situations. Some were only inconvenienced by the storm. A two-day wait for the roads to be cleared by the highway department was not a problem. It only meant another night in Motel 6. Some, however, really needed chains, as it was for the Biz Bucks family. The market worked. The supply of chains was properly allocated to those who had the greatest need. Those who had to get out of Barstow got out. Those with flexibility enjoyed the downtime.

What if the governor had immediately passed a law capping the price of chains at $14? The supply of chains would have sold out very quickly. The first persons to call would win and leave Barstow, but the first callers were not necessarily the ones who needed to leave Barstow the most.

The government cap would have caused a shortage. Some people who really needed to get out of town would be unable. Price signals are distorted by government intervention to the detriment of the demanders who needed chains and to the detriment of the suppliers who took a business risk and were not allowed an honest return.

How would the suppliers act when it's time to order chains for the next storm? Many would leave the risky tire chain business. During the next storm, supply would be much smaller. More travelers with critical needs would be stranded. No thanks, politicians, please don't meddle in the market Gouging is undefined in economics. Do the statesman-like thing and explain these principles to your constituency, rather than pander to them for a few votes next election.

HOW TO GET THESE
QUANTOIDAL BUSINESS SMARTS

The Biz Bucks Guy encourages all those who feel the need to improve their skills in the SAFE subjects to get into a classroom, if possible. If you have a high school diploma, you can get all you need by taking the first course in each of these subjects at a local community college. If you have a college degree, you can take the 500-level courses that would count toward a masters degree in business. The best option, but one which few can accomplish during life's challenging journey, is a full MBA program. Many universities have night courses, online courses, and executive (weekend) courses that may fit the needs of those fortunate to be able to devote such time and treasure.

To help those who cannot attend a college curriculum, or those who are already in leadership and need the basic business skills quickly, The Biz Bucks Guy has established an online alternative, www.BizBasicsOnline.com. It will be available in 2014. It will consist of a series of courses covering these SAFE subjects. It will be quick, affordable, and flexible. It provides for a self-paced learning experience.

RETURN FROM QUANTOID HEAVEN

Those with quantoidal tendencies may have felt something akin to a safe harbor from this chapter. These SAFE subjects provide a synaptic reinvigoration for our left brain.

We quantoids can really get into these subjects and conclude we are ready for leadership. Not so fast, Einstein. Yes, these quantitative skills of boss-hood are great differentiators. Only quantoids become adept at using them. However, like your high school math teachers used to say, for leadership, they are "necessary but not sufficient." If you can also become talented in the other eleven skills of leadership readiness, your future in boss-hood looks bright.

Leaving the SAFE-ty of this quantoid heaven, we now turn to softer skills, beginning with the subject of how to organize your group, department, division, or company. Remember, recalling chapter 1,

The soft stuff is the hard stuff!

QUESTIONS FOR CURRENT LEADERS

1. Do the reports you get from your accounting system help you run your department or are they for others, like top management or the budget department? If the reports are not much used, what information *do* you need to better run your department? With the advances in IT tools, why can't your company provide you what you really need?

2. Does your company use derivatives to hedge risk? How far out do they hedge? How does it help the bottom line?

3. If you do a financial valuation for a spending decision, does your company use overheads (a.k.a. burdens or loads)? If so, you need to understand if a given overhead is a relevant cost to your problem. Some overheads need to be divided into a relevant and nonrelevant portion for your specific problem.

TECHNICAL ANALOG FOR LIFE AND LEADERSHIP: TOP-DOWN DESIGNS

A talented civil engineer, Ollie Briggs, once taught a much younger Biz Bucks Guy that in civil engineering you design from the top down, then build from the bottom up. That certainly made sense to this new engineer. How would you know how deep to make the foundations and how strong to make the framing if you did not know the mass that the foundation and framing were going to support? You need to determine the size of each floor, top to bottom, in that order, before completing the design.

Construction on the other hand must obviously progress from bottom to top.

Organizations should also follow a logical top-down approach to design itself for the future. That is the purpose of strategic planning, which provides direction and vision. Only those leaders highest on the organization chart can do this organizational engineering. Once the direction is planned, the various functions can construct their infrastructure. Financial wherewithal can be assessed, operations can be modified, product development refocused, people hired or trained, all to realize the vision. Without an initial design, from the people at the top, these functions are left to guesswork and any coordination between them would be minimal.

CHAPTER 7

ORGANIZATIONAL BUSINESS SMARTS

ORGANIZATIONAL AMBIGUITY

Unlike the quantitative tools discussed in the previous chapter, much of these organizational skills can be obtained through self-study, practice, and experience, not only in a formal classroom setting. This should not belie their importance. No ardent quantoid should be misled. This topic is of supreme importance. People will praise you or vilify you based on your acumen in this area. Plus, it is profitable. As one CEO of a small but well-known food manufacturing firm said after completing his MBA curriculum, the field of organizational smarts "made me the most money of anything we learned."[49]

Quantoids who are new to this organizational world must learn to deal with organizational ambiguity. Life is different than their frontline experience. In designing and improving organizations, some of the puzzle pieces don't fit together. In fact, some of the puzzle pieces may not even be in the box! Try as you may, as boss, your organization will not fit together perfectly, as many of your creative efforts have in the past, such as a circuit design or a set of quarterly financial statements.

Your design experience will be more like the microbiologist who starts a cell colony and watches it grow, encouraging change, adding chemicals, removing cells, observing complexities, *and* being in wonder at the creations of the colony.

FIXING YOUR FINGER

To begin our journey into this organizational laboratory, let's consider the following absurd story:

You have cut your index finger and feel you need a few stitches. So off to the emergency room you go. After a long wait, you finally meet the ER doctor. Without looking at your finger, he haughtily informs you, "I am the best doctor in this entire country at taking out appendixes. I am scheduling you for immediate surgery."

What would you do?

No one wants a doctor like that. All of us would skedaddle. One creative participant in a Biz Bucks mini-MBA class said, "I would show him another finger as I ran out the door!"

This fictitious doctor's mistake was being so enamored with his skill that he forgot to diagnose before determining action.

In the medical realm, this scene is preposterous. Everyone knows:

Prescription without diagnosis is malpractice!

So why is it apparently not preposterous when *doctoring* organizations? Why is it that CEOs, other top leaders, and many consultants get so enamored with the latest management fad that they don't take time to diagnose problems before prescribing the solution?

Frankly, consulting firms can sway top managers with an effective presentation, and the organization is rushed to the operating room for *fad du jour* surgery.

ORGANIZATIONAL DIAGNOSIS: FROM FAD TO FIT

To avoid such expensive, disruptive, and often unneeded interventions, managers should learn to diagnose organizational problems first, then second, fix the problem. If necessary, search for a consultant that has experience in the particular area of need.

The major reason for not using this diagnose-then-fix approach is most leaders do not have an understanding of how to diagnose problems in an organization. To diagnose organizational problems, leaders need a framework for understanding all the elements of an organization and the ability to analyze how the elements fit together. With such an understanding, a leader can evaluate the effects on the entire organization when a change is proposed. Without a framework, a leader is left to wing it and be at the mercy of a consultant's marketing efforts.

This powerful tool is sometimes called *systemic fit* or more simply *organizational fit*. The process of doing it is fit analysis.

The result of fit analysis is a list of issues or organizational pathologies called *misfits*. Fit analysis provides a logical way to identify pathologies that reduce the effectiveness of an organization and then to eliminate or at least mitigate them.

Consider the following not-completely-fictitious example of a misfit in a small group setting.

Work Unit 14

Work Unit 14 consists of five multiskilled craftworkers in a large manufacturing facility that covers several thousand acres located in a warm climate. The warm climate makes it advantageous to build the manufacturing process outside with little weather protection. Unlike other departments, Work Unit 14 has a seasonal peak in its workload. The peak is tied to the local weather, which is historically stormy during July and August. During this period, members of Work Unit 14 put in much overtime, around the clock, outside, in wet and windy conditions to keep the manufacturing facility's process infrastructure intact. The firm, however, has a one-size-fits-all policy of rewarding performance for all employees in January, after the end of their fiscal year, five months after the action has subsided for Work Unit 14.

Common sense indicates rewards should not be delayed too long after meritorious performance to provide the intended motivation and continued good performance.

A new supervisor of Work Unit 14, who was previously a plant engineer, diagnoses his work unit and discovers a misfit between two organizational elements: the corporate rewards policy and the seasonal work processes of Work Unit 14.

Recognizing this misfit, the new supervisor writes his manager who, in turn, involves his boss, the VP of plant services, and the human resources (HR) VP. A meeting is proposed to deal with the misfit.

At the meeting, three options are brainstormed:

1. The VP of plant services makes an impassioned plea to liberalize the rewards policy for the entire company to allow flexibility of rewards timing.
2. The new supervisor suggests allowing Work Unit 14 to have a special policy allowing it to have a "Storms 'R Us" party in September each year where special team and individual rewards are presented. The January pay for performance process would remain intact.
3. The HR VP suggests keeping pay as it is and move the stormy weather to December where it should be, by golly! This means there is no real chance to change the corporate approach at this time.

After some discussion, the second idea is adapted. This represents a compromise and at least mitigates the misfit of delaying rewards long after the natural performance period. The supervisor did well. He diagnosed a misfit, proposed a solution, worked through the chain of command, and was a leader in solving an organizational issue.

MODELS, MODELS, AND MORE MODELS

So what are the elements of an organization?

Big problem here! There is no one accepted answer to that question among scholars. For us practitioners, therefore, ambiguity reigns in this field. There are many models—or graphical representations—of organizational elements. They differ in shape, the number of elements, and in their definitions. Most models can be reconciled to another, given a jargon transplant. It is no wonder that most leaders cannot diagnose organizational problems.

Each organization should select (or develop for themselves) an organizational element model to use. This can be part of the strategic plan discussed in chapter 4, the "Organization and People Strategy." With such a model, employees will better communicate organizational issues, develop consistent and integrated management systems, and be able to perform fit analysis.

Some of the existing models are quite famous and highly useful...and copyrighted. By the numbers, The Biz Bucks Guy's favorites are:

- The five-point Star Model from USC's Center for Effective Organizations (CEO)[50]
- The Six-Box Model of Marvin Weisbord[51]
- The 7-S Model from McKinsey[52]
- The eight-element L-Model from Llewellyn Consulting in Figure 9
- The eleven-point road map of Larry Greiner.[53]

So given their copyrighted nature of these other models, we will use the L-Model for our discussion.

THE ORGANIZATIONAL FIT L-MODEL

Figure 9

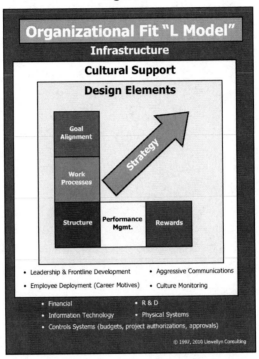

Here is an eight-element framework for organizational effectiveness and assessing fit. It is even more motivating and useful, as mentioned above, for an organization to have a team of interested people develop a homegrown model for their organization.

The first six elements of the L-Model are the design elements. These are the key management systems that leaders can and must design to work in an integrated way. The final two elements support the design elements.

Before discussing the eight, we need to visit the word swamp again. A *management system* is defined as a tool, technique, or process used by management for implementing strategy. This is not from a textbook. This is a practical definition developed by The Biz Bucks Guy. It differentiates the word *system* from the IT world's *information system*. Management systems are synonymous with the organizational elements of the L-model and all the sub-elements discussed below. Each element or system provides the means to develop and implement strategy. That is the emphasis. No tool, technique, process, or project should be done unless it develops or implements the organization's strategy. This text uses *management system* and *organizational element* interchangeably.

So let's consider these eight elements individually, beginning with the primary focus: Strategy.

Strategy

The arrow represents strategy or direction. Whether called a strategic plan, a business plan, vision, mission, strategic intent or group charter, every effective organization must have a direction.

The people throughout the organization know the direction and are both enthused and challenged by it. Accomplishing this is crucial and is part of a successful communications intervention.

Goal Alignment (Vertical and Horizontal)

Once the parent organization develops its strategic direction, subordinate organizations should set goals that are aligned with that direction. When the various levels of the organization are linked with cascading goals from top to bottom, the organization has accomplished *vertical* alignment.

When goals of the various functions support one another, they have accomplished *horizontal* alignment.

It is difficult to obtain vertical alignment. It is more difficult to obtain horizontal alignment.

Work Processes and Projects

The entire work of the organization has been formally listed. Every process and project is tied to the strategy. No process or project is done unless it has this fundamental fit to strategy.

All work is either recurring work (called processes) or onetime efforts (called projects). Work-process managers are assigned to each key process. They ensure work-process-improvement tools are being applied, as appropriate. Each process and project is tied to cascading goals or must fit with the overall organizational strategy.

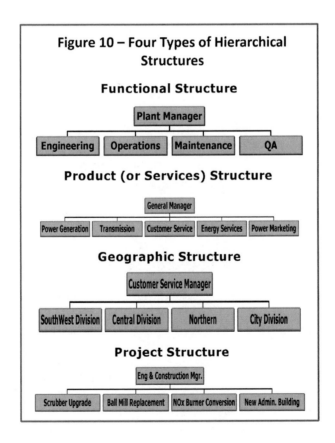

Figure 10 – Four Types of Hierarchical Structures

Organizational Structure

For this discussion, structure refers to the organization chart. The four basic structural hierarchies (pyramids) include *functional, product, project,* and *geographic* (see figure 10). Large organizations have combinations of all these hierarchies.

A fifth nonhierarchical organizational option is *matrix,* which blends two or more of the first four. Matrix requires employees to have more than one boss. While difficult to implement, matrix organizations can be very effective when implemented in a planned way in mature organizations. More on matrix structures below.

Ultimately, structure depends on how certain issues of importance play out in their marketplace. These include centralization versus decentralization, strategic initiatives, and metrics. In the end, the organizational chart must fit with the work processes and projects (the previous element).

Performance Management

Leaders are able to enhance the performance of their direct employees through a recurring three-step process. The third step is the performance review. But there is much more to do before that final step, as discussed in chapter 10.

Performance metrics for individuals should fit with the organizational metrics of that individual's organization.

Rewards

Rewards include tangible (dollars) and intangibles (time off, personal development, or job satisfaction). Timing of rewards should fit with the work processes and projects. Types of rewards should fit with the strategy and the culture.

Cultural Support Systems

This set of programs helps grow the desired culture identified by the strategy. All of these culture programs must be tied to strategy. They are the responsibility of staff departments. These departments should do *nothing* unless it is tied to strategy. This is the point of "Wasting the Covey Ticket" in chapter 4.

Some staff groups, like human resources, are famous for introducing programs that are not tied to strategy. Often this happens because the top leaders have not developed a strategy in the first place.

Primarily, this element includes employee deployment using Career Concepts and motives, leadership and employee competencies for development, internal communications, and culture monitoring. These are amplified in chapters 3, 11, 12, and 16, respectively. More on employee deployment below.

Infrastructure

Infrastructure is defined as an underlying foundation required for performance. The infrastructure items to consider include:

Financial Health – Without the financial resources, the most elegant of strategic plans will never be successful. Leaders must assure the financial power is available to fund the plan.

Information Technology – Many strategic initiatives will require or be supported by changes or improvements in IT. That functional group must be included in the establishment of such initiatives.

External Communications – The strategic plan provides the road map for external communication programs.

Research and Development – Initiatives for R&D must fit with the strategic plan.

Control Systems – Controls such as budgeting, compensation programs, project authorizations, and staffing approval systems must fit the work processes and the strategy.

Physical Systems – Room arrangements, building designs, and department locations and other physical layout issues must fit the work. These often forgotten points deserve some additional attention. See more on physical systems below.

Each of these infrastructure items must be tied to strategy, work processes or projects, and organizational structure.

GREEN OR BROWN?

When doing a fit analysis, one of two environments can exist, commonly called *green field* and *brown field*. A green field application of organizational design exists when a truly new organization is being developed. An example is an auto manufacturer opening a new plant. The management systems are not yet established. There is only an overall direction envisioned by a few decision makers. All of the elements can be constructed to fit with one another from the get-go.

A brown field application is the opposite. The organization has been in place for some time. Management systems have been established. Strategy may or may not exist. Work processes have evolved without much direction or fit to strategy. Staff programs from HR, communications, and IT have evolved to fight fires or to track the latest innovations but not tied to strategy. Pay and benefits are usually a one-size-fits-all approach. Many misfits exist although many have not been identified by top management.

Because a true green field application is rare, much of this chapter relates to brown field applications. Unless a new boss is starting a new function, most new bosses will be entering a brown field world on day 1. Because most applications of this model are brown field, leaders should not expect to redevelop the organization in a mechanistic way, following the eight elements in a set order. Yes, there is some general logic to the order, but improvement in brown field situations will probably flow back and forth between various elements of the model.

USING FIT ANALYSIS FOR DIAGNOSING

As noted above as the concept of fit was introduced, managers should consider two steps in applying these elements: (1) diagnose the organization to identify misfits and (2) deal with misfits.

Diagnosis requires two broad activities. The obvious first one is to review the current state of an organization in relation to these eight elements—one by one—independently. This is an assessment of each management system. How long has it been in place? What problems does it have? Has it been process-managed?

However, the real power of using this framework comes from the second activity, studying the interrelationships or *systemic fit* between each element. The math shows twenty-eight pairs of elements to consider.

Here are only a few of the myriad of questions that should be considered when comparing various elements in a large organization:

Do the company's work processes support the strategic direction?

Does the structure fit with the work processes?

Does the pay system fit the structure and the processes?

Are we developing our leaders with skills needed to meet the strategic direction?

Do we have the physical systems arranged to support the work processes?

Has our internal communications program been developed to support the strategic direction?

Does the performance period used in the performance management system (usually taken to be annually) motivate performance of employees working within a department's specific work processes?

In each of these questions, the diagnostician is relating two of the eight elements to each other. The answers to these and a myriad of other questions that a fit analyst team may develop will provide a healthy list of pathologies in the organization. Voile, a list of misfits!

This analysis process works for small teams, as well as large organization. A competent supervisor should be constantly on the alert for misfits and should regularly review the relationship between pairs of organizational elements.

As noted above, the same questions can be restated for smaller environments:

Do the work processes of our department support my boss's organizational objectives?

Does my department organization chart fit the work processes?

Would I pay my people in the same way if I owned this outfit?

Do I have a development plan for each of my people based on the future needs of this department and the company?

Do I have to have my people in cubicles? It that the best way to do our work?

Have I communicated the direction of the organization and our bosses' division?

Do I have any needs to recognize performance beyond the corporate way?

Whether in a large organization or a small department, systemic fit analysis provides a powerful way to identify misfits.

INFERENTIAL THINKING

Diagnosis is tough, particularly for many of us quantoids. Our left brains will be in full gear, but much of the art in diagnosis is more a right brain activity, one in which The Biz Bucks Guys is admittedly not gifted. It requires a talent called inferential thinking. This is the ability to see ties, trends, relationships, nuances, or subtleties between seemingly unrelated elements. Consider the following two examples of inferential thinking or the lack of it.

The Culture Questionnaire

A large company conducted a survey to assess the baseline for culture change intervention. The survey contained five questions.[54] The company received the following scores (based on a 1 to 6 scale, with 6 being the best):

Customer Focus—4.3
Empowerment—4.8
Teamwork—4.2
Driven by Vision—3.1
Creativity and Innovation—4.3
Can you infer anything particular from this data?

Left brainers may say, "Well, look at that *vision* thing. It is the lowest score. That is where we need to start."

This is a decent but not revelatory assessment.

Inferential thinkers can make an even stronger story. They might say, "This is an organization that already has a high degree of autonomy among its workers. They feel free to do what is right for the organization—that is, *empowerment*, our highest score. However, these same empowered people are the same people who don't know where the organization is going. Being driven by vision is our lowest score. This is a prescription for chaos! We have many people running around loose making daily decisions but are clueless regarding the direction of the company. It is urgent and critical that we start communicating our vision better."

Putting the two scores together makes a much different story for that same issue, improving our company's understanding of our vision. Which argument do you think creates the most motivation, the most change, and the most executive attention? Inferential thinking is an important skill. If a quantoid does not feel talented in this area, she should hire people or borrow people who might provide that perspective in crucial moments.

Here is another example of a misfit that was not discovered until it caused a morale problem in a large company.

The New Deal Misfit

About twenty years ago, a large company of several thousand employees became enamored with a fad called *The New Deal*. This was related to employee expectations for continued employment. The so-called old deal was this, "If you come to work for us at Good Ol' Amalgamated (GOA), you are here for life, unless you steal something."

The new deal was this, "You can be let go, even in the light of good performance, any time. But we promise to develop you while you are here so that if you are in the wrong place at the wrong time and we need to say good-bye, you will leave with many more skills in the marketplace than what you had when you joined us."

The company developed teams of people who understood this new deal to communicate its inception and to explain to others in the company this was the necessary reality in a competitive market. But throughout that period, something was rumbling in many people's stomachs. It was a sense of fairness or the lack of fairness that was bothering people. Everyone understood the necessity of the new deal. However, no one in GOA's HR department did an assessment of the ramifications on morale. The problem was the pension plan.

At that time, much of corporate America was using what is called *defined benefit pensions*. Such pension plans were designed to keep employees, having much of the pension benefit tied to seniority. Because of this, these plans are often referred to as the *golden handcuffs*.

So when the new deal was communicated, it set up a misfit, which disappointed people and reduced morale. The employees were interpreting the new deal as: "We, the leadership, can jettison you any time, but you, the employee, can never leave us! Ha ha ha, gotcha!"

No one involved with the change to the new deal inferred the misfit.

The problem was not corrected until the company introduced a *defined contribution* pension plan a few years later. Employees could then take their pension with them.

MISFITS: WHAT TO DO?

Once a fit analysis is complete, managers will have identified several misfits. No organization is misfit-free. For each misfit, the decision then is one of three choices:

1. Live with the misfit, and implement a plan to mitigate its effect on the organization.
2. Using internal resources, fix the cause of the misfit by redesigning particular elements.
3. Call in experts in the field of "organizational doctoring" to redesign the elements.

Fit analysis puts management in charge of where the organization is going, strategically and systemically, and avoids the management-fad phenomenon. The next time a consultant prescribes an organizational appendectomy, you won't need to run for the doors but will be able to explain your organizational needs, succinctly and confidently.

KILLING TEAMS

As noted above, the fit analysis can also help in avoiding "fad surfing." An example is insightful.

In the mid-nineties, yet another management fad was launched by one, then several large consulting firms. Books were written, speeches given, conferences organized, and presentations made. The seemingly all-inclusive answer to workplace problems was the detailed implementation of *teams*. This meant morphing intact work units into something different than they have been for generations. Once again, without an organizational diagnostic tool to determine fit, corporate America had fallen in its *management-by-best seller* mode.

In spite of the many other companies who were going down the *teams* route, even in their own industry, one company did not implement teams. Why?

Because it didn't fit.

To implement *teams* meant not only to change the structure in a work department but to have team goals set in the performance-management system, and team pay at the end of the performance period. One big misfit showed up in a detailed analysis before any serious consideration of team implementation grew.

For teams to be effective, the existing work processes for a proposed team should be both *interdependent* within the team and *autonomous* outside of the team. Why would you reward a team for its successful work if they didn't have to behave as a team to get results? Also, if a team was rewarded for success when other departments played a major part in their success, what would it do for morale and motivation in the other departments? Over five hundred work units were analyzed. None were found to have both interdependent and autonomous work processes. The fad was rebuffed. The team concept, while appropriate in other situations, was a systemic misfit for this firm with the work at hand.

HOW TO DEPLOY YOUR EMPLOYEES

A leader can display unusual powers of insight when doing an organizational change by using the Career Concepts (and motives) discussed in chapter 3.

For review, Career Concepts breaks careers into four paths—linear, expert, spiral, and transitory.

Consider a typical organizational redesign wherein information technology has allowed certain functions to be combined. Instead of having people do one function and become very good at it, employees are now going to be multi-skilled so they can do several functions with the aid of online information.

Because of this information technology innovation, the new bosses will have an increased span of control. This means instead of having five or six employees, each supervisor will have twenty or more. This reduces the available supervisory positions.

Now apply the four career paths to this new organization. What will be the effect on morale when the new organization is announced?

The linears are really distraught. Their chances for upward mobility have been greatly reduced.

The experts are also distraught. They have become widely known as experts and now will be forced to abandon that expertise to learn new functions in which they have no interest.

The spirals are thrilled! They get to move away from the expert area they have been in for some time and learn new things.

The transitories are also thrilled. They only hope for more such change in a couple of years.

Now recall the distribution, from a motive's standpoint. The four are about equal! This new organization will benefit about half of the people (spirals and transitories) and will harm the morale of the other half (linears and experts). Is it a fit? The financial and, possibly, the customer impacts if everyone were enthused with this change could be substantial. At least you know you are headed for trouble.

The Biz Bucks Guy has lived this type of trouble when a major reengineering consulting firm recommended such a change without being knowledgeable of the four career concepts. The implementation was a disaster for many and thus for the firm. The change had less-than-expected impact on the customers and the bottom line.

So how could you forge ahead with the redesign and mitigate the effects on 50 percent of the valued, previously motivated workforce?

One idea might be to create a few lead positions under each supervisor for the linears. These would be quasi-boss functions but also with frontline responsibilities.

Also, creating an expert position for each function to handle development issues with IT and to keep abreast of industry trends may remove the sting from experts.

Pollyanna says everyone will get a position that fits his or her career concept. In reality, some will not, but the Career Concept framework will help them realize the emotions they are feeling. This should help them gravitate to different parts of the company instead of being disgruntled for years and eventually leaving for somewhere better.

The key is to know who is what from a career concepts standpoint. This will be discussed in greater depth in chapter 11, "Developing Your People." Nonetheless, knowing the ramifications of organizational restructuring before you do it is a tremendous boost on mitigating problems.

MATRIX MADNESS—THE "TWO BOSS" STRUCTURE

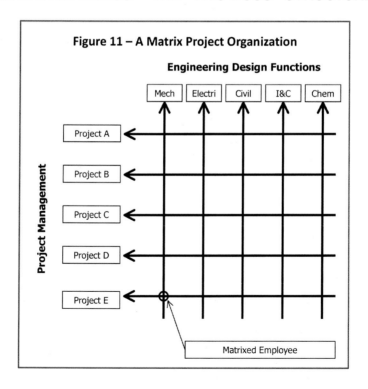

Figure 11 – A Matrix Project Organization

Many concepts in this chapter are further amplified in other chapters. However, a couple of topics will not be discussed later that deserve more detail: matrix organizations and physical systems. Concerning the former:

"Matrix management" is a phrase that has been used for good and ill for decades. Properly implemented matrix organizations can turn the culture of a firm around, provide amazing flexibility, and meet the needs of a diverse set of stakeholders from customers and employees to shareholders and regulators. Improperly implemented, matrix will cause valued employees to leave an organization, create enormous discontent, thwart productivity, and ruin careers of many.

What is this organizational option really like? Is it worth the risk? How do I implement one? All are good questions for the quantoid becoming a new boss and the top executive with aspirations of a total organizational transformation.

Matrix, simply put, is the *two-boss* theory. Matrixed employees report to two people (In fact, there are successful examples of reporting to more than two, but we will limit ourselves to the basics). The company has two competing needs to serve its customers well. So enter the matrix structure in an attempt to meet both needs. For example, an engineering company needs to design everything with top adherence to technical standards. They also need to complete designs on time and within budget. By placing engineers in a matrix, one boss for engineering design quality and one for project management, both objectives can be met. A picture of such an arrangement is figure 11.

There is much to consider before announcing such an organization. The respective bosses must know their divided responsibilities (The notion of shared responsibilities is a prescription for disaster and should be avoided).

The matrix employees must know who to go to for specific issues.

The matrix employees must know when to stop and call for a ruling when one boss provides direction that is contrary to the other.

Who will sign performance reviews?

Who is responsible for determining who is on what project team?

Where do matrixed employees sit, with their function or their project team? The Biz Bucks Guy is amazed by this simple question. It brings out the worst behaviors in some bosses' personality. Maslow's self-actualization level is often abandoned by some otherwise wonderful people when this question is raised.

What training in matrix theory is available for bosses and frontline employees alike?

Given all these issues and others that arise, it is clear that a matrixed organization is not for the faint of heart. Can it ever really work? Yes.

Most large engineering, architectural, and construction firms thrive on such a structure. Most big infrastructure projects are built using some version of matrix. A budget specialist in the field has a financial guru at the home office who directs his activities from a quality standpoint imposing corporate standards and providing expertise. The budget specialist also works for the project manager to roll up project estimates and provide analysis of budget variances.

Not all matrixed people are frontline employees. A branch manager of a bank will report to multiple bosses. She reports to the executive of all the branches. She also reports to the credit card executive for implementing various credit card programs, the safe deposit box guru at corporate for policy on rates, and other functions and services that each branch provides to customers.

At various times and in varying settings, matrix has been used in business schools, global manufacturing companies, utilities, and banking.

Many quantoids with linear or spiral career motives will develop themselves into project managers after a stint as an expert in a functional area. For them, a point of art about matrix will be important.

When a matrix is diagramed in the format shown in figure 11, the function with the most power tends to be across the top of the chart, with the weaker side down the left. In figure 11, this means the traditional supervisors for the engineering functions are more powerful organizationally than the various project managers. The project managers may be in developmental roles for a limited time and will be gone at the end of the project, as far as this organization is concerned. This means project managers, or anyone on the left side of a similar chart, needs to develop a skill The Biz Bucks Guy calls groveling with dignity.

An experienced project manager in a matrix knows exactly what this means. You need to maintain the importance of your role, but you have no real resources, little clout over performance reviews, and only the importance of your project to support you in battle with the across-the-top leaders. You will learn important communication skills from this *weak side* experience, including the improvement of your powers of persuasion.

PHYSICAL SYSTEMS

Every new boss should realize that physical systems count, big time! A few years ago, the world celebrated the fortieth anniversary of the discovery of the office cubicle, of which corporate America seems to have a love-hate relationship.[55]

Is a cubicle the right way to have people work? It depends. It is a matter of fit. If the work is highly independent, a cubicle environment is probably okay. If the work is true team-type work, where communications is important, maybe a bull pen is more appropriate. Some think a cubicle is a status symbol. Get over it. A commodity trader on Wall Street is in a bull pen.

They need constant eye-to-eye communication with their peers. They can make more moola in a few days than most engineers do in a year. Forget the status thing. Do what makes sense for your organization.

Physical systems refer to more than office space. One project manager, running a complicated process before much IT support had been invented, put an old bench in the middle of the office where everyone could see it. Seven old plastic in-baskets were lined up on the bench. Each represented a particular phase of the process. When team members would finish a step, they would place the folder in the appropriate in-basket. The administrative assistant would process each manila folder and move it to the next in-basket. Everyone knew by looking at the bench what work needed to be done that day. Each field person would simply take the next manila folder and leave for the field. The supervisor knew exactly where bottlenecks were as he walked into work. This physical system allowed the supervisor to work more in the field with his people. The administrative assistant really ran the daily work assignments. Even with today's digital environment, this system might be easier to implement than one online.

Proximity also counts. The relative location of offices improves or attenuates the communications between departments. While at USC, The Biz Bucks Guy was taught that studies show a mere one hundred feet is the key distance. If you want two departments to have better communications between themselves, locate them near each other, no more than one hundred feet apart. After one hundred feet, they may as well be in another county.

A leader of a large coal mining organization had a power plant as his only customer. Communications between his mine and his customer was strained. On learning about the one-hundred-foot rule, he visited the plant that was over a mile from his mining offices. He asked if the spare room next to the plant manager was still open. When the plant manager said "yes," the mine manager asked if he could occupy it for a few hours each day!

The communications between the mine and the plant opened up and improved.

_____

QUESTIONS FOR CURRENT LEADERS

1. Can you do a fit analysis of the eight elements for your organization? Particularly, is your organization chart supporting your work processes or does it create inefficiencies?
2. Do you intuitively know of misfits that exist under your responsibility or that of your boss?
3. Could you improve the physical system for your group without a major expenditure?

TECHNICAL ANALOG FOR LIFE AND LEADERSHIP: GIBB'S EQUATION

Some of you thermodynamic quantoids will recognize the following, known as Gibbs Free Energy equation.[56]

$$\Delta G = \Delta H - T \Delta S$$

In this case, ΔG represents the ability for a system to do non-mechanical work. ΔH is called enthalpy, or the heat content of the system. T is temperature in Kelvin. ΔS is the change in entropy. Entropy is the measure of disorder of a system. Thus ΔS is the change in disorder. Positive ΔS is increasing disorder.

By inspecting this formula and noting the negative sign between the two right side terms, we can gather that increasing disorder (ΔS) in a system decreases the work (ΔG) that can be accomplished. The reverse is also true. The more order in a system (decreasing ΔS), the more work the system can do. Hence, the ability to do work is reduced by disorder.

Extending this into our leadership world, the Gibbs equation is a metaphor for our organizational skills. Our ability to organize our human resources properly, moving from a state of disorder to a state of order, implies we will be able to accomplish more work. Gibbs got it in the 1870s, long before organizational theory was born.

CHAPTER 8

MANAGING WORK: PROCESSES

A CARTOON LESSON

Some time ago, The Biz Bucks Guy saw a cartoon worth remembering. It had three frames. In the first, two people were talking on a grassy hillside, overlooking a huge industrial plant. One man, the plant manager, spoke to the other, a management consultant, "You know, we have the most lazy, unproductive employees on earth!"

In the second frame, the consultant inquired, "Why did you hire employees like that?"

In the final frame, the plant manager responded, "Oh, I didn't hire them that way."

Okay, boss. You either acquired them that way or made them that way yourself. You can't hide from it.

This and the next chapter are about productivity and efficiency—doing things right. It is also about effectiveness— doing the right things. While the focus is on the work itself, mastering the tools presented will provide much motivation for your people. You can create great employees through these methodologies. Great employees create great customers. Great customers create very happy shareholders.

Conversely, not applying these skills and tools will help *you* create the most lazy, unproductive employees on earth.

THE WORLD OF WORK

If you consider the internal workings of an organization, all work can be divided into two broad parts. First are processes. Second are projects.

A process is a *recurring* series of tasks or steps that ends in a business result.

A project is *unique* series of tasks or steps that ends in a business result.

One repeats, sometimes a thousand times annually. The other will never happen the same way again.

The two are intertwined. In mature organizations, projects are accomplished through the use of established processes, but a particular project will never repeat in precisely the same way as before.

Processes flow horizontally across the organization chart and may involve several different groups. Consider the new customer hookup process for an electric utility. The process flows from the call center, to the scheduler, to credit checkers, to the meter installer, and eventually to the billing department.

Good bosses acquire the skills to manage both processes and projects.

We quantoids should be enthused with both of these skill sets. For the most part, the basic skills of both process management and project management are logical, powerful, data-driven, and process-oriented. In the end, though, both are about those pesky, squishy, right-brain-advanced skills, such as people, teams, organization, and motivation. This chapter focuses largely on just the basic skills, tools, and methods.

Let's begin with process management in this chapter. The next chapter will focus on project management.

IS YOUR ORGANIZATION PROCESS-MANAGED?

To make the point that few companies are truly process-managed, The Biz Bucks Guy has asked hundreds of leaders the following questions in class,

"Can you name a 'bread and butter' process in your area, one which represents the core of what your organization does?" ("Bread and butter" means a process that is the essence of the business you're in, a frequently used process.)

After we reach a consensus on a process, more questions follow, "Okay, now, how many times is this process used each year?" Reasonable guesses come forward. Usually, they guess the process is used several hundred times per year.

And finally, "So, what percent of time does this process cycle as planned, with no rework, slowdowns, nor bottlenecks?"

This final question is the gotcha question. Almost always, the leaders are stumped. They begin to fidget. The Biz Bucks Guy is not too charitable at this point. He takes guesses from the class. They usually vary widely from "It works right almost all the time" to "It's right about 20 percent of the time." There is no consensus. Strong feelings sometimes flare. Then, I ask them if they would like to know the correct answer. They all eagerly say yes!

Then the boom is lowered to make the point. "The answer is, 'You flat out don't know!'" Ouch!

With a pregnant pause, The Biz Bucks Guy lets it hurt a bit. Usually I am right. Few companies have mastered the art of managing even the "bread and butter" processes for their organization. Most companies have been pretty lax in becoming process managed.

A process-managed organization, whether a full company or a small department, can answer the following:

1. How many processes flow through the organization?
2. Regarding each process, what group within the organization owns it? One group should be designated as the owner for each process.
3. What is the name of the assigned process manager for each process?
4. Have the process managers been trained in process management?
5. Which two or three processes are currently designated for a cross-functional team to apply the tools of the training and make needed improvements?

Turning these questions into a guiding methodology, here are eight steps to becoming a process-managed organization.

1. Develop a Hierarchy of Recurring Work (The Process List)

Organizations are very good at developing hierarchies of important things. Consider these three examples. HR goes to great lengths in the care and keeping of the organization chart. Engineers maintain functional decompositions of plant systems, equipment, and parts. Managers of large projects develop work breakdown structures, hierarchies of the unique project work.

Why is it, then, that we don't think to develop and maintain an organized hierarchy of the recurring work of the organization? This is just another hierarchy. Such a process list can be useful in several ways.

a. Process Management: The process list is the starting point for an organization to begin managing their processes. This is the focus of this chapter.
b. Restructuring: When the organization chart needs revision, leaders should use the process list to make sure

all work has been transferred properly (see "The Lost File Cabinet" below).

c. Work Force Planning: Adding estimated resource requirements to each process yields a clearer picture of where the labor is being deployed and should it be modified.

d. Outsourcing: With resource requirements added, top management can more easily make strategic decisions about which functions should be included within an organization and which should be moved to outside service providers.

As a suggested taxonomy, consider the following four levels of the hierarchy (with a consistent set of examples in parentheses):

Level I – General Function (Engineering)

Level II – Management System (Project Design)

Level III – Process (Conduct Preliminary Engineering)

Level IV – Step or Task (Produce Piping and Instrumentation Diagram)

In some process lists, *sub*categories may be necessary, such as a subprocess of a parent process.

Level III includes both business processes and production processes. Business processes are largely people implementing strategy as part of a management system. Production processes are largely machines controlled by people.

The process list itself would stop at level III, the process description. The steps will be identified for each process, only when needed, on a process flowchart.

If feasible, the process list should be in an easily accessible online database.

Each process should be described using a consistent syntax. One that works well is "Number: Action Verb + Object." A numbering system should represent levels, such as 4.3.6, being the sixth process of the third system of the fourth general function.

Thus, one process in the database list would read, "4.3.6: Develop Annual Capital Allocation."

The database at the process level should include important fields, such as:

- Owning department
- Department leader
- Process manager
- Other involved departments
- Analysis priority
- Date of last analysis
- File location of last analysis
- Date of next analysis
- Estimated resources use (for selected processes, as needed)

2. Prioritize the List of Processes

Once the list is completed, each process should be assigned a priority for analysis. A simple ABC scheme may be sufficient: A for "Get it analyzed now!," B for "On deck for next year," and C for "Let it sleep."

Whatever the priority scheme, keep it simple. Almost any prioritization scheme is merely an organized way of quantifying gut instincts. The instincts in this case should be on resource availability and the potential for strategic improvements in safety, cost savings, sales, and customer satisfaction.

3. Train process managers

The tools and methods of process management were developed, honed, and refined over decades of use. There is no one way to improve a process. There are many useful tools, but different experts espouse different methods. The basic tools for process management are included in item 5 below. Regarding training, an organization has three options:

1. Self-taught: Many process managers with quantoidal tendencies should be able to learn the tools of process management through study and application. If your interest is for your own small group setting and there is no large organization initiative, this may be the best approach. Public seminars can speed your learning.

2. Independent consultant: There are many qualified independent consultants who have a strong pedigree in this field.[57] Compared to the next item, this option will reduce the financial resources necessary to start moving. A single consultant is a viable option for many organizations of many sizes.

3. Large consultancy: A number of humongous consultancies would be pleased to assist your organization with the training of process managers and the implementation of a methodology of process management for a nominal fee. For very large application, this will probably be appropriate. Each consultancy will have their version of these tools and methods. They go by many titles: Six Sigma, Total Quality Management, Lean, Toyota Production System, Business Process Improvement, and so forth. For the most part, these are the same melody, same chords, same key, with different orchestration.

As a reminder of chapter 7, such an intervention in an organization, large or small, must be a fit with the strategy and other strategic initiatives.

4. Form Process Improvement Teams

Based on the prioritization of the process list, top management selects two or three processes to work the methodology and use the tools. A cross-functional team of five to seven people is a powerful tool not only to identify process improvements but to implement the improvements once identified. Each functional department through which the process flows should be represented. Other staff groups such as information technology or human resources may also be needed on the team. The process manager leads the cross-functional team. The team should strongly consider using an independent facilitator.

5. Use the Methodology and Tools to Find Improvements

The main tools are few and are described below. However, several other supportive tools exist and should be in the process manager's toolkit. Process managers will find many references, which provide more details of tools and a methodology than this short overview. [58]

The overriding methodology for process improvement is the plan-do-check-act (PDCA) cycle, noted in chapters 2 and 4. In fact, this item 5 and the final three are essentially the PDCA cycle.

The primary tool for understanding a business process is the *flowchart*. The Biz Bucks Guy advocates a special format for flowcharting, known as *swim lanes*. This format flows from left to right and has a swim lane for each participant in the process. See figure 12 on which is a business case approval process (which relates to the next two figures also). [59] This format allows everyone to see his role and helps in training and implementation of the changes. (See tips on flowcharting below.)

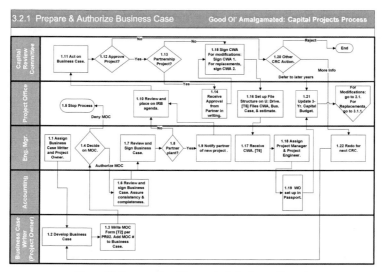

Figure 12: Process Flow Diagram in Swim Lanes Format

Recalling the future first principle in chapter 4, The Biz Bucks Guy advocates an unusual exercise next.

This is not typically included in most process management methodologies. With the flowchart complete and before working on improvements, the team should ask themselves cogent questions:

"How long *should* this process take?"

"What is world-class quality?"

"What would 'blow your socks off' performance be for this process?"

This gets the future envisioned from the get-go. If you want large-scale improvement, use future first thinking before you analyze the present.

From the flowchart, the team then focuses on the present. They identify the added-value steps versus the non-value steps. The team brainstorms ways to make the added-value steps more effective and efficient and to reduce or eliminate the non-value steps.

Before moving on, the team makes absolutely sure that the legal or social underpinnings of the process requirements are sound. The team does this by asking why about every aspect of the process. Some people call this the *Seven Whys Principle*. Peel the layers. Be annoying by asking *why* seven times if necessary. Get to the core basis for the process.

The team moves into the data gathering phase. Data is the lifeblood of process management. There is an old axiom of a process management:

> In God, we trust…everyone else, bring data!

The team collects data on the frequency, cycle times, and problems with the process. This answers the question asked earlier, "What percent of time does it cycle with no rework, slowdowns, nor bottlenecks?"

The team reviews the rework, bottlenecks, and slowdowns and again collects data on the causes of the problems. This is expressed as a Pareto chart, which shows the most frequent cause (see figure 13).

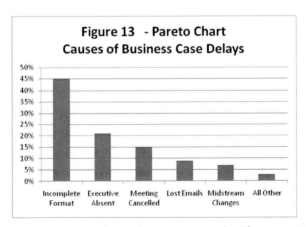

The team may need to do a cause and effect exercise that yields causes for the Pareto chart. This is best constructed and facilitated as a fishbone diagram (see figure 14).

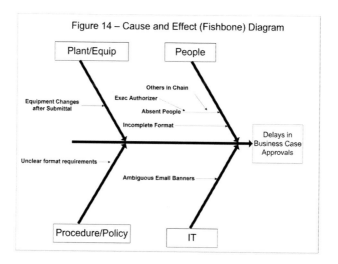

Figure 14 – Cause and Effect (Fishbone) Diagram

If the process is important, cycles frequently, and is easily measured such as a fabrication process in a plant, advanced tools of *statistical process control* may be appropriate. These include check sheets, control charts, scatter diagrams, run charts, and other quantitative tools.

Many other tools for process management and facilitation are available.[60] The key is to use the correct tool for the correct need. It is easy to overdo the methodology by falling in love with the tool kit.

Eventually, the team develops and plans a list of improvements.

6. Implement the Improvements

Depending on the nature of the changes, implementation can be the most challenging step. It may take project management tools noted later in chapter 9. It will always include the advocacy of the team members with the other members of the various departments. Communication should be formally planned, creatively done, and measured in tons not ounces.

7. Check on the Changes

The team assignment is not complete until the improvements are reviewed for effectiveness. The team should formally seek feedback from all the affected departments.

8. Revise as necessary

If warranted, the team may need to revise and reimplement the changes based on feedback and data.

TIPS ON FLOWCHARTING

For business processes, the flowchart is the fundamental tool for improvement. Here are some tips for improved flowcharting:

a.   Refer to flowcharting software for flowchart symbols. You can establish your own standard set of symbols. There is no single set.

b.   Do not think a business process flowchart must be as detailed as a flowchart for developing an information system. A *diamond* represents a decision in flowcharting. For information systems, every possible decision loop will need to be identified. For improving, training, and implementing managementprocesses, the highly infrequent paths are often not relevant. Use common sense, and use diamonds only when absolutely necessary.

c.   A highly useful symbol likely will not be in the software (see the lower right corner of a process step in figure 15).

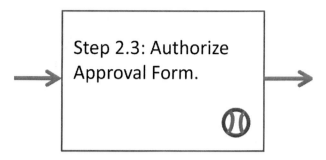

Figure 15 – Baseball Symbol

Yes, it is a baseball. It stands for iteration between the flowchart step where it is placed and the prior step. Think of playing catch. For example, when an approval form is routed, a boss may send it back to the originator several times before signing the form. Why put a bunch of diamonds, one for each possible iteration, when a simple baseball will explain the process and avoid the clutter?

d. The use of swim lanes allows for easy takeoffs for job descriptions, similar to how a designer does a takeoff from a drawing to develop an equipment list. A participant's involvement is graphically displayed in his swim lane.

e. Be sure to use the same syntax for steps as you do for titles of processes—Number: Action Verb + Object (see figure 12).

f. If you are writing a procedure for the new process, use the flowchart as the primary tool to convey the process steps. You then can follow the flowchart with amplifying comments by step. You can write as much as you need in the amplifying comments, but keep the flowchart steps simple.

g. Look for value-added steps as opposed to administrative steps. Maximize the former. Minimize the latter.

EXAMPLES OF PROCESS MANAGEMENT

Before turning to project management, a couple of process management examples, one good and one not so good, should be insightful.

The Claims Processing Posse: The Importance of Data

Some years ago, before the advent of outsourcing, a large company had a crack staff that processed medical claims as part of the employee health benefit program. Unfortunately, for some years, their service was less than perfect from most employees' perspective. The delay from the time of a doctor's visit to the time the doctor got paid was measured in months. Everyone knew the issue was those darn employees who couldn't fill out the claims forms properly. They were the processors' internal customers. History showed these annoying customers were untrainable. Fix the customer, and we will have no backlog, or so they thought. Frustrations mounted among the processors and the employees.

Then, the manager of the processors implemented a process improvement initiative.

The processor posse rounded up the data, developed a fishbone, and constructed a Pareto chart. The processors themselves did this fine work. It became clear the primary reason for the delays was not the misused claim form but a programming issue in a financial information system that allowed payments only in certain windows, which was infrequent. The finance department and IT were unaware of the issue. Finance was the primary user of the software. It worked fine for their needs. Once brought to their attention, finance and IT were very supportive. The change was made quickly and claims were paid in a couple of weeks, not months. Their internal customers were pleased. The processors were pleased. Data was the key to turning around this long, misunderstood problem.

The Lost File Cabinet: Missing a Process List

A supervisor of a small group at a large federally regulated manufacturing plant maintained some historical files concerning security off-site at a company warehouse. After a reorganization, the small group was disbanded, and their work was divided and assigned to other supervisors. None of the new supervisors knew about the warehouse filing cabinet.

The warehouse was eventually sold, and when the files were discovered by the new owner, a journalist was more than happy to inspect these sensitive documents. Much bad ink came of the unnecessary incident.

If the plant leaders had been working from a process list when the reorganization was designed, a process of Maintain Off-Site Historical Files would have been assigned to one of the new supervisors, and the problem would never have happened.

The K&HH Meeting Revisited: A Lesson in Why

In chapter 5, a newly promoted engineer-manager learned what was important from their internal customer by holding a series of *kiss and hold hands* (K&HH) meetings with them. In one of those meetings, the finance department related the need for the capital budgeting process to include the board of directors' approval for every line item. The notion was this was part of corporate law of the state. The budget team asked where that was written, effectively asking why. The team needed to know the legal underpinnings of the process to be able to improve it without breaking some little known law. After interviewing, six top managers who all espoused the same sentiment, the manager went to the chief *out-house* (as opposed to an *in-house*) attorney for the company.

When asked about where this law was written, the attorney asked, "Where did you hear that idea?"

"Oh, nowhere. Just every top officer of the company believes it! You mean it's not true?"

It turned out there was an old notion that had been propagated for decades within that company that the board must approve all capital line items each year. When that was identified as false, the team was able to simplify the capital process dramatically. The key was asking *why* multiple times until the truth was found.

QUESTIONS FOR CURRENT LEADERS

1. Have you determined the list of processes that flow through your department?
2. Have you determined who should have responsibility for continuous improvement activities for each process, the process owner? Is that person in your department or elsewhere in the organization?
3. For those process owners in your department, have you taught them the tools for process improvement? Have you given them performance goals to apply these tools?

TECHNICAL ANALOG FOR LIFE AND LEADERSHIP: PRISMS OF PROCESSES AND PROJECTS

Dating from the mid-nineteenth century, lighthouses have been able to magnify their lights through the use of Fresnel lenses. These are not typically shaped lenses like a camera or the human eye, but an array of carefully milled prisms each calculated to perform a specific refraction of light. At the Yaquina Head Lighthouse on the Oregon coast, the Fresnel lens is a circular cylinder about six feet in diameter and about eight feet high, including a conical top. It is a catadioptric system, made of 258 separate prisms and a parabolic mirror. A single 1000-watt lamp located in the hollow center of the lens emits light rays which diffuse radially in every direction. Because of the prisms, the light is refracted into a horizontal parallel alignment. These prisms bend the rays of the single-point light source of the lamp to appear as a vertical rod of light about seven feet high, much brighter than the original bulb. Ships at sea can see it twenty miles away, providing safety for navigators in the rough seas around that cape.

In an important way, these prisms are like the middle managers of an organization. Top management provides the light of strategy. First line supervision directs the various functional teams, but between these two levels are the middle managers. Largely, they are the ones that both manage the business processes and also direct the key projects of the organization. Throughout the organization, middle managers align, sharpen, and coordinate the strategic light of top management's strategy. The middle managers transform unfocused strategic light into targeted, efficient processes and successful, value-creating projects. These organizational prisms are essential to develop and produce the organization's products or services for customers who are navigating the uncertain waters of the economy.

CHAPTER 9

MANAGING WORK: PROJECTS

PROJECTS: THE PRIME MOVERS OF ORGANIZATIONAL CHANGE

Let's turn now to the other skill set to manage work: project management.

Projects are the engines (or *prime movers* in mechanical engineering terms) of change. To implement any idea, to change any culture, to improve any customer satisfaction score, to clean up the air or water, a project is required. They may be inexpensive and short-lived. They may take billions of dollars and a decade to complete. Regardless, each project takes skill, coordination, dedication, and focus. Like their first cousin, processes, the tools for project management are many. The art is in selecting the best set of tools for the particular project. It is easy to overshoot. Too many how-to books on project management advocate tools that have their place but present too much horsepower for most projects. The Biz Bucks Guy was the controller of a six-billion-dollar project, which was done before most of the computerized project management tools were in existence. While it would have been great to have them, they did much with little automation.

Project management is a critical topic for quantoids with leadership aspirations. Projects become the mode of travel for them. After gaining a degree of functional expertise, many quantoids of the linear, spiral, and transitory persuasion use project management for their first step into leadership.

PROJECT UBIQUITY

Projects exist in almost all functions and all walks of life. They are everywhere. Here is just a smattering of examples:

- Designing a new air pollution control system
- Constructing a bridge
- Building a dam
- Fabricating a new semiconductor chip
- Describing the human genome
- Hiring a new 401(k) plan administrator
- Implementing a culture change survey
- Replacing merit pay with pay for performance
- Changing the culture of a firm
- Designing a financial model to valuate capital projects
- Strengthening a balance sheet
- Upgrading the phone system
- Implementing a new training program
- Establishing a program to lead a multiproject environment
- Improving relations with a troubled customer segment
- Implementing a work management information system
- Adding a new wing to a customer service office
- Taking an alleged criminal to court
- Establishing configuration control for a chemical plant
- Moving to a new home
- Raising good children
- Getting a ring on your left hand
- Taking a ring off your left hand

The common trait of each item in this list is that the work is a one-time effort. It will never happen again in exactly the same manner. This is the key aspect of a project versus a process. One might say that a dam project recurs every time a dam is constructed. Not so. Every dam is different. Every design is unique. Every river is one of a kind. A new dam is certainly a distinctive project, never to be done exactly in that manner again.

With the ubiquity of projects, it is utterly amazing more organizations don't require basic project management skills in all their employees, particularly leaders. What follows is an overview to give a budding project manager a head start. Many references and public training courses abound to increase one's expertise.[61]

THE PROJECT MANAGER ROLE

Often a quantoid will seek the opportunity to lead a project as a career step. A project manager is the sole person responsible for the scope, cost, and schedule of the project. A more accurate term for this role would be project leader, but our culture is not as adept at using that phrase. Clearly, this role requires both leadership and management skills.

In some matrixed project organizations, the project manager has few, if any, real people reporting to him. This makes for a challenging assignment. He has full accountability but no ability to control resources. To survive this environment, successful project managers are able to wield power not from organizational position but by argumentation, by shear force of personality, and by the criticality of the project.

The Biz Bucks Guy was once a lonely matrixed project manager. Fortunately, the US Environmental Protection Agency was intensely interested in his project. Top management was therefore intensely interested in his project. This helped him get things done although for him the power of position was next to nil.

ORGANIZATIONAL APOPLEXY

Project managers are not necessarily born; they usually are made. Managing a project can be daunting. The Biz Bucks Guy once knew a wonderful guy who was perhaps the smartest person—in terms of academic smarts—in a large part of a company, a straight-A kind of guy. He ran a large and complex function successfully for several years. (Anonymity is required here.)

Then, tragedy struck. He was asked to redesign a major part of his operation to make it fit with the new corporate strategy. The project duration was more than a year. He immediately went into organizational apoplexy. He was not able to deal with the responsibility rationally. He did not know the skills and, for that matter, the fun of project management. In a few months, he took early retirement. It was a sad sight. He was a tremendous resource for the company but did not have the skills, educationally or emotionally, to handle this highly risky and visible project. The company did little to prepare him. It was a significant loss to both.

Project management skills are crucial in this changing world. No one should be given a project without at least basic training in project management processes and tools.

THE GOLDEN TRIAD OF PROJECT MANAGEMENT

In musical composition, a triad is a set of three notes that when played together form a melodious chord. The first, third, and fifth tones of a major scale form a major chord, the primary building block of orchestration for most songs.

Project managers will make beautiful music if they can balance three key objectives. These are the scope of the project, its cost estimate, and its timing or schedule. Scope, cost, and schedule are the golden triad of projects—the three primary objectives of any project. A successful project strikes a strong major chord for an organization.

For many long-term projects, a fourth objective is also important. That is the expenditure flow for each year of the project. In fact, in some instances, monthly expenditure flow is an important objective to manage. Although it is not technically correct, industry usage calls this *cash flow*. This will be the term used in this chapter. Strictly, booked expenditures may include accrued costs. Thus, cash flow is not actually pure cash.

When assigned a project, a project manager should ask top management which of the three objectives are most crucial to the organization. Project managers may have to sacrifice one objective or another during the course of a project. The most crucial objective should be held firm throughout the project life cycle, as long as possible.

THE *BIZ BUCKS* PROJECT PROCESS

The basic steps of project management differ by author or consultant.[62] Given the disparity of consensus, The Biz Bucks Guy has developed a unique project process that is more practical than many because it recognizes the reality that project understanding improves as the stages progress. Much can be learned for the new project leader from this process (see figure 16).

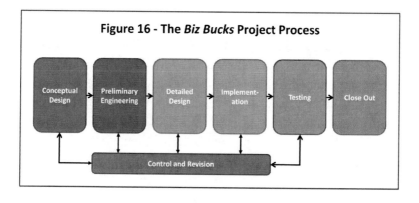

Figure 16 - The *Biz Bucks* Project Process

One important way this project process differs from traditional models is there is not one point for project planning. Project planning is repeated at various stages, as needed.

Also, there is not one step where a project manager is assigned. The project manager should be assigned as soon as possible in the process. Sometimes that is well into the second stage.

The following explanations for each stage will use two examples. First is a technical project to install a scrubber (an air pollution control system) at a power plant. Second is a softer project, the design and implementation of a training program.

Conceptual Design

After a problem is discovered or an issue has arisen, general management and their technical support propose an initial solution. There are no details. One person who may be the sponsor of the project or her representative will do a conceptual project plan.

Up to 50 percent contingency is added to the conceptual cost estimate. Conceptual authorization typically allows only the next stage, preliminary engineering, to proceed. Any cost estimate at this conceptual stage is based merely on open discussion with experts because no details are available.

In effect, top management is buying an option when they approve a conceptual design (the result of the first stage) and authorize preliminary engineering. They will not authorize the entire project until there is much more detail after the second stage.

A scrubber may be the conceptual answer to solve an air pollution issue concerning sulfur dioxide, but many details remain to be determined. How much can be removed? What kind of scrubber? When can it be completed? What kind of reagent to use? How many contracts will be needed? What will the project organization be? What permits are necessary? Will the reagent be prepared on a continuous or batch basis? All these and many more questions need to be answered in the next project stage.

A training course is the conceptual answer to improve some needed skills in a certain employee group, but again, many details remain. How many can be taught in one session? What type of discovery experience will fit these employees? How long will the course be? Who will deliver it?

Preliminary Engineering

For the scrubber project, this stage is the *real* engineering. It is where the main decisions are made. Operating philosophy is determined. Resources identified. A contracting strategy is developed. All the questions posed in the prior section are answered. Key drawings that define the technical philosophy of the project are developed, like piping and instrumentation diagrams, electric one-lines, and general layouts.

With this greater definition, a cost estimate can be completed with up to 25 percent contingency. A project Gantt chart is made. A formal scope statement is written.

For a training course, an outline with timing is developed. A class size proposed. Creative thinking yields a discovery experience. Delivery options are brainstormed and one selected. A cost estimate is completed, and a pilot program and the full rollout are scheduled.

Whether a large construction project, like a scrubber, or a soft project like a training course, the project manager takes the added definition and produces a *preliminary* project plan. Top management, if convinced of its appropriateness, authorizes the entire project at the end of preliminary engineering.

Detailed Design

This stage of a scrubber project is where a talented design firm produces the detailed drawings, equipment and material takeoffs, construction scopes for contracting, and field training requirements. Procurement for long lead time equipment may begin.

At the end of detailed design, the project plan is updated. The cost estimate is refined with added details. Only 10 percent contingency is allowed. If the detailed cost estimate exceeds the preliminary cost estimate, the project manager must receive additional authorization to proceed.

For a training course, the designer produces a digital presentation, a simulation, handouts, or a set of flip charts. Pilot participants are calendared and committed to attend. The pilot is conducted, and the course is tweaked.

Implementation

The scrubber system is constructed. All equipment is procured. Mechanical, electrical, and instrumentation and control systems are installed.

For the training course, the materials are reproduced. All the sessions are conducted.

Testing

For the scrubber, all components are rung out electrically. Systems are tested individually. Water is pumped. The entire scrubber system is put into initial operation. Air quality is measured.

For the training course, the effectiveness is measured by survey or by a skill improvement assessment.

Closeout

For any major construction project, like the scrubber, the project manager has a long list of activities to accomplish to complete the project. These include such things as closing all purchase orders, doing a lessons-learned report, reviewing the final report of actual costs, making sure all spare parts are procured, and reviewing any materials that could be returned to contractors for credit to the project.

For the training program, costs are summarized and a final lessons-learned report completed.

Control and Revision

At any time throughout the various stages of the project, the project manager may learn of variances from the project plan. This initiates a control sequence. Typical steps for control are:

1. Collect data on status
2. Produce a status report on project objectives
3. Produce an impact report if nothing is done
4. Develop corrective actions to mitigate the impact on project objectives
5. Implement the corrective actions
6. Check to see if the corrective actions were effective.

For the scrubber project, if the actual cost for a portion of the project is exceeding the estimate, the project manager must quickly determine the cause. If it is labor productivity, for example, perhaps some contingency can be used to add craft people.

If the forecasted costs are exceeding the authorized cost estimate, the project manager must communicate that to top management with a plan to bring the project to a close within the project objectives.

For a training course, it is possible the testing shows the course is not meeting the required improvement in skills. The project manager must determine why and make immediate changes to bring the course into compliance with the objectives.

This six-stage project process is common for most projects. Perhaps the nomenclature is different in various organizations, but the six stages exist in some way.

Let's now examine a few more details for developing a project plan.

THE PROJECT PLAN

The Work Breakdown Structure

The work breakdown structure (WBS) is a hierarchy of the entire work of the project. The hierarchy must cover the entire project scope and all activities related to accomplishing the project. The art of the WBS is to have only as many tasks as necessary to plan and control the project, not too many and not too few. That goes for the number of levels of the hierarchy. The lowest level of every vertical chain of the hierarchy is called a task (or an activity or a work package). The WBS can be expressed graphically as a hierarchy or in outline format (see figure 17 and figure 18 for an example of each). For projects of more than a few tasks, the outline format is best. Figure 18 shows an additional level for one stage of the project (tasks 3.1.1 through 3.1.6). More WBS levels can be shown using the outline format.

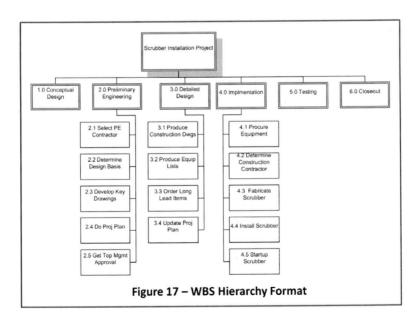

Figure 17 – WBS Hierarchy Format

WBS	Task Name
1	**Conceptual Design & Approval**
2	− **Preliminary Engineering**
2.1	Select Preliinary Eng Contractor
2.2	Determine Deisgn Basis
2.3	Develop Key Drawings
2.4	Do Proj Plan
2.5	Get Top Mgmt Approval
3	− **Detailed Design**
3.1	− **Produce Construction Drawings**
3.1.1	Produce Pipe Isometrics
3.1.2	Produce Foundation Drawings
3.1.3	Produce Grade and Drainage Plan
3.1.4	Produce Wiring Diagrams
3.1.5	Produce Control Panel Diagrams
3.1.6	Produce Caisson Design Drawings
3.2	Produce Equipment Lists
3.4	Order Long Lead Items
3.5	Update Proj Plan
4	− **Implementation**
4.1	Procure Equipment
4.2	Determine Construction Contractor
4.3	Fabricate Scrubber
4.4	Install Scrubber
4.5	Start up Scrubber
5	**Testing of Scrubber Performance**
6	**Closeout Project**

Figure 18 – WBS Outline Format

Project Scope Statement

A fundamental part of any project plan is a well-oiled statement of what will be accomplished and, even more importantly, what will not be accomplished. This statement is a project manager's best friend when those external to the project start advocating additions to the project scope.

Project Cost Estimate

The WBS is used to estimate the project costs and to schedule the project tasks. Estimating is an art in itself. When necessary, use experts with experience in this specific type of project.

Project Schedule

The project schedule is made by estimating the duration of time to accomplish each task, then, interfacing each task. Typical interfaces are finish-to-start, start-to-start, and finish-to-finish. Some interfaces have time lags built in. When a foundation of concrete is poured for a large column for a building, the column cannot be installed until the concrete has cured. This cure time might be expressed as a lag between the two tasks.

The path of interfaced tasks that defines the end date of the project is called the *critical path*. Any delay of any of those tasks will push the end date of the project unless mitigating action is taken. Other tasks, not on the critical path, are said to have *slack*. This gives rise to the term *CPM* (or *critical path method*) as a nickname for this planning process.

Two formats are useful in expressing a schedule. The most popular is the Gantt chart (based on critical path). This is a bar-chart format, but the interfaces between tasks drive the placement of the bar. They are not simply drawn using wishful thinking (see figure 19).

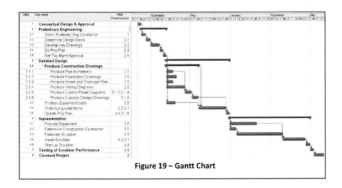

Figure 19 – Gantt Chart

A second format is the network. This format is useful largely for debugging the WBS tasks and interfaces and for producing large wallpaper charts that impress people who enter the project manager's office. See figure 20 for a partial network of the scrubber installation project.

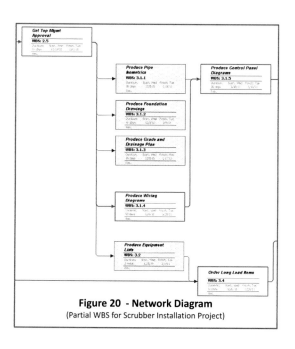

Figure 20 - Network Diagram
(Partial WBS for Scrubber Installation Project)

Earned Value and Percent Complete

Percent complete of a project is sometimes mistaken to be the percent expended of the total cost estimate. A project may have spent 90 percent of its planned expenditure and be only 50 percent complete! The percent complete is calculated by using a planned cost or an arbitrary, but consistent, point system. Points are totaled in the initial plan. Actual earned points are received only when the activity is completed. The actual earned points divided by the planned total points is the percent complete. The project plan for larger projects should have an earned value plan.

SOME REALITIES OF PROJECT MANAGEMENT

There are a few realities that new project managers should be cognizant of as they launch into their first project.

Scope Creep

One of the primary reasons for projects not meeting the cost or schedule objectives is *scope creep*. This happens when the project manager allows more work to be done and charged to the project than the originally agreed upon scope statement.

Consider a project at an existing manufacturing plant to change out the controls from analog to digital. The plant manager convinces the project manager (who is not one of his reports and may have much seniority) that a new floor in the control room is necessary after the equipment panels and screens are installed. He also makes the point that those pesky motor-controlled values should be replaced with newer ones, or the entire new digital controls are a waste of money. Pretty soon, the project is grossly over the budget. The plant manager is happy. However, top management is considering a poor performance review for the project manager who was not strong enough to avoid the scope creep.

All the new scope could have been bundled into another project keeping the original project objectives intact.

Lack of Timely Information

Many companies do not have managerial cost systems developed to provide timely information for project managers. This means the project manager is required to spend valuable time searching for data to determine the status of her project. This reality is particularly true when one IT system provides actual costs and another IT system provides information on committed costs from supply chain. Commitment reporting is a project manager's best friend when it is timely and in a WBS format that a project manager can easily track.

Project Communications

A primary failing of most project managers is the lack of formally developing and implementing a project communications plan. One way to do this is to analyze the schedule bar chart and put a mark where key progress is made. These are communication-point milestones. For each milestone, the project manager preplans the announcement, the audience, and the communication channel to be used. In addition to milestones, the project manager should have frequent staff meetings and customer meetings to communicate progress and solve problems.

No Project Process

Some companies do not have the organizational maturity to have a defined project process. The project manager may be the one to blaze that trail. The project manager will be *rowing* the project "boat" while *building* the project boat at the same time. This is a challenging but rewarding task but not for the faint of heart.

IT Support Systems for Project Management

Like any other field of endeavor, information technology for projects has developed greatly in the past decades. Recently, new, more graphically simple, more powerful, and even more inexpensive tools have become available. Some must be purchased. Others are available on a rented basis. The traditional IT vendors will be replaced by new competitors if the traditional tools don't keep evolving. Nonetheless, project managers should be wary of too much power for too little project. It is intoxicating to see some of these new tools perform. Sometimes, a creative use of an electronic spreadsheet is sufficient to run a fairly large project.

MULTIPROJECT CONTROL

Before concluding this discussion of project management, one final topic must be considered. In some organizations, the challenge is managing a portfolio of projects, sometimes called *multiproject control*. It is not unusual to have over one hundred such projects running in various stages at any point in these multiproject environments. In addition to individual project processes and tools, there are important multiproject processes that must be implemented concerning capital budgeting, project prioritization, resource leveling, contracting, and combined sourcing of materials, equipment, and services.

The issue typically for the multiproject environment is not to confuse project management tools with the common sense tools needed to manage the entire portfolio. Often, top management desires to control the overall budget of the portfolio. To do so, they bring in detailed project management training for everyone who touches a project. This is ineffective without a master schedule, a priority system, a monthly review board, and an integrated cash-flow forecasting spreadsheet. Much improvement to managing the portfolio comes from these tools, not the project skills needed to build a new nuclear plant or submarine.

THE ABILITY TO INNOVATE

Returning to a high-level view, this and the previous chapter are about managing work. Processes and projects are the work. Developing the ability to manage both in an organization is a key to one of the biggest differentiators in business. That is the ability to innovate. Some scholars have forecasted that as the internet takes economic friction out of our capitalist system, the *only* competitive advantage one company will have over another is the ability to innovate. Innovation is that important. What will we innovate?

Our processes and our projects.

- The order fulfillment process
- The product development process
- The customer recovery process (when we "hose it up" with a valued customer)
- The project to move into a new geographic area or to acquire a new company or to build a new engine

All these and many more are the fundamental building blocks for success in our future. It takes more than creativity. It takes the ability to put our creativity into action…through process and project management. Thus, we should conclude:

Innovation = Creativity + Action.

Action is our ability to implement our creativity and make it useful.

QUESTIONS FOR CURRENT LEADERS

1. Which employees in your area should be trained in project management? Do they have performance goals to obtain these skills?
2. How did the last project under your responsibility go? Was it brought in on time and within budget? Did you do a lessons-learned report at its completion?
3. What tools of project management fit the particular projects in your department? Which tools are over-kill, meaning too involved for the small size or complexity of your department?

TECHNICAL ANALOG FOR LIFE AND LEADERSHIP: THEVENIN-NORTON, MAKE IT SIMPLE!

In electrical engineering, a technique is used to reduce a complex circuit of many elements to its most basic electrical equivalent. Called a Thevenin or Norton equivalent, depending on whether the resulting equivalent is expressed as a series or parallel circuit, the resulting Thevenin or Norton circuit (which in reality is made of several components of voltage sources, current sources, and impedances) has only two elements. For a Thevenin equivalent, the circuit has one voltage with a single impedance in series. For a Norton equivalent, the circuit has a single current source with a single impedance in parallel. From this simple equivalent circuit, engineers can easily calculate and understand the effects of the complex circuit on a separate element, often called the *load*.

Leonardo da Vinci has been attributed as saying (most likely in Italian), "Simplicity is the ultimate sophistication." Some wise consultant once added two more words, "In technology, simplicity is the ultimate sophistication."

Thevenin and Norton have this simplicity thing figured out. When we deal with processes, we should do much the same. Reduce a complex business process to its value-creating tasks, and see how many steps are really necessary to accomplish the business purpose of the process. Nonvalue-creating tasks might include reviews, approvals, tracking, testing, validation, rework, postmortems, filing, and other administrative functions. While not all nonvalue-creating tasks are unnecessary, many can be reduced, simplified, improved, or just plain nuked.

In addition, decision-making, with seemingly complex situations and assumptions, often can be boiled down to a few items of pros and cons. Leaders must develop a knack of making as many decisions as straightforward as possible.

The Biz Bucks version of Leo's famous statement is therefore, "Simplicity, both in technology and leadership, is the ultimate sophistication."

CHAPTER 10

MANAGING INDIVIDUAL PERFORMANCE

DOES MONEY MOTIVATE?

In the mideighties, The Biz Buck Guy was a middle manager on the construction of a nuclear plant. The project was in trouble. The commercial operation date had slipped multiple times. While the magnitude and the complexity of the project was largely the issue, there was one elephant in the corporate boardroom that was not openly discussed. The project team itself was not cooperating with one another.

Multiple factions had developed. Operations fought with start-up. Start-up fought with construction. Construction fought with support services. Miniwars broke out all over the organization. Many were vying for future positions in the smaller operating organization that would exist after commercial operation was declared. Parochialism was rampant. Some higher managers forbade their direct reports to cooperate with other managers on the project because they were the enemy. In the vernacular of the school grounds, some fifty middle managers were not playing well with their peers.

The backlog of work was not being worked off. The commercial operation date was once again in jeopardy. The financial ramifications of these delays were significant to the consortium of owners. Some feared bankruptcy if the project— already a decade long—was not finished soon.

The top officers had to do something creative and immediate to get the project team, particularly the middle managers, working together. They called a meeting of the project management team.

At the end of the typical day of speeches and work group reports, the CEO unexpectedly appeared. He told the group that he doubted that they could meet the key date, called *initial fuel load*, for the first of three generating units. The scheduled fuel load was six months away.

He told them if they made that date, they would all get a bonus. The meeting was getting better by the minute. He said the bonus would be equal to... *one...year's...salary!* (About then, the meeting really got better.)

"Did he really say one year's salary?" the shocked group whispered to each other.

He continued explaining that if they missed the specific date for fuel load by one day, he would still give them a bonus: one year's salary times 179 divided by 180. If they loaded fuel two days late, the bonus would be a ratio of 178 divided by 180. So in other words, the sooner, the better. After six months delay, no bonus.

They all walked into that meeting, warring with each other. They all walked out like the Rockettes! All in perfect lockstep, smiling, focused on a single goal, and resolved to work together. A large backhoe was necessary to bury all the hatchets.

Feel the love!

After a tremendous effort of cooperation and sacrifice, the project team loaded fuel about three months late, and each manager received approximately a six-month salary bonus! The tactic worked. The mission-critical objective was accomplished.

However, as soon as the fuel load was accomplished, many, unfortunately and not unpredictably, fell back into their old ways.

Nonetheless, the desired objective was met. Such an intervention was unheard of in that industry. Clearly, money motivated performance.

This chapter is about managing performance of individuals. Organizational performance was discussed in chapters 4 and 7. Process and project performance were discussed in chapters 8 and 9. Now we focus on *individual* performance, beginning with the skill of hiring and ending with disciplining. Between these two topics are the primary skills for this chapter of managing and rewarding performance of individuals.

FINDING GOOD PEOPLE

After several years of boss-hood, each successful leader will review her boss-hood career and know success was largely a function of finding, leading, and developing good people. Finding means the skill of hiring top people. This crucial skill is quite intuitive not mechanistic. The standard HR hiring processes your organization will impose will only help marginally, if at all, to find really outstanding people.

The key is to find people that are honest and street-smart as well as a good fit with others and yourself. They also will need to be teachable. Unfortunately, these are attributes that you will not be able to assess easily from resumes or even interviews.

When possible, leaders get input from others. However, in this litigious society, you will not be able to get data from past employers. If you are considering a person internal to your company, their current boss will be biased. So beware. Not all current bosses are high on Maslow's hierarchy or on the honesty scale for that matter. The boss may downplay the candidate's skills if the boss wants to keep them. They may provide glowing reports for someone they want to jettison.

Nonetheless, to be a successful boss, you will need to develop a sixth sense to smell competence, potential, and integrity.

One tip is to be a great people developer. If you are known as such, good people will be clamoring to work for you. This is part of the next chapter.

Sometimes you are handed a team of people that someone else selected. You will need to do an assessment to determine if this is the team to get the job done. If certain members are not right, you have tough duty to transition them elsewhere and find people who are the right fit.

THE *BIZ BUCKS* PERFORMANCE MANAGEMENT CYCLE

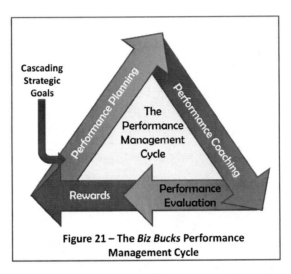

Figure 21 – The *Biz Bucks* Performance Management Cycle

Once you hire them or inherit them, you will need to manage your people's performance. We will use, as an organizing framework, the following model, figure 21, The Biz Bucks Performance Management Cycle. This cycle essentially has three parts, each representing different times within a performance period. They are: performance planning, performance coaching, and performance evaluation and rewards. Note that the final part is bifurcated into two separate entities. The reason will be discussed later.

Before proceeding with the details of this cycle, we must remind ourselves of some past discussions and assumptions about organizational fit.

ASSUMPTIONS FROM THE L-MODEL

In chapter 7, we discussed the organizational fit L-Model (figure 9). The last two Design elements were (individual) performance management and rewards. This performance management cycle covers both of these two final design elements of an effective organization. This cycle assumes the other design elements are complete:

- an overall organizational strategy exists,
- the middle and first level leadership team has aligned themselves, both vertically and horizontally, with the top organization's strategy,
- the work processes and projects are aligned with leadership goals,
- the organizational structure fits with the work processes and projects.

What remains is to align frontline employees work plans with that of the organization. This is called cascading strategic goals, flowing down all the way from the top of the organization to the individual frontline contributors.

THE PERFORMANCE PERIOD

To apply this model correctly, a leader must first determine the most appropriate period to measure performance for the individual. Most companies simply use an annual process, assuming that one size fits all. While the annual approach is most common, leaders should not necessarily buy into this performance period. The performance period should fit with the work at hand. If the work has a culmination annually that coincides with the company fiscal year, so be it. However, if the work culminates on a quarterly or annual basis, but ending at a different time than the fiscal year, leaders should encourage their HR department to allow a performance period that fits the actual work.

PERFORMANCE PLANNING

Individual Performance Objectives

At the beginning of the performance period, the leader should work with the frontline employee to prepare a list of objectives for the performance period. As noted in chapter 4 for organizational goals, these objectives should be SMART (specific, measureable, achievable, responsibility assigned, and time bound) and not DUMB (dubious, unbelievable, minor, or boring). Each objective must be tied to a cascading strategic goal of the leader herself or someone in her chain of command.

Some objectives are process related: "Reduce rework for the product Y4 fabrication process to two standard deviations by year end."

Some are project related: "Develop and implement a streamlined budgeting process by September 1."

Each person should have between eight and twelve such objectives. Each objective must either be a business result or an activity that is tied to a business result. It is appropriate to use a weighting system to indicate the most important objectives.

Key Performance Areas

Each objective should be written within one of many key performance areas (KPA), among them:

- Cost management
- Customer management
- Environmental Compliance
- Marketing/sales
- People development
- Process improvement
- Product development
- Project management
- Safety
- Strategy
- Technical competence

Key Performance Areas are useful in several ways. First, KPAs ensure that performance objectives are written across a broad spectrum of organizational needs. Also, top management can turn a company's direction by indicating which of the many KPAs are crucial for the next performance period. In addition, top management can also steer the organization by issuing new KPAs.

Enabling Resources

Many individual performance objectives will require some added resources. For each objective, the employee should identify any such needs. This is an important component of enabling results in setting the performance plan. In addition to funding, such resources might include office space, additional labor, decisions by management, software, and so forth.

Individual Development Plan

In addition to a set of performance objectives for the next performance period, performance planning also includes long-range performance planning that relates to personal professional development. This is more commonly known as an individual development plan. Each employee is responsible for their own development. The plan should be based on one's career concept, as discussed in Chapter 3. Taking time to plan for it is crucial. The next chapter brings out this important role of leadership more fully.

PERFORMANCE COACHING

Throughout the performance period, leaders must coach employees to enhance their performance. Coaching is done both formally and informally.

Formal Coaching

Formal coaching means a set time is established during the performance planning phase for the employee and her boss to meet. As a formal coaching meeting is accomplished, another one is set. If the performance period is a year, at least three such formal coaching meetings should occur. This does not mean quarterly. The boss should review the performance objectives and calendar the next meeting to fit with the work at hand.

During these formal coaching sessions, the boss should help the employee diagnose problems and develop corrective action to get any lagging objectives back on track. The boss is truly a coach. The employee should not be relieved of the responsibility for results.

After a formal coaching session, the boss must document the performance results discussed, both for completed objectives and those still in progress.

Informal Coaching

While formal coaching can improve performance, informal coaching can be even more powerful. The leader should maintain communication with his employee throughout the performance period. He should develop an open and trusting relationship with the employee so the employee is confident about keeping the boss informed. Watercooler discussions to discover issues, provide feedback, and enable performance are key.

The Biz Bucks Guy was once in charge of the design and implementation of a corporate performance-management process. He had the opportunity to implement this leadership intervention through a large company of whom many employees were in a bargaining unit. When union employees were asked if they wanted individual feedback on their performance, the results were 100 percent in the affirmative. Leaders should not be afraid to give feedback in a professional way when issues arise whether the employee is a chemist, a doctor, an electrician, or a supervisor.

Coaching should also include ongoing review of the individual development plan established during performance planning.

PERFORMANCE EVALUATION

Separating Evaluation from Rewards

At the end of the performance period, the leader evaluates the performance of the employee and, in a separate meeting, provides meaningful rewards for good performance. This is why the model (figure 21) separates the performance evaluation from rewards. The review of performance is less effective if the employee is waiting for "the number." It is best to separate the discussion of performance from rewards by at least a few days.

Evaluating Objectives

Performance evaluation is about the employee's performance objectives. It is not about how hard someone tried. It is about results. It is not about the cookies the employee provided every other Friday. It is objective. It is not subjective. As much as possible, it is about measuring. It is not about personality.

As mentioned above in formal coaching, it is important to document coaching sessions. Without documentation of performance along the way, a boss is left to remember how things went when it is time to evaluate performance at the end of the performance period. If the performance period is a year, most bosses without good coaching and documentation remember only about sixty days of performance. Her people are evaluated on just the last two months of the year! Not a fair system, but it is the truth more often than one might think if one has not been in boss-hood.

Evaluating Individual Development

In addition to performance objectives, the leader should include performance evaluation concerns regarding how well the employee implemented his individual development plan. This evaluation should answer these types of questions: Were the activities in it accomplished? Were the activities effective? Does the individual take ownership of the need to continuously development himself?

The Overall Summary of Performance

Many large organizations require the boss to do a final assessment of performance by assigning an overall score. Most of these systems have five gradations. The words differ from

HR department to HR department. Here is a somewhat cynical version to make a point:

5. Jumps over tall buildings in a single bound
4. An above-average employee
3. An average employee
2. Needs improvement
1. So dense light bends around him

Regardless of the creativity of wording, two things tend to happen with this scoring:

1. The employee knows his salary adjustment depends on this score. He is listening for that final score instead of focusing on his results.
2. The safe score is 4. The above average is the average. It is not unusual for 80 percent of an organization's employees to get the not-so-highly-acclaimed 4 score. Bosses will get criticized if they give out too many 5s, but a 3 will demotivate the employee. Thus, 4s are used. To what end? See forced ranking below for more on this.

Here is one creative solution. How about eliminating the overall score? It is useless in most business environments. Isn't the reason for performance management to enhance performance? Or is it to make the labor attorney's job easier? Is it to help create shareholder value? Or is it to make life easy for HR? If the goal is to enhance performance and create value, perhaps more straightforward feedback on a well-planned series of objectives would be better than boiling down a person's annual effort to one grade. This isn't public school, Toto.

REWARDS

Nonmonetary Rewards

Before discussing pretty much everyone's favorite reward, we should focus first on the other reward type, the nonmonetary reward. It can be given in many forms.

1. Recognition: This may be a trinket, such as a coffee mug or trophy. It may simply be a sincere thanks in a staff meeting or a larger venue. Leaders must be aware of individual idiosyncrasies. Some people might be embarrassed if recognized in a large setting.

2. The Opportunity to Learn: Growth and learning opportunities can motivate many.

3. The Opportunity to Contribute in a Larger Way: Some people will relish the assignment to work with the boss or even her boss to do a special assignment.

4. Independence: As a reward for high performance, some would savor the opportunity to work without the usual amount of supervision.

5. Flexible Hours or Time Off: This may be generational. The baby boomers might view time off as not being needed. Some, perhaps of the younger variety, would be happy not to be needed so much. Again, leaders need to know their people.

6. Merchandise: Some employees love to pick from a catalog of semiprecious power saws, tool boxes, GPSs, and jewelry.

7. Special Opportunities: The Biz Bucks Guy once facilitated a team through an important process to improve group results. When asked about what rewards they would like if successful, the group agreed they wanted to meet the people they work with on the phone every day. This group constantly talked to people throughout a fleet of plants, but they had never met them. The company plane

regularly flew the four hundred miles to the primary plant. If successful, the team wanted to individually take a spare seat and visit the plant and talk with their faceless colleagues. Another team wanted the company to make a small gift to the charity of their choice. The key is to ask.

Monetary Rewards

As noted in the fuel load bonus story at the beginning of this chapter, money can motivate performance. However, there is a principle that is still popular among some HR experts that is inherently wrong. The principle states, "Money isn't a motivator. It is a demotivator!" This statement comes from studies of Fred Herzberg, an early scholar in compensation theory. It is internally wrong. Demotivation is motivation in the wrong way. Thus, if this principle were true, it means pay does motivate, just in the wrong direction.

The statement has certain face validity, nonetheless, because *the way we pay* often is not a motivator. For decades, businesses rewarded performance by increasing pay as an annuity. This is the proverbial 2.4 percent base pay increase for top performers and 2.3 percent for average performers (or whatever the economy and inflation factors are). This is known, among compensation experts, as merit pay. How motivating is that? Not much.

Variable pay is pay at risk. Each year, there is an incentive available. It may represent rewards for results of large organizations, small teams, or individuals. Depending on the size, this might be motivational...and it might not.

Line of sight is an important concept when discussing rewards for large organizations. Line of sight implies an individual feels she has made a difference in the large organization. If not, she feels estranged from the results that drive the rewards. If the line of sight is too far, the incentive pay is not motivational.

Thus, Dr. Herzberg may have had a point. The way we pay is often not very motivational. You only need to review the fuel load bonus story to know pay *can* motivate. Most new leaders in large organizations will be held hostage by the corporate policy on pay. But, nonetheless, leaders should strive to find the best way to reward performance consistent with policy. [63]

DOES PERFORMANCE MANAGEMENT MATTER?

Over the years, there have been many studies done by dedicated researchers on performance management. One in 1994 showed a direct correlation between companies that focus on performance management and profitability.[64] Other studies are based on opinions of top leaders about performance management. They say a good performance management system builds a culture of accountability, drives alignment between employees and company goals, improves decision-making, and even enhances collaboration between departments.[65]

Regardless of the research, good, old-fashioned common sense tells us that tying one's objectives to the organization's goals will produce results. Yes, performance management matters.

PERFORMANCE MANAGEMENT ISSUES

Here are seven items of advice or tips to assist in applying performance management with your employees.

Time Requirements for Performance Management

One of the oft heard complaints about performance planning, coaching, evaluating, rewarding, and long-term individual development is it takes too much time. This is simply a cop-out. If a person is to be a true leader, they *must* commit to these principles. This is only possible through effective delegation. The key is to stop doing frontline work. Let your frontline employees do the frontline work. It boils down to a simple question: If you are not going to manage performance of your direct reports, what *are* you going to do with your time as a leader?

If you are not yet in a leadership position, you may not understand how middle and upper management expands the time required for you to do frontline work after you are promoted. It is a constant combat between you and your bosses to limit your frontline work. They want your input on all sorts of things. The boss stuff gets done in the interstitial points.

Let the Employee Draft the Evaluation

One hint to reduce the time for performance evaluation is to have the employees draft their own evaluation. This often provides useful information. Often, employees are harder on themselves than the boss might be. You can always amend the draft before it is finalized.

Appraisal Forms

Regarding performance management, driving commitment or becoming compliant is the conundrum for many bosses. HR requires certain forms, on certain schedules, with certain phrases. Learning the ropes of your performance appraisal system may be teaching principles that do not enhance performance of your direct reports. A simple text narrative following the performance management cycle may be superior to your organization's forms.

IT and Performance Management

Likewise, automation does not ensure enhanced performance of your direct reports. Yes, automation can reduce the burden of time to do performance management properly. But unless the software is developed using solid basic principles, the tools may be counter to enhancing performance. Automating a bad system yields a bad system done efficiently.

Forced Ranking

Some organizations still impose a forced ranking system. If a five-point rating system is used, the mode must be a grade of C with a normal distribution of something like 5-20-50-20-5. Such a system is usually counterproductive.

Forcing such a distribution across a midsize part of the organization requires bosses to meet and argue the merits of individual contribution. It becomes an issue of: Do I work for the best arguer? Morale is jeopardized.

Forcing a normal distribution on a small group is even more dysfunctional. It forces the preponderance of the group to be average. It also says there is always someone who is a bad performer. What a whopping good motivator for high performance that is. Imagine an outstanding group of people who work well together being forced into a normal distribution.

Coaching versus Micromanaging

The Biz Bucks Guy ran a performance management survey of seven thousand employees about three times in the midnineties. Regarding one of several questions, not one person said, "My boss overcoaches." Everyone wants feedback and coaching. No one, however, wants micromanaging. What is the difference? It is simply a matter of style. The micromanager takes the fun out of reaching goals by dominating the employee. The coach has more fun seeing his employee achieve the success.

Peer and 360 Reviews

Not all positions are easily measured. A senior staff engineer who consults with less experienced engineers provides a valuable service. The best way to measure her success is to ask her customers. This is known as peer feedback. It is invaluable to evaluate many positions. How about the administrative assistant who is perfect in supporting the boss but also is not too responsive to others in the department? The boss thinks he is wonderful. The other members think he should walk the corporate plank. The boss will never figure it out until he asks the others in the department.

If such feedback is for a leader and if their subordinates are asked to provide input, this is sometimes called 360 feedback. It also assumes people who work with the individual as internal customers and suppliers are queried.

GO GET A COMPANY CAR

Regarding rewards, The Biz Bucks Guy did something right once.

He and his department were responsible for a major corporate culture survey. This was long before automated and online systems were available for doing such things. Four thousand employees responded to a forty-question survey. Two women in the department did a perfect job of hiring a dozen temporary employees, directing the key stroking sessions, checking the resulting input, producing reports for five hundred supervisors and roll-up reports for their many managers and officers. They hit it out of the park. The hard copy reports stood in a pile about five feet tall. They were mailed exactly on the date promised to top management. All their quantoid manager had to do was write some simple software to collect and analyze the data.

Everyone in the department contributed in some way to the survey project, so it was clearly time for a luncheon celebration at the local Chinese establishment. Everyone in the department knew the two women had pulled off the impossible. Not one supervisor or manager got the wrong report. All the data was solid. The project was done exactly on time.

During the project, The Biz Bucks Guy overheard the two discussing the new outlet mall that was built about an hour away in a less populated part of the state. They chortled about how much they would like to go down to this mall some day and spend themselves into oblivion.

At the celebration lunch, The Biz Bucks Guy brought two envelops. Before dessert, he gave them to these two outstanding performers. He told them there was a really important letter that needed to be hand delivered to a remote company office (which conveniently was only a few miles from the aforementioned outlet mall). He told them the letter was so important that he wanted two people to protect it in route. This really confused them. The Biz Buck Guy was known as an efficiency nut. Never would he want two people to do the job of one.

As they opened the envelopes, they discovered checks for $100 for each of them. He told them, "I don't want to see you again today, and by the way," he added, "isn't our office near that new outlet mall?" The confused look turned to, first, disbelief, then shear excitement, and finally the fierce look of the focused shopper.

"Go get a company car."

Two wonderful, deserving women flew out of that Chinese restaurant without even opening their fortune cookies. It is impossible to measure the motivating value of that experience, but it was the right thing for a lot of reasons.

Some lessons: Listen, and know your people. Have fun. Be creative. More types of rewards are possible than you think.

YOU'RE FIRED!

A vice president of a large highly technical manufacturing complex hired a talented person from outside the company to handle a major set of the VP's many functions. He was given an impressive title and was given responsibility of various staff functions so the VP could focus on his line functions. The new person had a resume of success in similar assignments.

After a year, the new person asked for a performance appraisal. The VP was reluctant, saying he was just too busy, and he would let him know if there were any performance issues. After the second year, the now-much-less-new person requested again a formal time to discuss his performance with the VP. Again, he was rebuffed.

About thirty months into his assignment, the VP called and summoned him for his first performance review. The meeting was pretty much two words, "You're fired!" No real warning. Not much detail. The person was stunned. He really didn't know what he had done wrong. The first indication of performance problems was "Hasta la vista, baby." A few minutes later, he visited with The Biz Bucks Guy simply for solace. Sadly, he was never seen again.

DISCIPLINING AND FIRING

Every new leader should resolve never to be like that VP—one who treats people like so much cannon fodder, or as expendable, replaceable pawns. Remember, the first quality of leadership rightness is love of people.

Of course, there are sad times when, after your best efforts, you have not been able to enhance the performance of an individual above minimums. You will need to work with your HR team to start a process of discipline, which may eventually lead to termination or placement in a spot that is a better fit. This is difficult for both you and the employee. You should strive to do this with respect for the individual. You may need some emotional support yourself, particularly if this is your first such episode. In many cases, except such things as a gross breach of ethics, a boss should accept part of the blame. The boss has failed to motivate better performance. This does not mean the boss admits that to the individual in counseling sessions.

New leaders should commit to allocating ample time for individual performance management. Managing performance of your direct reports takes time. Lots of time. But it pays in the long run. More on how it pays is in the next chapter as we segue into the six behavior-based skills of leadership readiness.

QUESTIONS FOR CURRENT LEADERS

1. How would your direct reports answer the following ten questions about performance and company direction? Instead of guessing, why don't you get their real input.

    a. I know my company's goals for this year.
    b. I know my department's goals for this year.
    c. I understand the mission/vision of my company.
    d. I plan my contribution to department goals each year.
    e. I know what additional skills or resources I need to accomplish my performance objectives.
    f. My leader spends ample time coaching me without micromanaging me.
    g. In this organization, good performance is rewarded, and bad performance is not tolerated.
    h. My leader has a good system to identify the good performers.
    i. My leader is a people developer.
    j. My leader is known for giving timely performance evaluations.

    Answers to these questions will help a supervisor improve their performance management. Furthermore, these questions could be used in a survey for a company to assess the overall effectiveness of their performance management system.

2. Is there any good reason that you can't creatively reward outstanding performance?

3. Is the performance period one year for your company? If so, does that fit the work? If you were the big boss, what period should it be? By the way, you *are* the big boss for your small part of the world. Ask HR to help. Today, many HR professionals understand the one-size-fits-all approach does not always hold true.

TECHNICAL ANALOG FOR LIFE AND LEADERSHIP: INTERSTICES

Interstitial points are the small spaces between larger objects. Consider soil. How can groundwater exist in soil? It is because sand and other minerals have finite volumes. There are always small interstitial spaces between grains of sand. Water can find its way into these interstices. If the water carries a solution of soluble minerals, the water can fill the interstices with valuable microdust deposits.

A key to informal coaching is to use the daily interstices of time in which important interaction between you and your direct reports can happen. These are teaching/coaching/mentoring moments. These valuable interstitial points are often where the real coaching is found.

PART III

WHAT DO GOOD BOSSES DO?

CHAPTER 11

DEVELOPING PEOPLE

DON'T YOU KNOW WHO YOUR NEW BOSS IS?

Many years ago, while working for General Electric, The Biz Bucks Guy accepted a new assignment requiring a move across the country. He didn't know the reputation of Tom Skinner, his new boss, until the word got out that he was going to work for him. The congratulatory phone calls often included words to this effect, "Don't you know who your new boss is? Why, Tom Skinner's the best people developer in GE!"

The best people developer! A lasting legacy for an outstanding boss who knew the importance of building his direct reports. For two years, I was part of his crop as he demonstrated the simple but powerful art of people development.

Some years later, then GE CEO, Jack Welch, claimed GE's major core competence is the ability to develop its people. He wrote, "Crotonville [GE's leadership development center] became, in fact, our most important factory."[66] This is from a company that is arguably among history's finest.

Here's how a new boss can become known as a great people developer, like a Tom Skinner or Jack Welch.

DEVELOPING YOUR PEOPLE—OUR WORST SKILL!

First, we need to realize good people developers are in short supply. A good subtitle for this chapter would be "The Missing Leader." One might think people development is an obvious characteristic of all successful companies and their managers. Actually, the opposite is true. Lominger—a leadership development think tank and consultancy, now part of Korn/Ferry International— reports of their sixty-seven leadership competencies; developing direct reports is rated dead last, in terms of skill of leaders, out of all sixty-seven competencies in their leadership research.

That's right—sixty-seventh out of sixty-seven!

The Lominger study has been repeated over the past two decades. Each time, developing direct reports was dead last.[67][68] We can conclude we are not only bad, but we are also not improving.

Okay, so what? Is developing your people that important? The same studies indicate managers generally believe it is a "middle of the pack" skill in terms of importance, certainly not low. The remainder of this chapter supports the idea that developing your people is smart, even crucial for leaders and their organizations. Consider the words of Warren Bennis, who is among the leading theorists on leadership in the world:

> Since the release and full use of the individual's potential is the organization's *true task*, all organizations must provide for the growth and development of their members…This is the *one true mission* of all organizations and the principle challenge to today's organizations.[69]

Why aren't managers better people developers? Let's discuss a few drivers and tips representing the perspectives of both companies and their individual leaders.

REASONS TO BE A PEOPLE DEVELOPER

The following six reasons should be sufficient to drive bosses to be passionate people developers. They should be a people developer to:

- Improve Productivity and Effectiveness: While developing a direct report may cause some temporary reduction in productivity, it will pay dividends quickly in your department, team, or crew.
- Maximize Long Term Potential: Developing direct reports improves the long-run success of your entire company.
- Keep Your Sanity: Good people developers usually go home on time. Developing your people not only improves their capacity to perform but improves your capacity to delegate. Dreading the forthcoming budget preparation? Delegate much of it to a budding quantoid!
- Attract Talent: When the word gets out that you are a people developer, the up-and-comers in your company line up to work in your department, crew, shop, or division.
- Plant Good People: When people leave your area, they know your department's function, your methods, and your needs and can help you be successful from their new position.
- Get Promoted: Being a great people developer differentiates you from the pack. People say good things about you. People realize you are a more complete leader, not the usual commoditized manager.

The People Hoarder

Consider the following example of a non-self actualized boss.

An engineering manager refused to help his people get promoted because he felt he could not stand to lose them. It was pure selfishness. One of his people came to a job interview with The Biz Bucks Guy. He was not qualified for the particular available position, but this young man was quite impressive. So much so, that The Biz Bucks Guy talked to the engineering manager about him. The engineering manager hemmed and hawed and wouldn't give a straight answer. Finally, when pressed for more specificity, the engineering manager blurted out, "Okay. Okay. He's my best employee. You don't expect me to tell people that, do you? I might lose him."

A funny thing happened. That young man eventually found a way out of that department and eventually left the company. His motives were different than his manager's. He did not want to be an engineering expert. At last sighting, he was the chief financial officer of a large company and very successful. The engineering manager was unsuccessful in keeping his star.

Lesson: You may as well advertise your good people. They will eventually leave you anyway, particularly if they are linears, spirals, or transitories. Good people developers attract good people to their area, making up for losing others.

SOME TIPS ON BEING A PEOPLE DEVELOPER

What do great people developers, like Tom Skinner, do? Here are a few tips and ideas:

- Be convinced you can make a difference with people. Clinton Duffy was a famous warden of San Quentin prison. Several decades ago, his love of the inmates and his successful actions caused a change in corrections philosophy nationally.[70] When a critic asked him if he knew that leopards don't change their spots, Duffy responded, "You should know I don't work with leopards. I work with men and men change every day."[71] Your work can change people too.

- Be the motivator not the Mom. Convince your employees that *they* are responsible for their own development. Each must have a written development plan, including both short- and long-term development goals. Remind them that capitalism is creative destruction and their jobs may dissolve without notice. Corporate maternalism breeds unhealthy dependence on the company and minimizes self-reliance. A Tom Peters's metaphor indicates, people need to be the CEOs of their own career.
- Recognize that development is more than going to training. While training courses are an important aspect of development, so are rotations, special tasks, complex projects, reading assignments, informal brown bag discussions, and even successful staff meetings.
- Coach with a passion. Most people can remember a coach, teacher, or mentor that dared to confront behavior when it was less than optimal. People developers confront—in a private, professional, and respectful way—when needed. Tom Skinner did this particularly well. The old phrase "You praise in public and criticize in private" should not be forgotten.
- Delegate incessantly. Make assignments with development in mind.
- Know your people, particularly their career aspirations.
- When interviewing potential hires for your department, discuss an estimated time for them to move on (assuming this fits their career aspirations). Make moving on a goal and promise you will help them find their next position in the company when they have developed to your

expectations and performed in their current job for a reasonable period.

- Creatively reward people who actively develop themselves. Money is not always the right answer (as noted in the previous chapter). Know your people and reward them with a motivating intangible. For some people, it's a trip to a distant company plant, a donation in their name from your company's foundation to their favorite charity, or a gift certificate to a local hardware store.

CAREER CONCEPTS AND DEVELOPING PEOPLE

As boss, you must strive to understand your people's motivation. The Career Concepts framework introduced in chapter 3 can help you. Recall the four basic concepts: linear, expert, spiral, and transitory.

The individual development plan mentioned as part of the performance management process in chapter 10 should be tailored to the motives of the person. Hewitt's research shows the number one driver of performance is job challenge and fulfillment.[72] This means different things to different people. Using the Career Concepts framework, leaders can be more effective in providing the desired challenge and fulfillment.

The Career Concepts framework helps you know what kind of work to give them. You can help them with life navigation. You can help them to understand better both you and their colleagues. How should you help each to develop? Here are some ideas.

A Linear's Development Plan

A linear has motives of power and achievement. They yearn for the power that comes from positions on the organization chart. What could you do for them?

1. Let him know you understand his need to grow up the chain of command. Set a date at which you will begin helping him transition to his first or next leadership assignment. This assumes good performance in his current job.
2. Delegate to him leadership-like assignments. Could he organize the next all-hands department training seminar? Could he assist you in doing parts of the budget that does not deal with salaries of others? Could he represent you when you are on an extended trip away from the office?
3. Allow him to be a project manager for an important project. Coach him on the people side of project management, including selecting, motivating, evaluating, and rewarding project team members.
4. Send him to leadership schools and training courses. Nominate him for pre-supervisory courses. Send the midlevel engineer-linear to project management school.
5. Encourage him to read the latest book on leadership and, perhaps, to do a book report to the team.

An Expert's Development Plan

The expert has motives of gaining a deepened expertise and personal security and applying it to make a difference. They want to make a contribution by applying their education and experience but only in their chosen field. How should you direct an expert's development plan?

1. Assign her the technically complex problems.
2. Give her the role of the top technical person in the department. Develop the role of project engineer, chief engineer, or principle engineer (or analogous positions in other fields of endeavor).
3. Encourage her to write technical papers for conferences.

4. Send her to schools that deepen their understanding of her chosen field. Send the expert physical chemist to an organic chemistry seminar.

A Spiral's Development Plan

The spiral values creativity and growth, but unlike the expert, the spiral's growth is largely broadening, not deepening. How can you help a spiral to navigate?

1. Assign her a variety of projects or problems to solve.
2. Let her meet with other departments, particularly with internal customer or supplier departments. This allows her to understand the workings and processes of other functions.
3. Discuss the optimal time for her to transition to a new boss or function. This, as before, is contingent on good performance in her current job.
4. Send her to training that broadens her. For spirals, leadership may represent a step in broadening. For a spiral accountant, send her to financial decision-making training. For a not-so-new mechanical engineer, send him to project management school. Remember, the next step for a spiral is related to their current job.

A Transitory's Development Plan

The transitory's motives are variety and independence. These are people who live and love to move. They are often misunderstood and often not valued. How can you help develop a transitory?

1. Let him know you understand his motives. Discuss the reality of workplace duties, and tell him you are on his side, but investment in him may be limited if he thinks his next move is outside of the company.

2. Discuss his past work life. Brainstorm other possible assignments/jobs/moves. Plan the next move to occur in two years from the start of his current position. Discuss two or three other moves after that change.

3. Provide opportunities for a variety of projects, assignments, challenges, or teams.

4. Look for assignments that others may not want. Sometimes transitories are willing to relocate or move to a less secure department.

5. Assuming he has a general commitment to the larger organization/company, send him to training that is much different than his current assignment but which has value to the department. Send the medical-assistant transitory to database training related to the department's information system.

EMPLOYEE DISCIPLINE: CAN PEOPLE CHANGE?

People development also includes dealing with performance issues that are not solely part of the objectives in the performance plan discussed in the prior chapter. This is the disciplinary track. Sometimes, employees exhibit behavior that is not conducive to themselves or others getting the job done. Their behavior becomes unacceptable.

An experienced leader knows when to let a person go who has exhibited aberrant behavior or whose productivity is lacking and unsavable. However, each leader must be sure he has taken all possible steps to alleviate the problem before planning a thirty-something's early retirement. Most large organizations have employee assistant programs if there are psychological, emotional, financial, or addiction issues driving the behavior. Such programs are much appreciated by anyone who has had to deal with an employee with personal difficulties.

However, sometimes direct feedback and a stern and honest warning is sufficient to help the person deal with their issues. Two stories will illustrate the importance of providing discipline when necessary.

The Unexpected Rattlesnake

An experienced manager once inherited a valuable employee that we will call Andrew. In the past, Andrew was always cordial and professional in customer settings with the inheriting manager.

At the initial team staff meeting, however, Andrew went on a tirade. Andrew did not like the method the manager was suggesting to accomplish a step in the process this internal team was implementing throughout a five-thousand-employee organization. Andrew was sure he knew the best way. It was not his facts; it was the heavy-handed and pernicious way he packaged them that was the issue. The manager was shocked and disappointed. Other team members complained privately later. Some even advocated flushing Andrew immediately.

At the next meeting, he injected more venom into a seemingly tame issue. This pattern went on for several weeks. It was hurting the team and killing the effectiveness of training meetings. He had become the quintessential rattlesnake, fangs flaring at every possible situation.

After counseling with HR, one Friday afternoon, the manager lowered the boom in a professional, respectful, and direct way. Andrew blew up, accused his boss of grievous personal biases, took issue with the boss's religion, and indicted him as socially unfit to serve. The boss reminded Andrew that this meeting was about Andrew, not the boss.

Monday morning, in walked Andrew. He was different. He sat down with the boss and said he was deep in soul-searching all weekend. He said he had even broken down in tears a few times.

He did not realize how awful he had been. Andrew came to the realization that he was the one who needed to change.

He told about his ability to break an alcoholic addiction many years earlier without any help from therapists. He fessed up that the things that bugged him were something he alone had to conquer. Most of his issues were things he brought with him from his last position. He promised to turn over a new leaf.

And indeed, he did!

Over a year later, the company offered an early retirement for certain employees. Andrew took it. It was sad for the team to have him go. He had become a very cordial, engaging, professional, and effective member of an internal consulting group. He had made a difference and ended his career on a high note.

Yes, people change. Paraphrasing Warren Bennis's earlier comment, good leaders strive for the release and full utilization of the potential of each of their direct reports for the betterment of the organization and the individual. Sometimes, that means doing hard things like confronting unacceptable behavior.

Instant Maturity

The Biz Bucks Guy once worked at a company where his father had been a top executive. A successful midlevel manager once shared with The Biz Bucks Guy the fact that he owed his career at that company to Daddy Biz Bucks. This manager, many years earlier, was a craftworker with a history of bad attendance and unreliability. He was young and headstrong and worshipped fervently at the "shrine of the grape," causing much of his performance issues.

After many attempts to change the young man's performance, his boss gave up. The young man was sitting on the cold concrete outside of his boss's door near a loading dock as the boss was calling the union steward and the HR department to fire him. He was feeling really low and wished he could have acted better.

He really needed this job, and the gravity of his behavior had finally settled in. The prospect of starvation has a way of assisting in one's maturation.

At that moment, around the corner came their VP, Daddy Biz Bucks, whose office was many miles away and rarely visited this dock at the company. The VP asked him why he was sitting on the cold concrete. After hearing the young man admit his problems, the VP went into the supervisor's office. Some wise counsel was provided to the supervisor. The supervisor decided to give the young man one more try. The young man was not terminated. This experience caused him to mature in the moment. A successful career ensued, eventually ending in a prominent managerial position.

People change. Good bosses can help. Discipline, meted out professionally, can go a long way to help the transformation process.

THE BEST YEAR OF MY ENTIRE LIFE

Being a people developer is a wonderful, rewarding skill as shown by the following:

A seasoned leader, who was also a known people developer, was quite enthused when he discovered that a highly effective administrative assistant, who we will call Jaylynn, had a four-year college degree in business communications. This presented an opportunity for the boss to help this talented person move into a position that could leverage her skills, allow her to broaden her influence, and also cause her to have considerably more, much-needed pay. The people developer was frustrated however when she refused opportunities for advancement. She was fearful of change and didn't want to take the plunge into such a position.

After three years of subtle prodding, Jaylynn accepted a single assignment to facilitate a group, as an internal consultant, for two hours. It took an improbable set of circumstances.

Another frontline employee had a doctor's appointment and could not facilitate an important team meeting. The boss who usually would provide the backup himself had a mandatory meeting with top management at the same time. The boss asked Jaylynn to facilitate the meeting. Luckily, she knew the manager of the department who would preside at the meeting, another woman. This emboldened her. The boss called the department manager and set up the meeting.

The boss returned from the meeting with top management and heard his phone ringing. It was the other manager. The conversation went like this:

"So…to be honest I thought you were crazy sending Jaylynn to facilitate my meeting. But now that she has been here and done her thing, there's something I want you to know…she was a whole lot better than you would have been!"

Both laughed. The boss took the occasion to share that phone call with Jaylynn. She was emboldened by this early success. More opportunities came. Eventually she took the plunge as a valued analyst or facilitator.

Some months later, Jaylynn left for a week's vacation at the end of the year and left a Christmas card on the boss's desk. It simply read, "Thanks, this is the best year of my entire life!"

Lesson: Need one more reason to be a people developer? Simply put,

> Being a people developer is the best part of being a boss!

TWO QUESTIONS

Tom Skinner left a legacy among his peers as the best people developer at GE. This begs two questions for any new or seasoned leader in any company or organization. First, who is known among *your* peers as the best people developer in your organization?

And second,

Why isn't it *you?*

QUESTIONS FOR CURRENT LEADERS

1. Do you understand the motives of your employees? If not, what can you do to get better acquainted?
2. Do you have the intestinal fortitude to discipline when necessary? Have you fallen short of that in the past? How has it affected the future?
3. Which one person of your direct reports do you want to develop and mentor? Why? How can you start? How about mentoring two people or three?

TECHNICAL ANALOG FOR LIFE AND LEADERSHIP: PEOPLE AS PROJECTS

In chapter 9, figure 16 illustrated a project process with six steps (plus a control loop). Two examples were used: the development of a new scrubber at a power plant and the development of a new training course. This process might be nicknamed the development process. If it can be applied to technical projects and to training projects, could it be applied to people? Most of us have heard the phrase, "Joe is one of my projects." However, we should not use the word *project* in a pejorative manner when referring to people who deserve to be respected. Indeed, the six project process steps (figure 16) can apply to the development of people as well as things.

Step 1:   Conceptually, you decided as his boss to help Joe develop. Initial conversations ensue.

Step 2:   You help Joe formulate preliminary ideas for development.

Step 3:   You help Joe become very detailed in his development plan. He commits it to writing.

Step 4:   You help Joe implement his development plan.

Step 5:   You check to prove that Joe got the skills, tools, and competencies desired.

Step 6:   You close out the performance year and return to conceptual planning for his development for next year.

The first three steps are the keys. Driving from conceptual through preliminary to detailed planning makes the development project work. Step 2 is the often forgotten step. Every concept needs to be fleshed out with hard preliminary thinking before jumping into the details. Step 2 is where the why of the ideas is determined. Adults need the why to buy-in.

CHAPTER 12

DECISION-MAKING

TRUMAN AND THE BOMB:
A BIGGER DECISION THAN MOST KNOW

Harry Truman has a special place in history for making a decision that changed the world. Some argue for the better. Some argue for the worse.[73] At what is now known as White Sands Proving Ground in New Mexico, on July 16, 1945, with code name Trinity, the United States conducted the first test of a nuclear explosion. A few weeks later, the world would witness the results of this successful test. A horrible war immediately ceased.

Many years ago, a physics professor in explaining quantum mechanics to The Biz Bucks Guy and fellow classmates[74] mentioned that the initial atomic test bomb was a bigger decision for Truman than most understand. Some physicists at the time were afraid that the Trinity explosion would raise the energy level of the oxygen surrounding the detonation above a certain quantum level making the oxygen atoms explode in a nuclear chain reaction. This, as the theory went, would trigger every oxygen atom in the world. The entire world would instantly be incinerated. Truman listened and made one of the toughest calls in history. His choice that fateful summer is oft debated. His guts, however, are without question.

Few leaders will need to make decisions approaching such magnitude or consequence. But decisions of all kinds will test the mettle of each person who steps into a leadership role. Decision making is more than merely being decisive. Leaders need to make the right decisions. This chapter provides some basics principles and also teaches a specific tool: decision trees. Before delving into the principles, let's discuss some workplace decisions.

DECISIONS IN THE WORKPLACE

Most quantoids whether engineers, accountants, chemists, plant operators, or financial analysts have been involved with a variety of decisions in the workplace. When you become boss, however, the nature of these decisions changes. The importance increases. Their frequency multiplies. Their ambiguity and uncertainty amplifies. To give those contemplating boss-hood a better picture, here is a representative list of decisions a manager or supervisor may be asked to make. This list is intentionally diverse on many dimensions, including ethics.

You might need to decide:

1. Whom to lay off during a reduction-in-force downsizing
2. Who should go to the important industry seminar
3. How to distribute scarce dollars for raises
4. If an employee should play in a vendor golf tournament
5. What product idea to develop next
6. What to do with a customer who is wrong about an issue (given your customer-support person has already dealt with the issue and it has been raised to your desk)
7. To lay off an employee who is not as guilty as he was made out to be, but the VP is forcing you to lay him off anyway
8. On giving an under-the-table benefit to your number 1 client as your VP has directed even though the legal department has advised against it

9. Whether to order the normal high fat, high calorie, high carbohydrate lunch for your training meeting participants or to support the new corporate health initiative and only have *rabbit food*
10. Which one person of many good candidates to select for your vacant position
11. To accept a warranty settlement or to litigate
12. What kind of contract to issue, time and materials or fixed price
13. To launch a product (or open a new store) now or wait for more market information
14. To fix the equipment that shows deterioration during your busy season or try to ride it out until the busy season is over
15. To bid a reasonable price or to buy the business with a low bid and hope you make it up on change orders later
16. To pad change orders to make up for a low original bid
17. To recommend a change to an organization chart that eliminates your close friend's job
18. Move a department closer to its major client, causing relocations and potential resignations
19. To close an underperforming customer office in a potential political hotbed
20. To buy a software package priced above your authority limit when your boss and his boss are gone for the holidays and the price is only good for another two days.
21. To use common sense and approve overtime (which will save money on retravel) when a new corporate policy requires overtime to be approved by a VP in advance
22. How to confront a valued employee regarding a "he said, she said" sexual harassment issue
23. Who to promote
24. Who to demote

25. When to start finding a new growth position (outside of your department) for a valued employee

If a work life filled with these types of decisions is unappetizing for an ardent quantoid, perhaps a leadership assignment is not the right path. For them, an expert career path will be fulfilling and exhilarating.

On the other hand, with your common sense and a few tools, you can learn to make most of your decisions well. Leadership, particularly when you hit decision-making home runs, is also fulfilling and exhilarating.

To assist new leaders, here are some decision-making tools, types, and tips.

SOME STARTING PRINCIPLES

There is much academic fluff available on decision-making. An online search will uncover digital reams of it. Some of it is interesting. Some is pretty useless in a practical sense. Here are several foundational principles of the more practical variety for new leaders.

Decisions are Hard

Why are decisions hard? There are several reasons that all play together to make decisions hard:

1. The outcome matters. The issues are important. The consequences of decisions affect people, their well-being, their income, their sense of self-esteem, and their safety. The higher one advances in leadership, the more people are affected by your decisions.
2. There is no clear choice. Several alternatives may exist. If one choice is obvious, it really isn't a decision.

3. There is no one generally accepted methodology to use to make a decision.

4. There are often many intangibles that are important regarding the potential outcomes. These tend to offset each other somewhat. The importance to place on a given intangible is a matter of personal perspective.

5. There are often multiple sources of uncertainty, like weather, sickness, equipment failure, cost, timing, economic cycles, or technological understanding.

Combining number 1 and number 5, anxiety is a function of importance amplified by uncertainty or in quantoid terms:

$$Anxiety = Importance \times Uncertainty$$

Avoid Suboptimization

The first principle of decision-making in larger organizations (like a medium or large corporation) is to make decisions that are best for the entire company, not a small part of the company. The problem is this: budgets and bonuses collude to cause people to do the opposite, to suboptimize their decisions. Suboptimization is doing what is best for a small part of an organization, not what is best for the overall organization. This may also apply to a large division, if it is a separate profit center. The Biz Buck Guy has collected many examples of suboptimization from students. Consider this one:

An outage manager at a nuclear plant was accountable for completing the outage on time and within budget. Early in the outage, a crucial component of the turbine generator was inspected and found to have very little life left. The component needed replacing. Fortunately, someone twenty years before ordered a spare component. It was still in great shape collecting dust in the warehouse. Accounting wise, normal inventory does not depreciate. So this component was still carried on the books at $750,000. When the component is taken out of inventory, the outage will be charged that much.

The vendor of the turbine got wind of the situation and got a price from the factory, which miraculously was only $600,000. He told the outage manager he could save him $150,000 on his outage costs by buying the new one from him. The company had already decided *not* to replace the component in the warehouse if it was ever used. The outage manager took the *Kool-Aid*. He saved his outage $150,000 but created a cash outflow for his company of $600,000. If he used the warehoused component, the cash outflow would have been zero. In fact, the property taxes would have been reduced every year from then on, an additional cash *in*flow. The suboptimization flu is very contagious. Many companies have a culture of suboptimizing. The loss of profit is substantial.

Growth Comes from Decision-Making

The greater responsibility you have in an organization, the tougher the decisions will be. At a supervisor level, you are being nurtured by the small decisions you make. If others perceive that you are able to handle the smaller decisions, opportunities for additional responsibility are possible.

There is an old political term, *mugwump*, that has come to mean a fence sitter. If you are unable to see shades of gray and postpone decisions that are needed to be made now, you may be labeled a mugwump, someone who sits on the fence with his *mug* on one side and his *wump* on the other. This can be caustic to your upward mobility.

Your Values Count

To be a good decision maker, a leader must filter each alternative through her own set of values. Values are what we stand for.

They are non-negotiable. Without a good understanding of one's values, decision makers will be subject to vacillation and indecision. Subordinates will argue for their own self interest based on their values. The decision maker will be "tossed to and fro by every wind" of argumentation. Roy Disney, Walt's nephew and a top Disney executive, once said, "When your values are clear to you, making decisions becomes easier."[75] Get to know what you stand for.

Don't be Fooled by Analysis

A wise mentor of The Biz Bucks Guy, Joe Showalter once said, "An engineering evaluation is a precise mathematical expression of a biased opinion." Just because you have been given an elegant analysis, full of NPVs, cash flows, and cost estimates, do not consider that your final direction. Look for bias in the assumptions. Let your instincts help you make the choice.

Recommending versus Making

Most frontline quantoids have ample experience in recommending decisions to their bosses. Please be careful to realize that *recommending* and *making* are two very different things. When the responsibility falls on your shoulders, it is much different than using analytical tools to number out the decision's financial aspects. There are always intangibles that can override a financial decision. The decision maker earns his keep.

Making Decisions Right versus Making Right Decisions

Decisions may not always pan out as planned, but at least, the process of reaching a conclusion and implementing it can be sound. However, don't be confused. A decision that turns out bad is not a right decision even if you made the decision right. In the real world of decision-making, style points don't count. It is always better to be lucky than good. As a old saying goes,

> The world isn't interested in how many storms you encountered, but whether you brought in the ship!

To excuse a decision that went poorly with rationalizations of "But we did everything right!" only keeps you from growing and improving your decision-making skills. Honestly collect lessons learned and implement needed change any time the dice comes up snake eyes for you.

FOUR TYPES OF DECISION-MAKING FOR LEADERS

Like so many topics in the field of leadership, there is no one model that everyone subscribes to about decision-making. There are many lists, many tools, and many focuses. The Biz Bucks Guy has used the following model for approaching decisions, particularly when you are a boss with good people on your team.

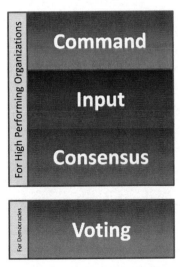

Figure 22 – Four Decision Types

As shown in figure 22, decisions can be made by command, input, consensus, and voting.

Command

The boss simply makes the decision with no input from the group. This is used often in emergencies. A fire captain does not typically call a group meeting to determine how to fight a raging fire. Some leaders are only able to use this method of decision-making. They exhibit a *heroic* management style, thinking they must always be the hero and make the call. However, if the heroic leader will give them a try, many decisions can be made using other decision-making types, particularly the next two, input and consensus. Better decisions will ensue.

Input

The boss makes it clear to everyone that she will retain the final decision authority, but she would highly value the professional input from the group. Everyone else feels respected, respects others in the group, and openly provides data, information, opinion, and argumentation. The boss expresses appreciation for counsel from the council, then makes the call. This method fits particularly well when the decision has large ramifications, and there is sufficient time to contemplate as a group.

Consensus

The main difference between input and consensus is, with consensus, the boss abdicates the responsibility for the decision to the group. The boss can facilitate the group to a conclusion, or he may have an outsider or a member of the group facilitate the discussion. The boss's opinions, in theory, carry no more weight than anyone else's. This is a unique, high-performing group when this ideal is reached.

Consensus building can lead to unanimity, where everyone agrees. However, consensus does not mean everyone agrees in the end. Reaching consensus recognizes a small part of the group may not fully agree with the larger part's alternative, but the minority is not willing to fall on the sword for their position. They agree to be supportive, even though they think a better solution is available. The larger group's approach is sufficient. In motivational theory, this is called sufficing.

Voting

Whether by the raise of the hand, a voting booth, or any method in between, the group agrees that majority wins. The group must also decide, if there is more than one option, if plurality wins or what the rules of a runoff are going to be. Nonetheless, the numbers make the decision.

High-Performing Organizations and Decision-Making

Here's the revelation: high-performing organizations use only the first three! Without question, voting has its place in a democracy or another political entity like a union. But most organizations are not and should not be ran as a democracy. There are those in authority who are paid to make decisions. They have perspectives that come largely from their position that are more long reaching. Simply put, they are at the top of the palm tree and have the longest view. Others certainly may help, but decisions must be made quickly. Voting on anything but the smallest scale usually takes too much time, yields misunderstanding, and results in decisions that may not be really balanced.

Okay, voting on the place to have lunch is no big deal. But voting on working four ten-hour days each week instead of five eights, for example, may yield a start time that fits the majority but hurts single heads of families who rely on child care that is not available in wee morning hours. For some, it is not a matter of convenience but survival. A balanced decision may give more weight to single heads of families than the opportunity to tee it up for eighteen holes each Friday.

Simply having a discussion and then voting may seem appropriate for small groups. But requiring people to share their opinion, negotiate, and compromise builds strong decisions and strong groups. Whether it is by input or consensus, the group tends to buy into the decision.

THE JUSTIFICATION MATRIX

Many of the decisions made by leaders involve some sort of spending, whether capital dollars or expensed dollars. The following is a useful framework to help sort out spending decisions.

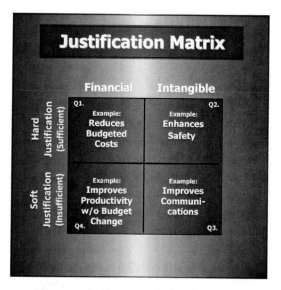

Figure 23 – The *Biz Bucks* Justification Matrix
for Spending Decisions

The justification matrix in figure 23 posits both financial and intangible areas of justification for spending decisions. The intangibles can include the improvement of safety, communications, employee satisfaction and development, customer satisfaction, brand equity, the environment, information, the community, and regulatory relations.

The matrix also shows both the financial and the intangible justification can come in two versions: hard justification, meaning sufficient to justify the recommended path, and soft justification, or insufficient to justify the path. There is nothing new regarding quadrants 1 through 3. We all know that some alternatives have strong financial justification (quadrant 1), some have strong intangible justification (quadrant 2), and some only have weak or soft intangible justification (quadrant 3).

Quadrant 4, however, may be more insightful to the new leader. Sometimes the financial numbers are also soft. Consider the supervisor who requests a new and expensive software package for her department. Everyone knows it will improve productivity of the department. However, if the department has twenty people, and she claims a 10 percent improvement in productivity, she should be willing to remove two people from their department to push the justification into quadrant 1. Otherwise, this is merely soft quadrant 4 justification, which does not justify much at all.

This productivity improvement may become quadrant 1 justification if the supervisor can make a firm case that the workload will be increasing soon and no additional positions will be needed with this software.

But unless a new leader understands the difference between quadrant 1 and quadrant 4, she will be pushing a rope to get her recommendations approved by upper management.

THE FUNDAMENTAL PHILOSOPHY
OF FINANCIAL DECISION-MAKING

In Appendix B, several principles of finance are listed. One bears repeating here:

F3. In making spending decisions, separate the financial data from the intangibles. Use the financial data to number out a financial decision, then and only then, weigh the financial decision against the intangibles. Let your common sense determine if the intangibles outweigh the numbers.

This is called the fundamental philosophy of decision-making in Biz Bucks training courses. To those who know how messy meetings can become when the person leading the meeting allows both financial and intangible considerations to be discussed together, not separately, no explanation of the principle is necessary. To those who have not been involved in such messy meetings, perhaps no explanation is possible.

When groups mix financial data and intangible data together in a meeting, The Biz Bucks Guy calls it *churning*. It is like churning butter; everyone throws their favorite ingredient into a decision-making butter churn, and then everyone discusses it in a random, disorganized fashion. Everyone is inadvertently colluding to move the handle of the churn up and down. There is much illusion of decision making, but mostly just motion and commotion of the churn. And worse, nothing is really getting decided. After much wasted time, eventually, someone proposes a direction. The group generally goes along, more to terminate the churn meeting, than to passionately support the direction. It is a soft, buttery decision at best. In addition, the degree of buy-in is often suspect.

There is a better way. Have someone do the financial analysis outside of the meeting and then review that analysis without bringing up intangibles. Only after the financial analysis is well understood by the group, allow them to consider intangibles. Use common sense to weigh the intangibles against the financial recommendation, and pick the direction that your common sense yields. An intangible weighing matrix may also be useful. This matrix will be discussed later in this chapter.

HANDLING UNCERTAINTY WITH DECISION TREES

A decision tree is a statistical tool that helps picture and weigh various aspects of a decision. It is among the finest group facilitation tools on the planet. It helps everyone stay on focus. It provides a balanced assessment of both financial and intangible considerations. It yields buy-in from most people.

Decision trees are also the Rodney Dangerfield of leadership tools. They "don't get no respect" from the uninitiated.

The Biz Bucks Guy has faciliated the devleopment of decision trees with clients who are facing incredibly complex decisions. The more significant ones have included a hundred-million dollar environmental decision, a control room layout, and an engineering system decision with three warring factions who fought for two years. In every case, all parties were able to reach a unanimous recommendation for upper management. Decision trees are powerful.

Decision trees help you deal with financial decisions when the assumptions are uncertain. That, by the way, is all the time in the real world. Engineers coming out of school are used to cranking numbers on word problems where the assumptions are always given. In the real world, the assumptions are picked by the engineer, the financial analyst, or the physicist. Decision trees allow you to shape a probablistic picture of the possible outcomes.

The steps to use a decision tree are summarized as follows:

1. Determine relevent sources of uncertainty
2. Draw the tree structure (from left to right)
3. Add the costs, revenues, or net present values (NPVs) for each terminal path
4. Add your best assessment of the probabilies for each outcome node
5. Work the tree (from right to left)
6. Only then, consider intangibles

After introducing an example, each of these six steps will be explained in greater detail. The example and all numbers therein are ficititious.

The Space Shuttle Decision

In honor of our now retired NASA vehicle of the last three decades, let's consider a fictitious space shuttle example. The space shuttle is nearing the completion of a long mission. They would like to land today at Kennedy Space Center in Florida, but the weather does not allow them to do so. They can land now at the first alternative site, Edwards Air Force Base in California.

Another option is to stay up and hope the weather clears tomorrow. They have two days of food and fuel, and then they must come down.

If they go to Edwards, it costs them $5 million to get the shuttle back to Kennedy. An extra day in space costs $3 million. Your NASA meteorologist believes there is a 55 percent chance of it clearing tomorrow and a 95 percent chance the second day. There are no weather concerns for Edwards for the next two days.

One of three fuel cells has failed. The other two are operating within specs. The shuttle only needs one to land safely.

What should you do? Land now at Edwards or stay up a day?

This problem clearly has a significant intangible. The safety of the crew may be jeopardized by waiting a day. The decision-tree methodology allows a facilitator to waive off any comments on safety until the financial aspects have been reviewed. Then, any intangibles can be weighed against the financial result of the decision tree, known as its *expected value*.

1. Determining Relevant Sources of Uncertainty

In this problem, there is one source of uncertainty for the decision tree—the weather. Yes, there is an intangible, safety of the crew, which is certainly an uncertainty, but that will not be reflected on this tree. The fundamental philosophy of decision-making requires us to separate the financial valuation from the intangibles.

In some decision trees, there may be three or four sources of uncertainty. This makes the size of the tree grow exponentially. The analyst should limit the sources of uncertainty to only the most relevant ones.

2. Drawing the Tree Structure

Decision trees have two shapes connected by lines. A decision is indicated by a square. It is called a *decision node*. Possible outcomes are indicted by a circle called an *outcome node*.

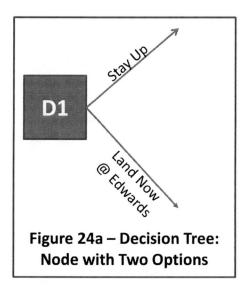

Figure 24a – Decision Tree: Node with Two Options

Referring to figure 24a, the decision tree always starts with a decision node, labelled *D1*. In this example, there are only two options, stay up or land now. If we land now, it will be at Edwards in California.

The next step is an important tip. The analyst asks a cogent question of each path. "If I take this option, can I control the outcomes?" This relates back to the relevant sources of uncertainty.

"Based on the weather, if I stay up, can I control the outcomes from the weather? No. It could clear tomorrow, or it could remain below minimums, and landing at Kennedy would not be an option." When the answer to this question is no, the analyst draws a circle, an outcome node, and describes the plausible outcomes. This is shown as the first outcome node in figure 24b.

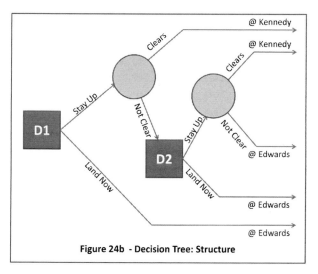

Figure 24b - Decision Tree: Structure

For the "land now" option, the answer to the question is yes because the decision was made to land, and the problem is over. The weather is not an issue. No outcome node is needed.

If the weather clears, we will land at Kennedy. If it does not clear, this leads us to another decision, *D2*. The problem repeats itself for the second day.

When completed, the structure has five *terminal paths*. Two indicate they would land at Kennedy with three for Edwards.

Just drawing the tree structure will provide the group a better understanding of the options available. This may occasionally be sufficient to make the decision without completing the tree methodology, particularly if most of the terminal paths can be rejected for obvious intangible reasons.

3. Adding the Costs

This space shuttle example is a *cost* problem. In cost problems, like golf, low numbers are good! Some problems are *revenue* problems, and others are *NPV* problems. For these, high numbers are good. This third step consists of calculating the cost of each terminal path, from D1 to the end. The top path shows we stayed up one day, cost: $3 million. Refer to figure 24c.

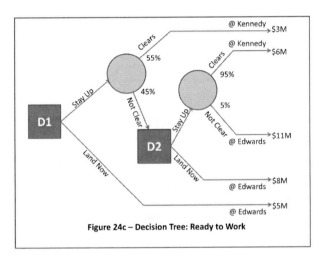

Figure 24c – Decision Tree: Ready to Work

The second path shows we stayed up a day and the weather did not clear, so we chose to stay up a second day, cost: $6 million.

The third path is the most expensive. We chose to stay up one day and the weather did not clear. We chose to stay up a second day, and again, the weather did not clear. We had to land because we are then out of fuel and supplies. That cost us $6 million for staying up two days *plus* $5 million for landing at Edwards—a total of $11 million.

The fourth path reflects staying up one day but landing at Edwards when the weather did not clear, cost $8 million.

Finally, the last path shows we just chose to go to Edwards now, cost: $5 million.

4. Adding the Probabilities

The final preparatory step, before working the tree, is to add probabilities to each outcome node. We will use the meteorologist's data for this example. In many real-life decision trees, the analyst does not have such convenient data to plug in.

Referring again to figure 24c, the chances of it clearing at Kenneday tomorrow are 55 percent. If that is the case, the chances of it not clearing are 45 percent. This gives rise to the Biz Bucks theorem of outcome-nodal completeness:

There is a 100 percent chance of something happening!

This insightful theorem is important, particularly when you have multiple outcomes from a given outcome node. They must all add to 100 percent.

For the second outcome node, we use 95 percent and 5 percent.

As shown in figure 24c, the tree is now complete and ready to be worked. The structure is drawn, the costs added, and the probabilites added.

Binary versus Full Distribution of Outcomes

The analyst must understand another important point about outcome nodes. This space shuttle example conveniently has *binary* outcome nodes. Either the weather clears or it doesn't. That makes life easy for the analyst. However, many problems have outcome nodes with multiple outcome paths. In fact, there could be an infinite number of possible outcomes. The analyst has the lattitude to determine how many paths are necessary to approximate all possible outcomes. Take a court room example.

Your company is being sued for wrongful discharge of an employee. If it goes to court, can you control the outcomes? No way. Juries are about as sure as the tables in Las Vegas. So what could happen? Almost anything. To capture the situation, perhaps the analyst uses four outcome paths.

1. We lose big (guess: $5 million).
2. We lose moderately ($2 million).
3. We lose modestly ($1 million).
4. We win.

When there is a full distribution of possible outcomes, the analyst should pick a representative number. The Biz Bucks Guy's experience says no more than four paths are necessary to represent the outcome well. How many outcomes to pick is as much art as science. After four, additional outcomes provide no added accuracy and definitely adds useless work.

5. Working the Tree

The analyst drew the tree from left to right. We work the tree from right to left. Starting at the most complex part, move back until you hit a node.

In this space shuttle problem, by inspection, the most complex part appears to be the second and third path. Moving back, the analyst comes to an outcome node. There is one rule for outcome nodes and another for decision nodes. Refer to figure 24d.

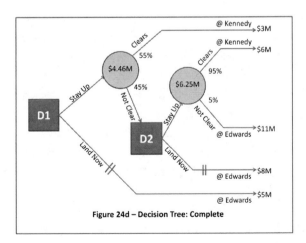

Figure 24d – Decision Tree: Complete

For outcome nodes, the rule is multiply and add. This is called calculating the expected value of the outcome node. In this case, you multliply all pairs of numbers, one cost with one probability, then add the results together. The two pairs are 95% × $6 million and 5 % × $11 million. The expected value of the outcome node is $6.25 million.

Moving back again, the analyst comes to a decision node, D2. The rule for a decision node is easier than the outcome node. Simply, make a decision. It is better to have $6.25 million than $8 million. The analyst uses a *double hash mark* to indicate the path that is not selected. If the decision node has twenty options, the analyst would add nineteen double hash marks.

Continuing, the analyst hits an outcome node. The pairs of numbers are 55% x $3 million and 45% x $6.25 million. The expected value is $4.46 million.

Finally, the analyst reaches the original decision, D1. The choice is clear. The amount $4.46 is better than $5 million. The double hash mark is used to indicate this final financial direction. Summarizing and rounding, it appears there is about a half million dollars in favor of staying up.

Sometimes the financial expected value is very sensitive to the probabilities selected for the outcome nodes. This means by wiggling the probabilities, the decision tree's recommended option changes. This is still good information. It should be intepreted that this decision is not a financial decision. The decision should be made by considering intangibles only.

6. Considering Intangibles

For this space shuttle example, a value judgment is needed regarding the important intangible in this problem: safety. Is it worth half a million of expected value dollars to risk the crew's well being given one of three fuel cells has failed? That is a matter of discussion for a group setting. Unless you are an expert at NASA, this may require some discussion of values and risks.

Coincidentally, a similar but real-life situation developed on a space shuttle mission many years after the Biz Buck Guy developed this simple example. In midmission, one of three fuel cells cratered. The mission was immediately aborted. They came down during the next orbit. If one cratered, perhaps there is a systemic problem with all three fuel cells. End of mission, land now before another fails.

When more than one intangible is important to the decision, the group may need to consider a separate calculation for intangibles as noted in the following section.

A DECISION TREE FOR INTANGIBLES

Often there is more than one intangible to consider. The Biz Bucks Guy has experience in doing a matrix to determine an intangbile score for each path. The score is run through the decision tree structure, replacing the costs with the intangible score. This yields an intangible expected value. If this intangible expected value is in the opposite direction of the financial expected value, the group still is left with a healthy discussion of which one overides the other.

The matrix of intangibles is based on both *importance* and *impact*. Use the *ten-point must system* for both. Each intangible is first weighted by importance, relative to each other. The analyst selects the most important intangible to this decision and assigns it ten points. The other intangibles are given other *importance* scores, compared to the most important one.

Then each terminal path is analyzed for impact on each intangible. Again, the analyst selects the path that has the most impact on a given intangible. That gets a ten-point score. Other impacts are considered relative to the one with the most impact.

The intangible score for each path is the sum of the *importance* score times the *impact* score for each intangible.

TWO TIPS FOR DECISION TREES

First, never use decision trees with the uninitiated. You will be instantly labeled *Geek of the Week*, particularly with normal people (nonquantoids). If you have a decision tree to show someone who is not familiar with the methodology, hold off! Spend some time with them first, explaining decision trees in general. Come back a few days later, if possible, and show them your recommendation using the decision tree methodology. You will have better acceptance.

Second, use progressive disclosure. In the training industry, the term *progressive disclosure* refers to building a diagram or graphic in front of the class, not just plopping some complex creation of yours in front of their eyes. It causes overload immediately, and you are in trouble with people absorbing your ideas. Take the time to build the decision tree. This can be done using PowerPoint custom animation or simply by using a flip chart. If you let them build it with you, you will have a much better chance of eliciting their buy-in.

THE REAL POWER OF DECISION TREES

An industry engineering expert in a large company had a track record of not being able to give firm recommendations when things were uncertain. He did not know the decision tree methodology. After attending a decision tree course, he returned and, in a few days, got some unsettling data on a major component in one of the manufacturing plants. It was showing signs of impending failure.

The company was just at the beginning of their annual season for making most of their profits. The season was four months long. The expert could recommend shutting down now and fixing the machinery or trying to limp through the season, hoping to fix it after the profit-making time was over.

If the company fixed it now, the planned outage would be three weeks. If they risked it, trying to get through the season without the three weeks of lost time, an uplanned outage might be as much as seven weeks. The lost revenue for the three weeks planned outage was $4 million!

The expert applied his new knowledge of decision trees. Using his best guesses of outcomes and probabilities, the decision tree indicated the company should take the risk and limp through the next four months. He presented his recommendation up the chain of command. Everyone had also been trained in decision trees. The top leaders understood his reasoned, balanced recommendation. They agreed to risk the consequences and try to limp through to the end of the season.

It was successful! This decision tree saved them $4 million. The Biz Bucks Guy did not charge them half that much to teach them decision trees.

The real power of decision trees is its ability to help a group of experts (and perhaps their bosses) agree on a direction. It is not merely a statitical tool. It is a group decision-making and facilitation tool. Decision trees allow groups to make tough decisions when the underlying assumptions are uncertain. As was stated earlier, that is all the time in the real world.

The decision tree is a quantitative tool. Many quantoids can become enamored with this methodology. However, this tool is only a means to an end, a well reasoned decision, balancing all key aspects of the decision-making environment. Of equal importance is mastering the four types of decisions (presented before the decision tree) and developing the wisdom to know what situations support their respective use.

Decisiveness is not a natural attribute for many new leaders. It must be developed. As Ron Seidel, a leader in the energy industry, has said, "People will forgive you for making a mistake, but they will not forgive you for not making a decision."

QUESTIONS FOR CURRENT LEADERS

1. Which of the four types of decisions do you use the most? Should you consider using the more participative ones (input and consensus) more often? Would it change the development of your people?
2. Have you ever been in a churn meeting? How did the final decision get made? Did the one with the most power make the decision?
3. Does your larger organization understand decision trees? What can you do to improve the use of decision trees?

TECHNICAL ANALOG FOR LIFE AND LEADERSHIP: CIRCUIT ANALYSIS AND JUMPING TO CONCLUSIONS

When The Biz Bucks Guy was completing his undergrad degree in electrical engineering, one of his mean old professors gave his class a lab problem. One of the challenges with electrical engineering, compared with mechanical or civil, is you are working blind when working with an electrical circuit. With a mechanical system, you can see what is going on. No such luck with electrical components. They stare at you innocently, giving no hint of what is happening on the inside.

Paired with a lab partner, each student was assigned to diagnose a circuit and report on the problem in the circuit. We had done similar assignments in the past. This seemed like a breeze. However, the more our dynamic duo poked the circuit, loaded with components of resistors, capacitors, inductors, with the oscilloscope probes, the more confused we got. We finally submitted an answer. We knew something was up. The professor was making a point. No team got the correct answer. At the end of the lab, he announced the solution. Unlike all the other lab testing we had done, there was not one element misbehaving, but two! It was so simple, but it threw a group of pretty smart dudes and a few dudettes off.

The Biz Bucks Guy learned something from that lab experiment that day, more than merely circuit diagnosis. Do not jump to conclusions. Look for all the underlying problems and issues. Solutions to problems do not necessarily come gift wrapped. Like the circuit with two bad elements, decision-making in business can be deceiving too.

Look for multiple reasons and seek the root causes. Don't think the first root cause is the only one.

CHAPTER 13

COMMUNICATING

DAT WHICH CAN'T BLOW UP AIN'T GONNA!

Several decades ago, the commercial nuclear power industry was regulated by the predecessor of the Nuclear Regulatory Commission, the Atomic Energy Commission (AEC). The AEC was politically bipolar. It had responsibility not only for ensuring safety of atomic power plants but promoting and advancing the construction of such plants. During the time of the AEC, a classic story in communication took place. Heard at an industry conference many years ago, The Biz Bucks Guy recalls the following account:

> A problem arose among longshoremen working at the port in New York City. These dedicated workers essential to the economic well-being of the area were quite concerned about the construction of Indian Point Power Plant several miles upriver from NYC. The mere mention of "atomic anything" conjured up visions of a mushroom-shaped cloud suddenly appearing on the horizon near NYC.

> In response to their concerns, the AEC sent a technical expert from their staff to speak at a longshoremen's union meeting to persuade the longshoremen to support the

plant's construction. The expert explained the technical reasons why a commercial light water reactor cannot blow up like a bomb. The enrichment of the fissionable uranium isotope U-235 occurs in nature at approximately 0.7 percent compared to the fertile isotope U-238. That percentage needs to be increased to over 90 percent for a chain reaction to occur at a rate sufficient to cause an atomic explosion. The uranium in a commercial power reactor has been enriched to only about 3 percent, nowhere near the 90 plus percent required to make a bomb. The expert explained reactivity coefficients, moderators, coolants, fuel rods, bundles, the fuel cycle, gaseous diffusion, and other esoteric terms. The more he spoke, the more the longshoremen felt frustrated. He was not connecting with them.

The expert left. The concerns stayed.

The AEC officials were perplexed. Hadn't they taken the time to properly explain the simple reasons that a plant cannot blow up? Hadn't they sent an educated expert? What was needed to change the thinking of these longshoremen?

Another staff member volunteered to go to a subsequent longshoremen meeting and try his hand at neutralizing the concerns. This man was not only qualified to speak on the safety of nuclear power, but he also came from Brooklyn. Furthermore, earlier in his career, he was a New York City fireman.

At the next meeting, after being introduced as a former local fireman, he was welcomed by the longshoremen. He spoke with his instantaneously recognizable Brooklyn accent. After listening to their concerns, he simply said, "Hey, youz guys, dat which can't blow up, ain't gonna!"

That was enough. He said it all. The meeting was largely over. The objective of alleviating the longshoremen's concerns had been met.

"Why didn't the other guy say that?" was the attitude of the longshoremen. The second expert knew how to speak the language of his audience. What sounded like a government snow job initially was transformed into a big win. The first guy beat around the technical bush. He never got to the point. The second expert was perfectly clear and succinct. The audience got the message from one with credibility. He was considered one of them.

THE GRAND COMPETENCE

This chapter is about communication. This skill could be called the grand competence. Most of an organization's problems can be traced to poor or nonexistent communication.

A department goal is not met. Yes, it was communicated at the beginning of the performance period, but was it reinforced multiple times?

A new company strategy has been developed. A top-down communication plan was rolled out. A few weeks later, the buzz never developed among the rank and file of the company. Yes, it was initially communicated through passive means, but was it communicated using "inertia breaking" aggressive tools appropriate for implementing a corporate strategy?

An employee breaks a new security rule at a manufacturing plant. Yes, the rule was discussed at an all-hands floor meeting, but was the employee in question on sick leave that day?

Most quantoids understand the importance of being a great communicator. Many quantoids may not understand the difficulty in being a great communicator. Each quantoid who is shooting for an eventual leadership assignment must realize:

> The danger in communication is assuming it has taken place.

Referring back to figure 1, the four skills of leadership, the third skill is communicate the vision. People know what the organization is all about. They know where the organization is going. When such communication is a permanent cultural norm across the organization, organizational miracles often occur, as illustrated by the following.

Johnny "The Baggage Handler"

When The Biz Bucks Guy was attending the USC Executive MBA program, he travelled weekly from Phoenix to LAX on Southwest Airlines. Near the close of the first year, he had racked up several free flights. He and Mrs. Biz Bucks wanted to take the entire family on a really great vacation during the summer break. But there was a problem. At that time, Southwest Airlines did not fly to that many hot vacation spots. The places on most people's vacation list were in relatively close proximity to their home. They had already vacationed at them. It looked like a wonderful week in Lubbock was all that was left! No offense to that nice Texas town.

On one of the last flights before the break, The Biz Bucks Guy got on late and sat in the back next to a young man in a brown uniform. His name, Johnny, was embroidered on the shirt over one pocket. Over the other pocket was embroidered Southwest Airlines.

The Biz Bucks Guy, in jest, said, "So…you work for Southwest, huh? So when are you guys going to open up a flight to Honolulu, so I can take my family on a cool vacation?" It was a joke, but it flew right over Johnny's head. Everyone knows if you want to take a 737 to Hawaii from the mainland, you will need to *row* the last thousand miles! It just doesn't have that range.

Suddenly, Johnny's personality ignited with some sort of corporate missionary zeal. The Biz Bucks Guy learned he had just joined the airline as a baggage handler. He had "gotten it" when they explained the vision and mission of his new company at his recent orientation training. He told me in recent years they were the only profitable airline in the skies.

Johnny began to explain that 737s, the standard plane of Southwest, did not have the range to make it to Hawaii, but he, Biz Bucks Guy, should be happy about it. He continued to speak before The Biz Bucks Guy could suggest his question was just a weak attempt at humor.

"The 737 allows us to standardize much of our business, and we are then able to pass the savings onto you in the form of lower ticket prices. You see we only have to train pilots in one type of plane. We only have to train mechanics in one type of plane. We only have to stock inventory for one type of plane.

"And by the way, do you know why we don't have real food on Southwest? Do you know how heavy all that food and the big carts are? That saves a bunch in gas per flight.

"And by the way, do you know we baggage handlers are in a contest with the gate attendants to see who can get their part of the turnaround done first? We get planes in and out, from nose-in to pushback, in only twenty-two minutes! That is much faster than any other airline. You know we make money when the planes are in the air, not at the gate.

"And by the way…yadda, yadda, yadda." The Biz Bucks Guy's new friend had a speech impediment. He had to stop talking every twenty minutes to take a breath! Finally, on approach to LAX, Johnny rested his dissertation on the strategy and future success of Southwest Airlines. And a fine job it was. They never met again.

By total coincidence, the next day's class included the first lecture from an internationally prominent professor, Dr. Alan Shapiro, the world-renowned political economist and author of many books and academic papers. We were all a bit in awe as the program leader completed his impressive introduction of Dr. Shapiro.

Dr. Shapiro walked confidently down the middle aisle, turned to the class of sixty, and began by saying, "Before beginning our study of economics, I want to first review the importance for a large organization to have an integrated strategy. We will discuss three cases studies. The first one is…(you guessed it) Southwest Airlines. Did you know they only fly one type of plane, the Boeing 737? Do you understand why they do that? Why they only need to train one type of pilot! They only need to train one type of maintenance staff! Furthermore, their inventory is much reduced!"

After about ten minutes of a scholar's description of the Southwest Airlines strategy, The Biz Bucks Guy took a risk with this eminent professor.

"Alan." He stopped abruptly, looking a bit annoyed that he was interrupted in midsentence.

The Biz Bucks Guy continued, "Do you know this is the second time in two days I have heard this lecture?"

Dr. Shapiro's eyes rolled back a bit as he contemplated what he did yesterday.

"No. Let me explain," said The Biz Bucks Guy. He took a few minutes and let everyone onto the joke, explaining Johnny and the prior day's "lecture."

Dr. Shapiro then regained control and continued, extending his arms out and turning his palms up. "Well, isn't that what it's all about?" he asked the class. "When a company cannot only develop a coherent strategy but communicate it throughout all levels of the organization, such that even a new baggage handler can articulate it with passion for forty-five minutes…well…that's when the magic happens!"

And indeed it does. World-class communication of strategic intent, goals, metrics, and results—throughout the entire organization—is the catalyst for not only performance but employee satisfaction. It is magic of which Houdini would be proud.

Here are six helpful tips or concepts to jump-start a leader's quest to become a great communicator within her organizational environment.

COMMUNICATE × 10

New leaders may not understand the amount of communication needed to capture the attention of their direct reports. One good rule of thumb is the *communicate x 10* principle. This means a leader should contemplate how much communication is necessary and multiply that by ten. That is a better estimate of how much is really needed. This implies you should use many channels of communication to get the message firmly implanted in the hearts and minds of your people.

BE A GOOD STORYTELLER

Another important channel in effective communication is the ability to relate anecdotes to your audiences. More simply, great communicators are great storytellers. It is a marvelous way to teach a principle and have it remembered.[76]

USE MULTIPLE COMMUNICATION CHANNELS

Channels of communication might include staff meetings, newspapers, e-mails, blogs, posters, mind maps, computer-based notices, wall-mounted charts, one-way speeches, and framed mission statements. All of these are examples of *passive*, not *aggressive*, communication channels.

Aggressive communication channels are ones that really make a difference. They might include, if done properly, roundtable discussions, town hall meetings, or even residential simulations (*residential* means a group goes away for a few days to a hotel to experience the future through an experiential activity).

One important communication channel is simply dropping in on key people to discuss the latest issue, project, innovation, or challenge. These face-to-face meetings may be calendared or on the spur of the moment. Unless overdone, this personal approach usually yields interpersonal dividends.

The Executive Speech Action Item

A top executive of a large company of seven thousand employees gave the first speech at a full day leadership meeting of all management. He provided a one-page list of bullet points for each leader and concluded his message with an assignment for every leader there to inform his or her respective supervisors of an important deadline dealing with the implementation of a new HR process. The bullet-point sheet clearly had the assignment indicated in bold letters at the bottom of the page.

Three weeks later, the HR manager who was implementing the new process decided to check if the message got to the company's five hundred supervisors. A sampling showed only 7 percent were told about the deadline from their boss! Lesson: Use multiple channels to communicate.

THE "WHAT WENT WRONG" MEETING

The Biz Bucks Guy once put a group of top leaders into a room at a hotel. Their division of their company was lethargic, having been a highly regulated company for several decades. A new competitive marketplace was being established by the state legislature. These leaders were not yet unified in how to react to these competitive pressures.

The room was decorated with some creative props to indicate the group had entered into the future by five years. The Biz Bucks Guy enlisted a talented, amateur actor from within the ranks of the company who played the role of the new CEO of an acquiring company who thanked everyone for their work and fired each of them. He told them that if they stayed for ninety days to help in the transition, then they would earn a modest severance package. Otherwise, they were free to clean out their desk after this meeting. The CEO indicated he was expecting results like they had never seen before in this division and none of them had shown the ability to lead this division to that level. He introduced The Biz Bucks Guy as the HR VP of the acquiring company. The CEO left abruptly.

In role, The Biz Bucks Guy asked the group if they wanted to cooperate or not. All said they would take the ninety days and the severance. Using only subtle facilitation techniques, The Biz Bucks Guy began to seed the ensuing conversation. "So what did you guys do wrong to deserve being on the wrong end of a hostile takeover?" After an hour, the group had charted a list of things that went wrong. This was easily turned into things that needed fixing in the real world. The team continued to meet for two days and one late night and produced the first integrated strategic plan that this division had ever seen.

This "what went wrong" meeting aggressively communicated the need for change. Simulations have a special way of getting the message through. Lesson: Use aggressive, not only passive, communication channels for the important things.

SELLING A BUSINESS CASE

One of the most important skills a leader must have is the ability to formulate and present justification for an idea or to justify a recommended alternative among several possible alternatives. In many organizations, the vehicle to communicate your thinking is called a *business case*. A business case is a written or oral recommendation, making the case for a business decision. Four key skills for successful business cases appear as figure 25 and are now discussed.

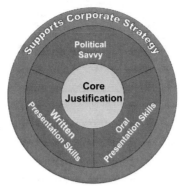

Figure 25 - The *Biz Bucks* Business Case Skills

Core Justification

The core justification for a business case, as detailed in previous chapters, includes both financial and intangible justification. Review the financial section of chapter 6 and figure 23 from chapter 12 for specific insights.

There are many financial valuation tools from which to pick, including net present value (NPV), profitability index (PI), internal rate of return (IRR), and minimum annual revenue requirements. Each large organization will use a particular tool. You must be skilled in the theory behind that tool to present the financial justification.

This financial justification must be based on reasonable assessments of financial benefits and also a reasonable assessment of any offsetting costs if the recommended alternative is accepted. This last point is crucial and should not be overlooked. For example, if a new set of flow monitors for a production process is installed to improve the failure rate of the current monitors, there may be increased preventative maintenance costs for the new monitors compared to the old. Business case recommenders should avoid "falling in love" with their recommended alternative without a balanced assessment of both improvements and future costs.

Written Presentation Skills

The cultures of organizations vary widely. One variance is the norms around communications for decision-making. Some organizations like written justifications. Others prefer spoken. Others prefer both.

For written business cases, some organizations have an accepted outline or format. If not, figure 26 provides a useful approach.

1. Title of Project or Strategic Initiative
2. Executive Summary
3. Statement of Problem
4. Recommended Alternative
5. Other Alternatives Considered
6. Core Justification for Recommended Alternative (Three Reasons)
   - Financial (Quadrants 1 & 4)
   - Intangible (Quadrants 2 & 3)
   - Tied to Strategic Planning metric/goal/initiative
7. Summary and Timing of Expenditures (capital, operations & maintenance, marketing, inventory, administrative)
8. Scheduled Deliverables and Implementation Date
9. Project Controls Philosophy
10. Potential Problem Analysis and Impacts (on people, culture, community, environment, etc.)
11. Suggested Assignments (top management sponsor, project manager, technical support, administrative support, "designated cynic")

Figure 26 – Business Case Outline

This outline provides some useful insights into leadership development itself. In contemplating the items on the list, a leader needs skills in political savvy, financial valuation, organizational theory and practice, project management, problem analysis, and strategy.

1. The title may seem trivial. It is not. Words matter. You should think about a title that connotes the intent without using phrasing that could cause concerns among the community, any regulators, or the public in general. The

title should be specific enough to help avoid scope creep. A good title might be "The Business Case for Implementing a Distributed Control System (DCS) on the control board of Unit Three." Scope creep could happen if the 'on the control board' phrase was omitted. DCS projects have a habit of growing beyond the original approved scope. Many other parts of a plant's control system could get upgraded other than the control board itself.

2. The executive summary should be less than a single page. One paragraph on a third of a page is a decent goal.

3. The statement of the problem will historically capture the issues and motivation behind the search for a solution. This should include data sufficient to know if the problem has been solved or the issue alleviated.

4. The recommended alternative should be discussed in as much detail as is available. Figure 16, the *Biz Bucks* Project Process, provides a framework to communicate the level of accuracy of the recommended alternative. It could be a conceptual, preliminary, or definitive (detailed) level of understanding.

   If this is a technical issue, a key engineering drawing or two might be appropriate.

5. Most top decision makers will want to know if you have honestly considered other alternatives, other than the "do nothing" alternative. You might engage the services of a designated cynic to help brainstorm alternatives. This person also can play an important role in bulletproofing financial benefits and intangible justification.

6. As discussed above, the core justification must include a balanced assessment of not only benefits but future costs.

7. The business case needs a cost estimate and an expenditure (cash) flow. This cash flow is not only based on accounting principles but also includes all expenditures caused by the recommended alternative, including inventory increases.

The business case should clearly indicate the level of accuracy of the estimate, conceptual, preliminary, or definitive as discussed in chapter 9.

8. If the recommended alternative has progressed past the conceptual phase, the business case should include key deliverables or milestones and a clear project in-service or end date.

9. Each new project will need some types of control tools to manage the project's objectives of scope, cost, and schedule. These may be a basic set or a more robust set of tools, depending on the complexity of the project. The business case should delineate the tool set. A basic set may only be a project cost analysis monthly and a Gantt (bar) chart for schedule control. More robust tools might include a critical path Gantt chart, with resources, costs, and earned value plans.

10. Almost all initiatives will have deviations from the plan as the implementation work progresses. The business case should include a brainstormed list of potential problems and mitigation plans should a problem arise.

11. In addition to the designated cynic mentioned above, the business case should include an organization chart or at least a list of people resources for the project. The key assignment is the project sponsor who usually is a member of top management.

Oral Presentation Skills

The Biz Bucks Guy believes most decisions in high-performing organizations are made from oral, not written, business cases. This requires the leaders who champion proposals to develop outstanding speaking and presentation skills, or suffer the consequences of getting few ideas approved.

A highly useful and practical framework for oral presentations is the Rule of Three.[77] For reasons that only really smart people with lots of letters after their name might explain, we seem to like justifications that total *three*. When selling any proposal, we should state the clear recommendation and then state the possible alternatives. Then suggest there are three reasons to adopt the recommended approach. After providing an overview of the three reasons, the presenter then digs in and explains each reason in detail. The presenter should summarize at the end, once again clearly stating the recommendation and ask for the order.

But what should a presenter do if there are more than three good reasons to accept a recommendation? Get creative, and combine them into three.

Conversely, what if there are only two reasons or even one good reason to take a certain path? Again, get creative. Consider not only financial justification but intangibles. As an example, the written outline in figure 26 shows the tie with strategy to be a third possible reason.

Another tip to successful oral presentations is to use *progressive disclosure* as discussed in chapter 12. This applies to business case presentations, not only decision trees.

The oral presentation may not be as formally detailed as the written version. Nonetheless, a business case presenter should be prepared to articulate every item in the business case outline presented in figure 26.

Political Savvy

In spite of the best presentation or write-up, business cases are sometimes doomed to rejection—not because of the quality of the argument but because of conditions, cultural norms, values, and frankly, personalities of the organization. Many possible organizational beehives exist, not the friendly honeybee types, but the killer-bee types. Good leaders who are proposing projects or strategic initiative must develop political savvy to be successful. They should ask themselves a series of questions before advancing a business case. A beginning list of such questions are:

- Has top management recently been burned by a similar proposal, one that did not yield the promised benefits?
- Are there other proposals that a sponsor has accepted that will require her full-time focus?
- Is the company in a severe capital rationing mode?
- How do the officers like to receive their proposals?
- Is there an internal guru on this subject that must be on board before top management will act?
- What is the pecking order for this decision?
- How much signature authority does each level have?
- Who has been successful in presenting a business case recently?
- What works?
- What doesn't?

If a group of top managers will meet to discuss the proposal, one tip is often useful. Meet with each off-line, one-on-one, and explain the business case. Ask for their support in the joint meeting. This is the "skid greasing" tactic and often makes for a smooth, nearly friction-free meeting.

Supporting the Strategy

Surrounding the other business case skills in figure 25 is the most important principle for successful business case development. The proposal *must* support the strategy of the organization. Nothing should be done in any organization unless it supports the stated strategy. The business case writer might choose to bury this link to strategy into the core justification (as noted in figure 26). He should nonetheless emphasize it appropriately. Doing so shows the business case writer really understands the strategy. This gives the decision maker a good reason to approve the idea. Again, no proposal for anything should come to top management without a direct tie to the organization's strategy.

INTERNALLY COMMUNICATE FOR EMPLOYEE SATISFACTION

Every organization should strive to have employees who are satisfied with their jobs, their ability to succeed, and their prospects for the future. For-profit companies should strive for this goal because of the service-profit chain[78] that says if you have satisfied employees, they will treat your customers well. If you have well-treated customers, they will tend to buy your products or services, which, in turn, treats your shareholders well. It begins with employees.

But high employee satisfaction is often an elusive goal. No organization can afford to lavish employees enough to buy their satisfaction. So how can an organization build employee satisfaction?

The Hay Group has identified seventy-five components of employee satisfaction.[79]

In their study, they discovered trust and confidence in top leadership was the single most reliable predictor of employee satisfaction. Furthermore, they reported trust and confidence were based on effective communications from top management on answers to three crucial questions:

1. What is the strategic direction of the organization?
2. How does my work contribute to the organization's objectives?
3. How is the overall organization and my part of the organization doing on reaching strategic objectives?

This is not only the role of top management. Each first-line supervisor must be the conduit for much of this communication on strategy and communication, particularly the status of progress on objectives.

PROJECT COMMUNICATIONS

Certain principles of project management were included in chapter 9. One principle, the project communications plan, was left for this chapter. Many talented quantoids will become project managers. This may be a stepping-stone to other leadership opportunities. An important but often overlooked skill of project management is planning project communications and then implementing the plan.

Without good communications, the stepping-stone to added leadership assignments may turn to clay, then butter, then fade entirely. How can this be avoided? Each project manager should develop a formal plan to communicate. Here are a few tips:

1. After a project schedule has been drafted (presumably in a Gantt chart format), the project manager should consider who are his audiences for the project. Depending on the project, these might include upper management, internal and external customers, the project team, contractors, regulators, operations, maintenance, HR, and other users of the intended change.
2. The project manager then reviews the draft Gantt chart in detail and marks key decision points, milestones, and deliverables in the project schedule. These are the communication points for the project. The project manager also identifies recurring communication points, such as project team meetings, monthly reports, and verbal updates.
3. For each communication point, the project manager determines what communication channels are best.

4. The project manager revises the Gantt chart with a new WBS item at the top level, entitled "Project Communications," and adds all the planned communication points as tasks under that WBS, tied to their predecessor dependencies.

These four simple steps yield a project communication plan. Every project, no matter how small, deserves at least a minimal version of this approach.

COMMUNICATING ACROSS THE GENERATIONS

Most new bosses will be in their twenties or thirties. They are part of the culture of their so-called generation. Communication will be easier with their direct reports of the same generation. However, new bosses should study the norms and values of each generation. Trends, events, movements, music, books, movies, politics, technology (both information and other), natural disasters, economic conditions, wars, and many other factors tend to shape thinking, motivations, behavior, opinions, and vocabulary of large groups of people.

It is also imperative that a boss understand such broad generational differences may not apply to individuals within a generation.

New bosses should not only learn the nuances of currently working generations but be aware that new generations will emerge that will see things differently. The new bosses of today will be the old geezers and geezer-ettes of an all-too-quick senior leadership team.

The Out-of-Practice Parent

The Biz Bucks Guy relearned the principle of cross-generational communication difficulties a few years ago. He and Mrs. Biz Bucks were asked to take two nephews, cousins to each other, for a week while their parents and grandparents were on a well-deserved adults-only vacation to the beaches of Hawaii. The patience-trying week began in the parking lot of a Mexican restaurant equidistant between homes and got off to a challenging start. After leaving the restaurant, The Biz Bucks Guy got Kaden, aged eight, and Conner, aged six, into the backseat of their not-so-family-friendly small car. The Biz Bucks Guy was barely able to avoid back strain as he helped the boys get their seat belts fastened. Just as the second belt clicked, Kaden looked up and said, "Uncle Bob, Conner's gotta wee!"

"Grumble, grumble," The Biz Bucks Guy said under his breath. "Okay," he said out loud, "both of you get out. Back to the restaurant."

Kaden got a puzzled look on his face, then repeated more emphatically, "Uncle Bob, Conner's gotta wee!"

"Okay, I get it. I get it," The Biz Bucks Guy said to himself, again under his breath. "I'm not too old to remember when we used those kids' terms, whiz, tinkle, leak. Been awhile since I heard 'wee', though." Then he said out loud, "Okay. Let's go. I heard you the first time. I wish you guys would have thought about this before we left the restaurant."

Again, the look on Kaden's face was one of puzzlement. After a third round of miscommunication, Mrs. Biz Bucks finally broke the secret code. "Grandpa, I think a *Wii* is a new computer game system!"

Once again, The Biz Bucks Guy learned the difficulty of being a world-class communicator, particularly across generations. As a leader, you will need to be mindful of generational differences in your communications. Sooner than you think, your generation will not be the latest generation.

QUESTIONS FOR CURRENT LEADERS

1. How often and how well do you communicate to your people the results of not only your specific group but the entire organization or company?

2. What channels of communication do you naturally use? Which others might improve your effectiveness?
3. Are all of your direct reports equal to the baggage handler?

TECHNICAL ANALOG FOR LIFE AND LEADERSHIP: THE VLSI CLOCK

The advances in semiconductor technology have allowed most of us today to have a communication device in our pockets that even Dick Tracy could not have conceived. Moving from single transistors to integrated circuits, to very large scale integrated (VLSI) circuits, to the ultradeep submicron (USDM) era, the half century of progress of this technology (and the products it has spawned) is nothing short of amazing.

One of the challenges of putting that many active elements on a single substrate is to have them all working synchronously. To do so, a VLSI clock must keep the circuitry working together. Getting all components to respond, communicate, and process together is an ongoing challenge for electronic engineers who design hundreds of millions of transistors on a single chip.

Leadership is much the same. How do you lead your organization so that every employee knows his job, every department knows their mission and the strategy of the total organization, and people provide timely and honest feedback so the whole works efficiently and effectively? Like the challenge of the VLSI clock, leaders must solve these issues to yield a synchronous organization. Focusing on the key management systems of strategy development, communications, team building, information delivery, project and process management, planning, budgeting, and change management is a good way to begin.

CHAPTER 14

DELEGATING

GOING HOME AT NIGHT

Three decades ago, a wonderful man mistook fear for talent and promoted The Biz Bucks Guy into his first managerial assignment. He headed up a new department. He inherited some good workers from a few other areas of the company. There were no business processes established for the work, only a rough mission to solve the company's number one internal problem at that time: He was to create a team to accurately set, monitor, and reforecast a capital budget that was out of control and totaled approximately $1 million per day, every day, 365 days per year.

The Biz Bucks Guy was unfamiliar with process management, budgeting, employee development, and most of the other topics of this book. He had ran a successful and complex project that had high visibility. Now, he poured his heart and soul into fixing this vexing problem for the corporation.

After many months of developing several processes and nuking many of the cultural norms that had impeded that function for years, he became a bit proud of his accomplishments. He had sacrificed his body for the home team. Yes, the capital budget function was improving. But he had spent many late nights and weekends developing the processes and implementing the changes. He thought he was making a name for himself by winning the change battle even though he was having problems remembering the names of his children.

Then came the day of reckoning. A top officer of the company, after listening about the many hours The Biz Bucks Guy was expending to be a success, slammed him down a bit.

"When are you going to build a team to delegate so you can go home at night?"

He was right! The job of a boss was only being done partially in the new department. Until then, *delegation* had not been a functioning word in The Biz Bucks Guy's lexicon. He changed and began to enjoy watching his kids grow up.

WHAT IS DELEGATION?

Delegation is defined as making assignments to subordinates, coaching them as necessary, and receiving their work. You delegate the authority to the delegatee but retain the ultimate accountability for the results.

In this chapter, delegation is about delegating to individuals. Delegating to teams will be discussed in the next chapter.

There are several possible shades in the spectrum of delegation. One representation, the Biz Bucks Shades of Delegation, follows as figure 27.

Increasing Freedom to Act					
Micro-Manage (Here is how to hold the pencil.)	Provide Alternatives (I will decide.)	Provide a Recommend-ation (We will decide.)	Develop a Complete Solution (I will review.)	Full Responsi-bility (I still care.)	Full Abdication (I don't care.)

Figure 27 – Shades of Delegation

Micromanaging

This is actually the antithesis of real delegation. The boss just can't let go. Perhaps this is needed to develop an employee. It should be used rarely. Micromanaging is not coaching. The difference is in the boss's style. If the subordinate thinks you are coaching, you are coaching. If he thinks you are micromanaging, you are.

Provide Alternatives

This relates to the *input* type of the four decision types in figure 22. You are allowing your subordinate to develop ideas and choices for you to consider. You retain the decision.

Provide a Recommendation

You are suggesting the subordinate brainstorm alternatives and select the best. Then you both will chew it around and make the best decision. This is similar to the *consensus* type in figure 22. Afterward, the subordinate will do the details.

Develop a Complete Solution

You delegate not only the recommendation but the development of implementation details. You notify the subordinate that you still retain the right to review and modify, if necessary.

Full Responsibility

You delegate both authority and responsibility to a trusted subordinate. Your brains are conjoined! You know they will do as good or better job than you would. The subordinate is fully developed in this area, and you have confidence in him. You can never eliminate your ultimate accountability from your boss, but they know you are allowing them to act for you. You let them know you care about the outcome and are there for advice, if needed. You still set a time to discuss the outcome. This is the nirvana state of delegation.

Full Abdication

You give full authority and responsibility to the subordinate, and you do not care about the outcome. Simply put, you are not acting as a leader if you abdicate. In fact, like micromanaging, this is not real delegation at all. You don't plan to review their work, recommendation, or implementation plan. You simply put your time into other things. Depending on the individual, full abdication might be motivating (because they have freedom to act) or de-motivating (because they feel their work will not be appreciated).

WHY SHOULD YOU DELEGATE?

Here are some good reasons to delegate:

- It builds your people for the long term.
- It expands your ability to get things done.
- It grooms your potential successor.
- You keep your sanity and you get to go home at night.
- It motivates your team members.
- Good people want to transfer into your department.

These are remarkably similar to the reasons to be a people developer in chapter 11. That is because people development and delegation are two companion skills. Like two wheels on the bicycle of leadership; things don't roll well without both.

WHEN SHOULD YOU NOT DELEGATE?

Yes, there are good reasons not to delegate. They should be considered short-term reasons.

- You don't have a person with the right skill.
- You don't have established processes.
- It will be faster and time is off the essence.
- The project is a corporate secret.
- It is mission critical, and you just can't risk anyone else messing with it. An airline pilot should not delegate the landing to a flight attendant for their personal development.

However, the I'm-the-expert-and-I-don't-want-to-let-go-of-my-power syndrome, is not a good reason to avoid delegating. This syndrome is, however, a good reason to doubt your rightness for leadership.

HOW DO YOU DELEGATE?

A casual online search of the word *delegation* will yield some exceedingly long lists of "Do's for Delegating." Mostly are common sense and relate to the SMART and DUMB objectives in chapter 4. Here are a few tips that might prove useful.

1. Pick the right person. You should decide if this is a slam dunk or a stretch for the person and plan to support him accordingly.
2. Communicate clearly which shade of delegation you are using from figure 27.
3. Unless you are using the full responsibility shade, set a date for them to return and report.

4. Keep a list of delegated items. In his earlier days, The Biz Bucks Guy has occasionally asked a subordinate to do something and forgotten about it. He has even asked someone else to do the same thing a few days later or done it himself. This is more than absentmindedness. A new department will generate many actions, changes, immediate crises, and special requests. The sheer volume can be overwhelming. Keeping a list not only helps the boss to keep delegated assignments straight, but it helps to communicate the time boundaries for the delegatee.

JETHRO'S NINE RULES OF DELEGATION

There is a priceless passage on delegation in the Old Testament. Whether you live by Biblical standards or simply consider the Bible to be good literature, the passage provides important insights.

After Moses led the children of Israel out of Egypt and after they were safely into the desert and Pharaoh had his last swim in the Red Sea, Moses tired of the burdens of leading the 600,000 men and their families.

In Exodus chapter 18, Moses was tutored by his father-in-law, Jethro of Midian, regarding delegation. Jethro saw that Moses was administering with the people "from morning unto evening." Moses was using the heroic management style. He felt obliged to deal personally with everyone's issues. He had to solve everyone's problems. Neither he nor the people were well served by this heroic approach. Jethro counseled his son-in-law:

...The thing that thou doest *is* not good.

Thou wilt surely wear away, both thou, and this people that *is* with thee: for this thing *is* too heavy for thee; thou art not able to perform it thyself alone.

Hearken now unto my voice, I will give thee counsel, and God shall be with thee: Be thou for the people to God-ward, that thou mayest bring the causes unto God:

What was Jethro's counsel? It can be summarized in nine points:

1. Delegate to unburden yourself.
2. Delegate all but the big stuff.
3. Heroic management doesn't serve the people well.
4. Teach correct principles, and they will govern themselves.
5. Communicate your vision.
6. Teach them their job skills.
7. Find the right people to be the leaders, then delegate to them.
8. Organize your people.
9. Without delegation, "Thou wilt surely wear away!"

Being a great delegator is the key to life balance, otherwise, you wilt surely wear away.

A NAVAL ACADEMY FINAL EXAM

An internet urban legend (that may be true) tells of an Annapolis professor giving his midshipmen their final exam in a leadership class. There was only a single question:

You have a twenty-five foot pole, two one-hundred pound sacks of cement, tools to dig and finish concrete, one-hundred feet of high strength line, one chief, five sailors, ten feet of three-eights rebar with a hacksaw, and an American flag. Describe how you would construct a flagpole so that the flag can be seen for four-hundred yards. You have two hours to explain your process.

After two hours, the professor collected the papers. He looked at each before dismissing the class. He announced, "There are many wonderful papers here, but only one A. Would you like me to read the A paper?"

The response was a unanimous. "Yes!"

It reads, "Tell the chief to put up a flagpole and then leave the area."

Most of us have some hero in us. We quickly think of how we would do things to solve a problem. It takes an enormous amount of personal discipline to be a great delegator and let others solve problems. The midshipman who wrote this paper understood delegation. He was the only one of that class who did. His answer freed himself up for more important work. His answer helped develop the chief's ability to lead and increased confidence in the sailors, themselves. He deserved the only A.

CONSIDERING PATTON

In the opening scene of the 1970 Oscar-winning movie Patton, the lead character, played by George C. Scott, made a memorable statement to his troops, the Third Army, "Now I want you to remember that no soldier ever won a war by dying for his country. He won it by making the other poor dumb soldier die for *his* country."[80]

So it is with working *hard* in your career in leadership. As a true leader, you should strive for balance in life. You should be able to fulfill your family commitments, provide service to others, have some recreational time, continue your life-long learning, *and* be a great leader at work.

Therefore, a benevolent top leader, in Patton-esque fashion, might say to a group of newly promoted managers, "Some of you managers think you are here to sacrifice your body for the company. If you do, we will really appreciate it. This company will send a wonderful bouquet of flowers for your grave when you work yourself to death... and furthermore, we will remember you fondly...for about two weeks. But you are not here to sacrifice that much. You are here to delegate and cause your subordinates to burn the midnight oil and sacrifice *their* bodies. Perhaps you will not reach that ideal, but at least, you might occasionally have a little company when you are working late."

Yes, this is a bit over the top. Likening your valued employees to the enemy is only for fun. However, it is almost that serious if you lose your life's balance over an extended period. If you lose the life balance war, the reason is starring at you in the mirror. It's better to be a great delegator.

QUESTIONS FOR CURRENT LEADERS

1. How would you rate your track record as a delegator? What are the reasons if it is not acceptable?
2. Is there anyone whom you should start considering more often for delegated assignments?
3. When you are given a special assignment, can you tell top management that you would like to delegate it? To whom? Why? Or does top management expect your personal work? In other words, they delegate, but want you not to delegate. If so, what can you do about that?

TECHNICAL ANALOG ON LIFE AND LEADERSHIP: THE THREE CYCLES TO COMPETENCE PRINCIPLE

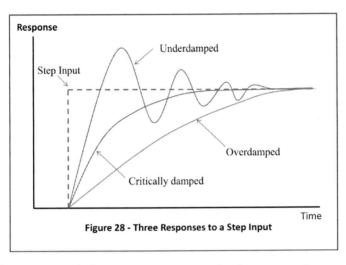

Figure 28 - Three Responses to a Step Input

In linear control theory, engineers study the responsiveness of a closed-loop system when a step function is inputted. The resulting output is often a decaying sine-like wave that eventually replicates the step-function input (see figure 28).

Engineers calculate several important factors of these response curves including the damping ratio (ζ or zeta), the natural frequency of the system (n), and the time for the output to settle within an agreed tolerance, say 5 percent of the step function (Ts).

Figure 28 shows three states of such a control system, the underdamped, overdamped, and critically damped. Each of these states has an underlying natural frequency of the system. Only in the underdamped state, however, can one see the oscillations that show the underlying frequency.

When the system is critically damped, the settling time can be calculated by

$$Ts = 3 \div n$$

Cycle time is the reciprocal of the frequency, n. So this equation could be rewritten,

$$\text{Ts}=3 \text{ } x \text{ the cycle time}$$

This can be interpreted as:

> The time required to make a change is three times the natural cycle time of the system.

Could this have application to organizations, leadership, and changes people experience? From forty years of observation, The Biz Bucks Guy thinks so.

Consider you have just received a promotion to lead an existing department. Some of the main processes of the department occur monthly, like closing the accounting books. It should take you about three cycles (three months) to become pretty good (settle in) at managing those processes. If, however, you also have a process with an annual cycle, say setting a budget, you will get better each time you do it, but it may be three years before you settle in and are up to speed on the annual process! Determine the cycle time of a business process that is new to you. Then, understand your native intelligence and hard work may not be the only determinants leading to your competence. Your learning curve is usually about three cycles.

If it takes you three cycles, shouldn't it also take your analyst three cycles for things you have delegated? This principle may help you develop patience when dealing with people you delegate to and also those experiencing a variety of other changes in the workplace, such as new hires, job rotations, reengineering, continuous process improvement, and the development of new management tools.

CHAPTER 15

USING TEAMS

STRATEGY IMPLEMENTATION TEAMS

Margaret Mead, the twentieth century cultural anthropologist, once said, "Never doubt that a small group of thoughtful committed citizens can change the world; indeed, it's the only thing that ever has."[81]

This relates back to our discussion from figure 1 in chapter 1. Recall that leadership's second skill is assembling a team to support the leader's vision. Professor Mead was on this same wavelength. The only thing that can really make a big change—in a small department, an organization, a country, or even on the world stage—is a small group of thoughtful, committed citizens. Such a team is an essential ingredient of leadership and the development and implementation of strategy. Consider the following example.

"His Last Name is Hard to Pronounce"

In summer of 1992, three candidates emerged for president of the United States. George H. W. Bush, the incumbent, was running for a second term on the Republican ticket. The Democrats had nominated a little known governor from a small state, Governor

Bill Clinton of Arkansas. In addition, a successful business executive from Texas with a hard to pronounce last name entered the fray as an independent, H. Ross Perot. Amazingly at one point in the campaign, Perot was close to Bush with Clinton far behind.

On one late night talk show, Jay Leno tried to help America. He remarked (in effect) "There is a third and little known candidate that is running to become president of the United States this year. Unfortunately, his name is hard to pronounce… so let me help you with that…it's *Clinton!*" Everyone laughed. But Bill got the last laugh.

Governor Clinton had built a super team, a highly organized group of thoughtful, committed citizens. And with this team (and admittedly the public's perception of a weakening economy), he successfully upended the incumbent, making William Jefferson Clinton the forty-second president of the United States.

This chapter deals with not only strategy implementation teams but teams in general: What are they? When should we use them? And how do you build them?

WHAT IS A TEAM?

A team is a group of people who work cooperatively to accomplish a common purpose. That's easy enough. But one of the biggest failures of organizational writers and thinkers on the subject of teams is that few really define what kind of team they are referring to in their academic pontifications. A team, in fact, can refer to many variations of organization. The literature of teams in the 1990s unfortunately added a large section to the business word swamp. To help us understand the broad subject of team, consider the following ten pairs of possibilities. A team can be:

1. *Permanent* or *temporary*
2. *Boss*-managed or *self*-managed

3. From a *single area* or represent *multiple areas* (such as product department A, location B, project C)
4. Comprised of *one type* of functional person (such as all mechanical engineers) or *interdisciplinary* (such as a mix of mechanical, electrical, and chemical)
5. Highly *interdependent* among themselves for success (such as a basketball team) or mostly *independent* from one another's work (such as a golf team)
6. Assigned to accomplish *projects* or work on continuous improvement/production of recurring *processes*
7. Staffed with seasoned *veterans* or *newly acquired* employees
8. A *long-established* group or a *newly formed* group
9. Represented by *one level* of employee or *multiple levels* of employees organizationally (front liners, supervisors, middle managers, and officers)
10. *Full time* or *part time*

A quantoid will realize the mathematical combinations of these ten pairs of team attributes is 210 or 1,024 possible types of teams. While some of these combinations may not logically exist in practice, many do. Each variation will have its own idiosyncrasies regarding leadership needs, staffing, logistics, development, success metrics, and pay. A good leader will fit the team to the work and design the management tools accordingly. For new teams, this fit process can be implemented quickly. For established teams that have languished without good fit, the time to create fit may be measured in many months or even years.

SEVEN SPECIAL TEAM TYPES

With 1,024 possible mathematical perturbations of teams, a handful of special types of teams are important to add to the leader's lexicon and tool kit. Here are seven useful variations of teams.

Strategic Implementation Teams

This chapter began with a short example of a strategy implementation team in politics. These are usually very high level teams, temporary, boss-led, representing multiple areas, part time, and interdisciplinary. In business, they are typically led by the CEO (or a division leader who owns and is implementing a division's strategy).

Intact Teams

Most teams are intact work units, ones that are on the regular organization chart. They are full time, boss managed, permanent groups doing assigned functions within established processes of the company or organization. All the principles of leadership discussed in the volume apply to this basic team setting. A wise leader will use the term team when referring to this intact group even if the corporate terminology may be different. Teamwork is always an essential cultural norm in any team, particularly intact teams. Even if the work of the team is highly independent of one another, like a sales force, some degree of teamwork will be required, if only to take calls for other associates.

Self-Managed Teams (Intact and Permanent)

Two decades ago, a rather new team phenomenon was widely discussed. It was the notion of *self-directed* teams. This short overview rejects the idea of self-direction. No team, with or without a boss, should decide what strategic direction they should take. All teams should be directed by strategy not serendipity. Strategy comes from upper management. However, when certain conditions exist, it is possible for an intact team to become *self-managed* (not self-directed), meaning there is no supervisor with authority over the team. The self-managed team meets among themselves to build consensus around issues that a supervisor would normally determine or at least facilitate with a team.

There is one overriding reason some top managers like the idea of self-managed teams. They require one fewer position—the supervisor. The Biz Bucks Guy suspects that was the core motivation of the fad two decades ago.

A self-managed intact team should be used sparingly but may be a good fit for a permanent team of seasoned veterans with mutual respect for one another's skills. When implemented, an advisor should be established to provide nurturing and advice to the self-managed team. It could be either the higher manager or an organizational expert from HR.

The concept of self-management for temporary teams is often a better fit and is assumed in the next two special team types.

Tiger Teams (Cross Functional Teams)

A popular approach to solving complex issues in large organizations, particularly when the issues cross multiple organizational silos, is the idea of a cross-functional temporary team. The Biz Bucks Guy refers to them as *tiger teams*.

Given they are usually self-managed, the motivation of tiger team members is usually high. They know they have been strategically formed for a particular purpose, and they appreciate the empowerment and confidence that upper management has given them. This approach came into vogue in the United States in the 1980s but became prevalent in Europe a few decades earlier. For example, they could be chartered to:

1. Determine the desired future cultural behaviors for a corporation to succeed in a changing marketplace
2. Write the specifications for a new product
3. Cut a proposed budget to meet corporate financial constraints
4. Implement a strategic initiative to improve customer satisfaction
5. Manage a critical construction project

6. Do a root-cause analysis of a technical problem
7. Chart a course to improve relationships with a regulator
8. Review a proposed technical modification to a plan for safety, environmental, engineering, operations, and maintenance suitability
9. Select a vendor for the next IT expansion
10. Design a recovery program after a difficult layoff

As should be clear from this list, the uses of tiger teams are limitless. Leaders can accomplish many organizational objectives by finding the right people to form tiger teams which will unite quickly, determine a specific charter, and accomplish goals.

Z Teams

A Z *team* is a type of cross-functional or tiger team wherein it is advisable to have various vertical levels of the organization's hierarchy represented. The Z implies the cross-functional members come from not only a horizontal slice of the organization chart but an angular slice, crossing various levels and functions.

The person with the highest level of leadership assigned as a member of a Z team must be careful not to become overbearing with the other team members. His position can carry much weight, and he might bias the team inadvertently. On a Z team, everyone is theoretically equal.

Z teams are used when a particular issue needs both frontline and leadership perspective to solve. For example, the last item in the tiger team list above (to design a recovery program after a difficult layoff) would need both frontline and leadership perspectives.

Matrixed Teams

Matrix management is discussed in detail in chapter 7. When a team is permanent (or at least long-term), cross-functional, full time, and boss-led, a matrixed team has been established. The members report both to a project boss and their functional boss. This is a common way to do engineering projects on complex systems. Refer to chapter 7 for helps, hints, and potholes associated with matrixed teams.

Change Teams

From time to time, top management of a large organization may desire to form a full-time, temporary team to push an important strategic initiative, a key organizational intervention, or frankly, the latest management fad. The Biz Bucks Guy is well aware of both the power and problems associated with such a change. These teams can be fun, make a big difference, and improve skills and visibility of many people who are named to the team.

Unfortunately, there is a downside for change teams. Consider the following not-too-unusual scenario.

Initially, there is a large push of excitement as the intervention is announced. Top producers who eat change for breakfast (spirals and transitories and maybe a few linears) desire to be named to the team. Top management promises that people who are named to this team and are successful will have a bright future with the company.

The work begins. The intervention is implemented. The results are impressive but perhaps never quite as grand as envisioned. Efforts continue as if the team will always be needed.

However, all such interventions have half-lives.

Eventually, some other initiative takes the focus off the first. It is time to disband the team. The promises from top management have been long forgotten. Perhaps many of the top managers who made the promises have retired, left the company, or been demoted. The shutdown process does not happen as smoothly as promised. As the smoke clears, some team members have found good positions, others were stuffed away in less wonderful spots, still others were encouraged to take early retirement or face the prospect of a reduction-in-force. It is never easy to wind these teams down.

One important word of advice to those contemplating joining this kind of team: Depending on your psychological makeup and your career concept (recalling chapter 3), don't hesitate to get involved in such a team. Also, don't forget to get the promises in writing *up front* from top management about the eventual disbanding of the team. As a condition for accepting leadership of such a team, the proposed boss should demand that the top officers provide this written document before recruiting begins.

BUILDING TEAMS

But how do you, the boss, build successful teams? Mutter this question out loud at the water cooler to a passerby, and because of the efficacy of the grape vine, in a few minutes your designated organization development (OD) support person will probably give you a call.

She will suggest your company's latest offering in team building. It may be a team game, a workshop, options for team pay, or a variety of outdoor events aimed at improving communications and understanding the importance of diverse skill sets in the workplace.

For the most part, such interventions, in the OD parlance, are admirable. However, like many staff department solutions, they are *half a loaf.*

So what's the other half a loaf to build a successful team?

Here are some tips.

Recognize the Four Stages

In 1965, Bruce Tuckman, a psychologist with research interest in group dynamics, published his Tuckman's stages of team development. This has been widely used for the ensuing four decades, and it is popular because it makes sense and because it rhymes. Each new team will go through four stages:

1. Forming
2. Storming
3. Norming
4. Performing

This implies that after a team is formed, there will be rough moments between the team members. There is always someone who has strong convictions of how the team should work and what their goals are. They may not match with other team members' views. There is necessarily a storming stage to get beyond these issues.

This is naturally followed by a period wherein team norms are hammered out. Norms are social rules, often unwritten. The team may not even know they are establishing norms. Some norms may deal with who leads discussions, how do decisions get made, how do team members back one another up, and when to ask for help from others.

Once the norming period is complete, the team begins to run on all eight cylinders—er, four cylinders for many cars today. While the performing stage is last, Tuckman's stages can recycle back to storming and norming.

Write a Team Charter Together

One of the best ways to start a team, to propel it through the storming and norming stages, and to get everyone focused on the common goal is to have the team write its own charter. A charter was described in figure 8 of chapter 4. It includes a vision, mission, metrics, key processes/projects, and key stakeholders. A facilitator may be useful to assist the team. When the team becomes worried about single words during the word-smithing of the charter, the team is getting close to the buy-in necessary to perform. Much can be learned about the various team members from this charter writing exercise.

Some bosses are tempted to write the charter themselves and present it to the team for editing and adoption. This is a foolish act of perhaps a good-hearted boss trying to help the team work efficiently. This is foolish on at least two planes. One, it robs the team of an important teaming activity early in its existence. Two, the charter produced by the team is almost always better. As Warren Bennis recently wrote, "None of us is better than all of us."[82]

Create Small Wins

Do real work together successfully. To build a real team, members must do real work together and work on a real-time project, dedicated to accomplishing a difficult goal. Real team building comes from a group of people hitting home runs together and accomplishing something.

To begin, help the team select a project in your function that is modest in size and shorter in timing. It should have about a 50-50 chance of success. Lead the team to a conclusion on the project. Your project management skills (or theirs) may have to be augmented with formal training. Success can't be a given. But with effort, a little luck, and a lot of air cover from you as their leader, hopefully your team will be a success on this smaller project. This prepares the team for larger scale change.

Talk Regularly

Meet regularly to talk. Communicating with the team is so obvious, but it hurts The Biz Bucks Guy to think how many newer bosses are poor at it. I'm not talking about the dull, standard staff meetings where everyone gets to speak around the table every Friday afternoon after weathering the boss's latest pontification. I'm talking about meaningful planning, reporting on progress, problem solving, communicating work objectives and vision. Meetings also provide an opportunity to do something many bosses forget—to say thanks to those who have done well recently and also to everyone who is rowing as hard as they can on their work objectives, projects, and processes.

Celebrate Success

Celebrate together. If you are successful at a particular project or work assignment, a key to build a strong team is to celebrate successes together. Make a big deal about what you have accomplished. Spend a little money. This may be outside the normal culture of your organization. If you don't have the authority to celebrate success and you get pounded down by the bureaucracy when you propose a modest group team building experience, perhaps this is a message to start sending out your resume. Good performance should be recognized. Bad organizations think it's an extravagance.

Watch Their Back

One of General Collin Powell's leadership principles is "Take care of the troops." The team needs to know you stand by them and are watching their backs as they do their magic on the front lines with internal or external customers.

Remove Team Members When Necessary

Sadly, not all teams gel. Unless you inherited an established team, you have usually been the one to select the members. Having to remove a team member represents a failure of yours. However, sometimes, it is necessary. You should do it with the utmost respect. Unless there are overriding attitude problems or ethical issues, make it a conversation of fit. One bad apple can certainly spoil the whole bunch. It is a necessary and difficult thing when situations dictate.

ADDITIONAL TEAM CONSIDERATIONS

Delegating to Teams

Refer to figure 27 in chapter 14 on delegating. When you use a tiger team, you should make it clear which shade of delegation you are using. Are you looking for input from them to help you decide or are you giving them full control for the decision? This will help them write their charter.

Team Size

Team size for tiger teams ideally should be about seven with a maximum of ten. Group dynamic issues arise with larger groups.

For intact teams, larger groups are possible and perhaps advisable. When reengineering was prevalent in the early nineties, intact teams of fifty or larger were advocated by some proponents of reengineering. Many super large teams were disasters.

Teamwork versus Team-Type Work

Every team, by definition, needs a degree of teamwork, however, no matter how independent individual work is when doing the business processes of the team, an air of cooperation is necessary and must be cultivated. Open communication, watching out for one another, honest concern for home and family issues, all build this sense of camaraderie and solidarity.

When the business process requires interdependence of team members, you have *team-type work*. This enhances the need for teamwork in the traditional sense.

Team Pay

Some years ago, there was a management fad of paying a group bonus check for team accomplishments. The Biz Bucks Guy once did a pilot program to see if it made sense.

It only makes sense if the team is highly *interdependent* among themselves to be successful and highly *autonomous* from other teams.

In a large company with over five hundred intact teams, The Biz Bucks Guy searched for an intact team to pilot team pay. He found only one that appeared both autonomous from other teams and interdependent amongst themselves. After the pilot, the team pay idea was abandoned because he had blown the analysis. The pilot team was actually quite reliant on other outside departments for success. The autonomy that was described at the outset of the pilot pay program was overstated, both by the leader of the pilot team and the bosses of the peer teams. You should have heard the peer teams squawk when the pilot team got paid for success of which other intact teams contributed.

Be careful to get the analysis correct if considering team pay. It is no wonder this fad has had its day.

Team Staffing, Diversity, Respect, and Race

It is highly advisable to staff teams, whether intact teams or tiger teams with a diverse set of people. Diversity means many things. It can mean its step cousin, affirmative action, intended to meet legal race quotas, or it can mean all types of diversity, including diversity of locale, diversity of culture, diversity of beliefs, or diversity of thought.

The Biz Bucks Guy was educated well on the important life principle of *respecting others* when he was only about eleven-years-old. His idol was a local college football coach, Frank Kush, widely known for his toughness and for winning, particularly when his team was the underdog. Coach Kush was only in his late twenties when he was hired as head football coach of the Arizona State University Sun Devils. He was able to recruit several talented players of African descent, particularly running backs. These black players did not look like many of the fans in the stadium. This apparently bugged a few boosters in that era.

In that regard, this being the late fifties, one booster asked an inflammatory question at a weekly booster luncheon, "Just how many [African American] runners do you have, Coach?"

As the local newspaper reported (at least as a former eleven-year-old recalls), the ever tough Coach Kush responded directly, "I don't know. I never counted. Everyone bleeds red on the football field!"

It silenced the bigot, and an eleven-year-old boy, reading the sports section, learned an important lesson about respecting others. Indeed, we all bleed red together in our various organizations as we unify and accomplish important goals. As Dr. King said, "Judge a man by content of his character, not by the color of his skin."

Everyone has bias. These biases aren't reasoned into us. Therefore, they aren't easily reasoned out of us. We need some significant emotional event—either personally or vicariously—which shows us our bias and causes us to change.

When staffing teams, be sure to avoid any biases and keep in mind all kinds of diversity. Avoid hiring everyone who looks, believes, dresses, speaks, or thinks just like you. You will get a better product, and you will learn, through experience, the importance of diversity.

However, also realize diversity is not the end-all principle as some have come to position it in business. There is an overriding companion principle:

> As important as diversity is, it is our unity that makes us strong.

That unity comes from the development and implementation of strategy as discussed previously in chapter 4.

IMPROMPTU TEAMS AND
THE EMBOLDENING PRINCIPLE

The final topic of this chapter is atypical to discussions on teams. Yet this topic is powerful, germane to teaming, and unfortunately esoteric, meaning understood only by a few. It deserves its place in the sun. This is about one person speaking out, emboldening others, which results in the coalescing and eventual difference-making of an impromptu team.

An impromptu team that flares into existence is often short-lived, cross-functional, and is usually led by a leader established by team acclamation. Impromptu teams form to make a difference in the highly pressurized environment of political battles. Such political circumstances can exist in families, companies large and small, non-profit organizations, charities, governments of cities, states, and countries, and even on the world stage.

A generic scenario is as follows:

A difficult or controversial issue exists in some forum, either an established forum or an informal one. A certain political and well-funded force has taken the time to prepare and use the liberty of free speech to advocate a position that a less prepared, unfunded majority is not in favor. The so-called silent majority is disorganized and perhaps is in a very unfamiliar, even hostile setting politically. Finally, one person courageously speaks and advocates the position of the majority. Others are emboldened by his speech and then advocate the same position. An impromptu team forms. The one who spoke first against the well-organized minority faction is often the leader of the impromptu team. They get organized. They work behind the scenes, where the political maneuverings occur; change begins. Finally, the wishes of the majority are upheld. This would not have happened if the initial person had not been courageous and spoken out.

A Mead-esque group of thoughtful, committed citizens may not even know they are about to become a team and make a big, even world-class difference. It starts with one person's comments, which emboldens others to also speak out. That is the *emboldenment principle*. It is like the breaking of a dam. The flow starts with one stick of verbal dynamite.

The leader must be skilled in leading a fragile impromptu team. They must form and perform without the luxury of the storming and norming stages, or at least, the leader may ease them through those two middle stages quickly.

Examples of situations that might lead to an impromptu team include:

- A town council meeting where a triple-X porn shop wants to open in a family neighborhood.
- The officers of a large company formulate a plan that ultimately will embarrass the company.
- A college professor who is teaching (or perhaps better said, preaching) radical values that are not held by much of the class.

In many ways such as these three, we have opportunities to speak up, which emboldens others, and to organize quickly an impromptu team to make a difference. The following story of the UN Habitat II conference and a single delegate is the best known example to The Biz Bucks Guy—and it occurred on the world stage.

Habitat II

A few years ago, The Biz Bucks Guy had the privilege of having dinner in a small group with Richard Wilkins, a constitutional law professor at the J. Reuben Clark Law School at Brigham Young University in Provo, Utah, and former assistant to the solicitor general for the US Department of Justice.[83]

In June 1996, Mr. Wilkins reluctantly attended the United Nations Habitat II conference in Istanbul, Turkey. After years of battling the anti-family movement, Wilkins had grown weary of the fight. One night, a spiritual prompting awoke him. He left the next morning for Istanbul even though he was staring in a community theater production that night. He was one of twenty-five thousand attendees. He was not representing a government. He was one of thousands from nongovernmental organizations (NGOs) at the conference. NGO is the UN's code word for lobbyist. Habitat II was the third in a series of international UN meetings to develop a written statement on families for UN use. In time, this statement could propel many nations to adopt its principles.

After getting the lay of the land at the conference, it became apparent to Mr. Wilkins that a well-funded and smartly organized minority from the United States was using the conference to promote values that for many are considered antifamily, antiparent, and Marxist. This single, dominant, and domineering NGO had loaded committees, established their people as moderators and session leaders, and had biased the content of the draft statement.

In one pivotal session, the dominant NGO attempted to bias the selection committee for future speakers at the conference. Mr. Wilkins listened to the ranting behavior and preposterous arguments of this NGO for some three hours. Eventually, he could not sit passively anymore. After eight attempts, Mr. Wilkins finally was able to command time from the chair.

"I am an American. I have been a law professor for twelve years, and never have I heard arguments that had such little appeal to either a rule of law or a sense of justice. There are limited speaking slots available and procedures to select a broad range of speakers have been in place and approved for some time." He continued for a few minutes, detailing the nonsensical behavior and arguments of the dominant NGO and the need for a balanced process. He concluded, "It's time to turn this attempt aside and get on with the established procedures."

He sat down. The audience erupted into a standing ovation. The dominant NGO members left the meeting in protest of his emboldening speech. The selection panel itself was emboldened. A more balanced selection of speakers ensued. To his surprise, Mr. Wilkins, himself, was eventually selected to speak to a large plenary session.

But the dominant NGO was not done attempting to influence the conference.

At that full plenary session, the moderator, who was selected by the dominant NGO, tried to cut him and other pro-family speakers out at the last minute. After the final dominant NGO speaker finished and time had expired because the moderator had allowed them to speak longer than assigned, a representative from Algeria rose spontaneously to protest the bias of the session, demanding to hear other points of view. A delegation from the Vatican seconded the Algerian. The moderator was forced to allow other speakers. Mr. Wilkins was last. He was allowed only four minutes. He spoke of the need to strengthen the traditional family unit and encouraged the delegates to not adopt policies that will lead to the disintegration of the traditional family.

As he concluded, he was thronged by the delegates. Many who had become disenchanted or demoralized began to have renewed energy for the fight.

One Arab delegate said to Mr. Wilkins, "Where have you been?" Most at the conference did not think any American believed in traditional family values.

The Islamic conference attendees were energized. As the arduous process of finalizing the formal document ensued, they stood their ground for traditional family values. The world's major religions became an impromptu team, working together for a common goal. Their newfound energy made the difference. Mr. Wilkins and the NGO that invited him[84] played an important leadership role in this coalition. The final version of the document supported the traditional family.

Mr. Wilkins's courage and the ensuing impromptu team changed the outcome of an important conference on the world stage. Few will have such an opportunity to make a world-wide difference. But many leaders will find using the emboldenment principle is one way to make a difference in their own sphere of influence.

As Mead said, "Never doubt that a small group of thoughtful, committed citizens can change the world; indeed, it's the only thing that ever has."

A leader's ability to form a successful team, whether an impromptu, intact, or tiger team, can make a difference in whatever environment the leader is placed.

QUESTIONS FOR CURRENT LEADERS

1. Is your current intact work unit functioning as a team? Do they have the cooperation and camaraderie necessary to flourish?

2. Do you have a vexing problem that a tiger team could help solve?

3. How many teams have you led? Regardless of their past outcomes, what skills do you need to use to ensure better or continued success in the future?

TECHNICAL ANALOG FOR LIFE AND LEADERSHIP: SYNCHRONOUS GENERATORS AND OUTPUT

In the electric utility industry, the subject of power generation is fascinating. For a typical turbine generator set at a power plant, a steam turbine turns a shaft that is directly connected to the rotor of the electric generator. Those not familiar may think that to produce more electricity, the turbine spins faster. This is not the case. Electric power systems are based on alternating current, which in the United States is set at 60 Hz (cycles per second). Mathematically, converting 60 Hz to mechanical rotating speed, the shafts of all the generators providing power to the electrical system must turn at 3,600 rpms (assuming a two-pole generator). All the electrons throughout an electric grid are all doing a sinusoidal two-step dance. They are sloshing back and forth together, sixty times a second.

So the generators are likewise turning together to produce this synchronous movement of electrons. What then allows a generator to produce more power without speeding up? It has to do with a technically complex relationship between the magnetic forces in the rotor of the generator compared to the forces in the stationary part of the generator (the stator). These two force fields must be dancing together. When the turbine provides more rotating force (in an effort to generate more power), the rotor's magnetic force two-step changes, relative to the stator's dance. The rotor force grabs the magnetic force of the stator and causes them to dance together again. This increases the power to the system, all the while maintaining the same speed (3,600 rpms). To the casual observer, nothing has changed. The shaft still rotates at the same speed. However, the output of the generator may have multiplied many times with no observable change, unless you are in the control room and can read the indicators.

Leaders may learn something from these synchronous generators. People have norms. Norms, our unwritten social rules, vary from department to department, from team to team, and from individual to individual. Leaders may not appreciate the speed at which some people or teams perform. A leader should be careful not to impose her own norms onto others. The key is output. If a team or an individual gets the job done—perhaps in different ways than the boss—that is what matters. Speed of effort is not productivity. Process, the way they get there, is not what is important, effectiveness is. A new boss should let teams and individuals establish a track record before the new boss intervenes into their processes.

CHAPTER 16

LEADING CHANGE

THE SHEPHERD AND THE COLLEGE STUDENT – PART 1

Consider the following fictional account.

A young college business student seated himself on a long bench in a tree-lined common area near his next class. It was the start of a new semester, and he wanted to peruse his new text. Before he could open the book, entitled *Management: Theory and Application*, an older man about sixty strolled up and sat a few feet away on the same bench to enjoy the sunshine of a fall day. A little annoyed, the student looked up and noticed the old man's face. It was weathered, wrinkled, and tan. Together with his strong, muscular frame, they seemed to say he had spent his life working hard outdoors.

Abandoning his study time, the curious young man spoke, "So…I presume you are retired. What did you do for a living?"

"I was a shepherd," came the matter-of-fact response. "Every year for twenty years in May, I would lead several hundred head to higher ground."

"That's interesting," said the young student. "How long were you a sheepherder?"

Now it was the older man's turn to be a little annoyed. "You didn't listen, young man. I did not say I was a sheepherder. I clearly said I was a shepherd!"

"I guess I don't know the difference. Can you tell me?"

"Son, sheepherders push. Shepherds pull."

After pondering this tidbit of wisdom, the inquisitive student inquired, "How do shepherds get sheep to follow, sir?"

"Well, let's just say you won't find it in that *management* book you're reading."

So where do you learn how to lead people, not sheep, to the higher ground? As noted in chapter 1, the only real training for leadership is leadership. However, there is a body of knowledge around organizational change that may help. This chapter contains a good starter set of knowledge and suggests additional reading.

If an organization is to grow, improve, become more effective and efficient, make new customers, make additional profits, install a different culture, learn to be strategically driven, develop its people better, improve its relationship with key regulators, move into other markets or countries, streamline its processes, bring more projects in within budget and on time, *it will need to change.*

To begin, several questions may arise in a new leader's mind.

- Can a person really change?
- Can a department really change?
- Can a large organization, even an entire company, really change?

The answer to each is yes. The only remaining question is: Can a leader really help each to change? The answer is:

It depends on the leader.

THE LAST SKILL OF LEADERSHIP READINESS

This last skill of leadership readiness is last for a reason. It requires all of the other eleven skills, and it represents the essence of leadership. The ability to lead change is tantamount to being an effective leader. It is difficult. It is rewarding.

Not all change is progress, but all progress is change. Leaders must be *change artists* to move their organization to higher ground, to have their organization progress, to raise the bar for a department's performance.

CHANGE: SOME DEFINITIONS

Unfortunately, *change* became a corporate fad in the early nineties. Like all other such fads, the residue once the fad is over is very powerful, and its importance should not to be minimized. During the fad, there was little in the way of precise definitions and methods. The change fad contributed several entries into the business word swamp. To avoid the same mistake, let's agree on a *change taxonomy* by defining five types of changes in organizations. This chapter will deal with the first three. The remaining two were covered earlier.

Strategic Change – This implies the organized change initiative of a *large* organization, perhaps an entire company. Such a change is a broad and balanced spectrum of objectives and metrics.

Culture Change – A specific change initiative usually for a large organization to improve the way things are done, the way decisions are made, and the way people treat one another. A culture change may be part of a broader strategic change initiative.

Single Department Change – Such a change effort is necessary if a leader inherits a department with problems. This may include a culture change in the way things are done or the change of several business processes. Sometimes merely the advent of better performance information will spur a department to greater heights.

Single Management System or Business Process Change – Management systems (a collection of business processes) often are broken and need mending. The skill of identifying improvements and implementing them were discussed in chapter 8.

Individual Change – Occasionally, a leader can take on an individual as a *project*. Such change may include a special development effort tailored to the individual. The skills of developing and, when necessary, disciplining individuals were discussed in chapter 11. Recall the story of Andrew, the unexpected rattlesnake.

STRATEGIC CHANGE: THE APS EXPERIENCE

The following case study is illustrative of a corporate level strategic change, which included a culture change.

Over two decades ago, The Biz Bucks Guy lived through (double entendre intended) a corporate change program that was wildly successful. At the time, The Biz Bucks Guy was an HR manager charged with supporting the corporate change program in several ways. He had a ringside seat for this case study. Much has been written in business literature about it. It is a classic story of change that frames the focus of this chapter.

In 1990, newly promoted CEO, O. Mark DeMichele, headed Arizona Public Service (APS), a nine-thousand-employee, investor-owned electric utility in Arizona. At that time, the company was severely in trouble. Consider the following nine metrics of success:

1. Nuclear Operations: APS owned the largest portion and was the operating agent of the nation's largest nuclear power plant, Palo Verde Nuclear Generating Station. All three units were shut down for eighteen months because

the Nuclear Regulatory Commission (NRC) was requiring a complete change of management. The financial loss to the seven owner groups can be roughly estimated at $50 million *per month*. Not only Wall Street, but the other six owners was very unhappy.

2. Environmental Compliance: APS were receiving frequent tickets from the US EPA for operating problems at its coal power plants.

3. Safety: Largely due to safety mistakes around high voltage electricity, APS was experiencing tragic deaths of its valued employees all too frequently. In addition, APS's all incident injury rate (AIIR) was among the worst in the industry.

4. Customer Service: Data from independent consultants showed there was a serious problem with relationships with its customers.

5. Corporate Image: A national rating firm determined that APS was among the poorest companies in Arizona in overall community image, both with the general populace and also with state leaders in industry and government.

6. Budget Adherence: APS had significantly overrun its operating budget each of the last several years.

7. Efficiency: APS was second to last nationally among its industry peers in the employees-per-customer ratio.

8. Stock Price: APS halted paying a dividend a few years earlier due to a poorly timed merger with a bank. The stock was so low that other electric utilities were interested in buying out the APS shareholders. Hostile takeover attempts were brewing.

9. Corporate Culture: APS began measuring progress on twenty cultural behaviors in 1991. The baseline was abysmal.

In October 1990 at an all management meeting, Mr. DeMichele set a vision statement for the company. We would be recognized as one of the top five electric utilities nationally by the end of 1995. The phrase *Top Five by '95* was introduced. Some people were planted by a VP in the audience to give a well-timed roar of approval. This contrived rah-rah moment was detected by many.

For example, both because of the bar being set too high and because of the contrived verbal support, The Biz Bucks Guy had his eyes roll back so far he almost saw his frontal cortex.

"Become top five in five years. No way! We just have too many problems," he said to himself.

Happily, The Biz Bucks Guy was wrong. He was glad he kept his thoughts to himself. What a great ride it turned out to be!

Four years later, in mid-1994, the company celebrated success in reaching the top five vision. The same metrics now showed:

Nuclear Operations—Palo Verde was setting industry records for power generation.

Environmental Compliance—The US EPA gave APS a special award for going beyond compliance of environmental regulations.

Safety—APS's statistics were leading its regional industrial safety group. The terrible string of fatalities had stopped cold some years earlier.

Customer Service—APS significantly improved its customer relations, exceeding that of other utilities in the state.

Corporate Image—APS became one of the premier corporate citizens in Arizona, per the same national rating firm. Often, APS was the top vote getter in this semiannual prestigious rating.

Budget Adherence—APS underran its 1991 operating budget by more than $22 million (not including a refinancing deal that saved another $20 million). In the beginning of 1992, Mr. DeMichele removed that same $22 million from the operating budget, challenging the company to do it again. At the end of 1992, the company had underrun that reduced budget by

$20 million. That is a pretax budget savings in two years of $64 million. No layoff occurred during those two years.

Efficiency—With a series of early outs, voluntary severance packages, and a forced reduction or two, APS had trimmed its staff to under seven thousand while their customer count increased. This improved the customer-to-employee ratio dramatically.

Stock Price—The dividend had been restored. Stock price was up six times over its previous low.

Corporate Culture—Measuring every six months, APS showed a constant and significant improvement in the twenty cultural behaviors.

How did this dramatic change happen? Many leaders in industry and government wanted to know the answer. The Biz Bucks Guy hosted many out-of-towners who came to learn about the *how*. Here are the high points in summary:

First, we (particularly our CEO) learned how to think and act strategically. Mr. DeMichele did not flinch once. He kept the vision alive.

Second, our top officers were united in making the strategy a reality. This was a strong team throughout the change.

Third, we learned how to communicate strategy internally.

Fourth, we implemented—and implemented well—several strategic initiatives.

Not surprisingly, these four points are a reminder of the four skills of leadership introduced in chapter 1.

The list of strategic initiatives included, among others:

- A division-level strategic planning effort similar to the corporate planning process. This was the first step in a vertical alignment of objectives.
- A horizontal alignment initiative, causing operating officers and their staffs to merge and correlate their respective strategies.

- A new individual performance management process, which completed vertical alignment from the corporate plan down to every individual, including union-represented employees.
- The development of specific leadership and frontline competencies and an intervention to focus HR and all training people on them.
- A series of interventions, which anchored the strategic plan throughout the company. These included a five-day residential simulation to live the future. This residential simulation was run over a dozen times with up to eighty participants each time. When that first series was complete, we designed and introduced other conferences, simulations, and seminars, which kept the energy up and the ideas flowing.
- A host of creative ideas from many people throughout the company.

One rather creative idea was the establishment of the APS clowns. The company hired a professional clown to train several dozen volunteers. These newly minted clowns would then attend many civic and community events, such as the Fiesta Bowl Parade with several hundred thousand in attendance. Soon, the clowns were noticed throughout the state and became part of the company's transformation as a premier corporate citizen. They began to realize a goal of our HR department to have two kinds of people in Arizona: those who work for APS and those who wish they did.

APS's corporate strategic change was focused on preparing the company for the impending deregulation of the electric utility industry. The Edison Electric Institute, the industry's trade association, gave APS the Edison Award in 1993, emblematic of the top utility of the year for this preparation for deregulation.

In 1990, no one could have guessed how far and how fast APS, a dusty, old electric utility, could change. They had, indeed, become top five in the industry. APS did it by focusing on three, often overlooked principles of change. Much later, The Biz Bucks Guy adopted a golf metaphor for them.

The Three Golf Balls of Change

Figure 29 - The Three Golf Balls of Change

Here's three practical tips on making an organizational change. When doing so, leaders must keep their eye on not one, or even two, but three golf balls at the same time. It is hard to hit a single golf ball, but three at the same time is a supreme challenge. Nonetheless, a leader must concurrently hit all three right down the middle when implementing a change.

First, every change must be tied to strategy. If your organization does not have a well-articulated strategy, your change may be viewed as flavor of the month. The need to tie everything to strategy may seem obvious to new leaders, but in reality, few companies have really learned how to develop an integrated, comprehensive energizing strategy.

Second, every change must be rigorously designed. We quantoids are pretty good at this second principle. We like things to fit together tightly. If a management tool is perceived to conflict in any way with another management tool, one or both are doomed before the organization has given the new tool a chance to prove its usefulness.

Third, the people involved often require significant emotional support. Every change elicits human emotions. Most are dysfunctional and can include fear, anger, depression, rebellion, even the desire for sabotage. One company that was implementing a reorganization provided ample opportunity for affected employees to talk to counselors. The company even educated a certain group of peer employees with basic counseling skills and allowed them to talk to individuals who were feeling overwhelmed with the prospects of the change.

These three tips are particularly important when a culture of a company needs overhaul. Some new leaders may not understand the deep rooted inertia of an organization's culture nor the importance of culture to organizational effectiveness.

DOES CULTURE COUNT? YOU BET!

Here's a provocative question. Which company typically makes the most profit, a company whose culture focuses on shareholders and their return or a company whose culture focuses on having a balance between the interests of shareholders, customers, and employees?

It may seem counter intuitive, but the balanced culture usually makes more return for shareholders than a company focused solely on shareholder return. This was the result of a study by John Kotter and James Heskett of the Harvard Business School.[85] A summary of their study is compelling (see figure 30). This study shows the balanced culture outperforms the shareholder-only culture in each of the four key measures.

Figure 30 – Culture Counts!
[Per Kotter and Heskett]

Companies with:	Balanced Culture	Shareholder-Focused Culture
Revenue Growth	682%	166%
Work Force	282%	36%
Stock Price	901%	74%
Net Income	756%	1%
[Increases over an eleven-year study period]		

HOW DO YOU CHANGE CULTURE?

Culture is defined as our norms and values. Norms, as noted earlier in chapter 15, are social rules often unwritten. Values are our bedrock principles, the things we stand for. The Biz Bucks Guy was deeply involved in the successful culture change of APS described above. Based not only on that experience but additional research and contemplation, he has developed a five-step process for improving culture in large organizations (see figure 31). It begins with the top officers. Without the rigor of these steps, officers are more cheerleaders than coaches in the culture-change game.

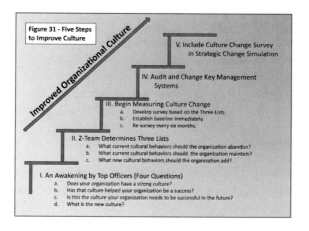

Figure 31 - Five Steps to Improve Culture

Improved Organizational Culture

V. Include Culture Change Survey in Strategic Change Simulation

IV. Audit and Change Key Management Systems

III. Begin Measuring Culture Change
   a. Develop survey based on the Three Lists.
   b. Establish baseline immediately.
   c. Re-survey every six months.

II. Z-Team Determines Three Lists
   a. What current cultural behaviors should the organization abandon?
   b. What current cultural behaviors should the organization maintain?
   c. What new cultural behaviors should the organization add?

I. An Awakening by Top Officers (Four Questions)
   a. Does your organization have a strong culture?
   b. Has that culture helped your organization be a success?
   c. Is this the culture your organization needs to be successful in the future?
   d. What is the new culture?

I. An Awakening

Changing culture requires an epiphany among the top leaders of an organization. The Biz Bucks Guy has had success in awakening such people through the use of four questions.

1. Does your organization have a strong culture? The officer usually responds in the affirmative.
2. Has this culture been a support to your organization's success over the past decade? Again, the response is a quick yes.
3. Is this the same culture that your organization needs to be a success in the future? Usually, they respond no.
4. Then, The Biz Bucks Guy lowers the boom with the final question: "Okay, so what *is* the new culture?" The typical response is "I dunno."

At that point, the top officers realize that they have not done the hard work of defining the new culture. That leads to three lists.

II. The Three Lists

The top officers should empower a Z team to develop three lists. The first list answers the question "What current cultural behaviors should the organization abandon?" Perhaps a company has paralysis of analysis and can't make a decision. If such behavior is no longer consistent with the corporate strategy, that cultural behavior should be abandoned.

The second list answers the question, "What current cultural behaviors should the organization maintain?" If a company has a stellar safety record and an equally outstanding safety program, such behavior should be reinforced.

And third, "What new cultural behaviors should the organization add?" If a company has to develop its people better, a new cultural behavior of *people developer* should be listed.

The Z team's three lists will be tentative, and the top officers will eventually need to refine the lists and come to agreement on the final version.

III. Measuring Culture Change

By answering these three questions, these lists make up the basis for a survey. All employees should be asked to participate. The survey should be run once to determine the baseline. From the baseline, goals should be set and progress measured by repeating the survey frequently. In the APS example, the culture survey was repeated every six months for several years.

IV. The Management Systems Audit

Once the three lists are complete, additional Z teams should be formed to audit key management systems. This is where the real change is found. For a given management system or process, does it grow the old culture or does it grow the new culture? Most of these audits will show improvement is necessary to the management system to support the new culture.

What are management systems? They include the elements of the L-model in figure 9. Management systems include any tools or processes that support planning, control, rewards, communication, employee development, and the often overlooked physical systems.

As each management system audit is complete, the organization should implement the findings.

V. The Simulation

The final step in a successful culture change relates to the overall strategic change of the organization. The best way to have the organization *feel the change* is through some sort of a simulation. By living the future in a simulation, employees will see the value of the change and how they can help implement it. As part of that simulation, a short culture survey, which resembles the real survey in step three above, should measure the culture of the participants as the simulation proceeds. This tactic helps employees understand why the survey is done so frequently. Simulations are expensive to develop and even more expensive to implement properly. They are often multiple days (and perhaps nights) in length and are best run as a residential, wherein the participants move into a hotel for the duration.

The need for a strategy simulation often separates those that give change lip service and those that truly see the need for dramatic, effective lasting change.

A SINGLE DEPARTMENT CHANGE— TWO KEY PRINCIPLES

For most new leaders, the challenge of leading a change will occur not on a large scale but within a small department. There are two key principles to effect change. First:

> Change management systems to change results.

This is nothing more than the core of step IV of the five listed above for large organizations. Our management systems are designed to work in the current culture. To change culture, we must at least tweak the systems before they pull us back into our old culture.

Second:

> Involvement is the key to buy-in.

Involvement can be done using special tiger teams or the entire department if warranted. Involving others teaches them you value their input, their intellect, and their creativity.

Consider the following example of a boss who used both principles.

The Transportation Transformation

Some years ago, a young man was hired to assist the manager of the transportation fleet for a large company. The transportation department purchased, outfitted, maintained, and sold heavy construction vehicles for a large construction-related company. Most of the department employees worked in the maintenance area, repairing engines, transmissions, and all other problems throughout the fleet of several hundred vehicles.

In a short time, the manager took an early retirement package, and the young man was promoted to be the manager.

Before joining this large company, the young man was the service manager for an auto dealer in another city. He knew the typical costs and prices for maintenance services. What he did not know was his own department costs to do the same work. The one-size-fits-all corporate budget system did not support him knowing such information. When budget season came the first year for him, he asked his budget coordinator who he was doing this budget for...because it certainly wasn't for him. The budget coordinator, to her credit, listened. While the new manager still needed to submit the typical budget estimate to fulfill corporate needs, the budget coordinator and the new manager worked together to design reports that would provide the new manager with the means to compare the costs of his internal department with competitive external companies that did the same work.

When the new reports arrived, the new manager was shocked. They showed unequivocally the absolute worst place for the company to have their maintenance work performed was their own internal department. Clearly, the employees of the transportation department needed to all be fired and the function outsourced to one of many local maintenance companies. The shareholders deserved better than they were getting.

The new manager knew his people were good. They knew their business. The new manager shared the data with them. Instead of an emotional backlash, the employees became engaged to solve the problem. They knew if such prices were the competitive benchmark outside of the company, they could beat them internally. So the entire team went to work to beat the outside world.

These workers had what is often called a *burning platform*. This analogy is based on a story about an oil rig worker who, during a fire, had only two choices: to burn or jump into the cold waters of the North Sea. He jumped even though he knew survival was unlikely. He was rescued and told how he was forced to accept long odds as opposed to certain death.

It only took about a year. From then on, the *best* place for the shareholders to have their vehicles maintained was their own internal department. Yes, there were company-planned reductions-in-force that were implemented during that time. But the remaining employees found ways to get the job done without replacements. Inventory was reduced. Overheads were slashed. Processes were streamlined. Innovation blossomed. Internal customers were better served.

To review, the change was necessitated by a change of a single management system, cost reporting by activity. The new data and a manager with confidence in his people evoked a permanent change that proved good for employees, internal customers, and shareholders. The solutions came from involved employees who contributed to their security with their creativity to solve a difficult problem.

This account is a beautiful example of the power of measuring the right things, the motivation that comes from creating a sense of urgency, and results from getting everyone involved.

THE POWER OF ONE

A new leader can make change faster than they may think. Consider the following study from family therapy.

Over three decades ago in Florida, a group of family therapists did a field study regarding understanding communications within intact, solid families.[86] Their goal was to discover what skills of communication these successful families had. Perhaps this would lead them to help less successful families overcome issues.

The study involved several thousand families. Each family allowed a researcher to be an observer and to do a tally of the amount of esteem-building comments that were heard compared to the amount of pejorative comments. The therapist were saddened to find out that, in these supposedly successful families, 80 percent of the comments were negative, esteem-lowering, pejorative comments. Only 20 percent were loving, esteem-building comments.

A second phase of the study was organized in response to this troubling finding. With the approval from the head of the household, one mature family member was selected to play a particular role for a few weeks and to keep it a secret for several months. Their role was, for a few weeks, to give one positive comment per day to another member of the family. They were not to divulge this assignment to other members of the family.

After a time, the therapists came back in and repeated the study. To their amazement, the statistics had flipped. Seventy percent of *all* comments in these families were now positive. Only 30 percent were put-downs. The researchers repeated the counting a few more times, a few weeks apart. After six months, the statistics were never worse than 60-40 in favor of the positive comments. The role play that was only for a limited time had caused a permanent improvement in the spirit of these families.

Is this study from family-relations research applicable to the workplace? Most would say yes.

Indeed, if one person would take the initiative to complement a coworker for doing a favor for someone or to deflect the all-too-frequent bad-mouthing behind someone's back, it can make a huge difference in the spirit of a department. Bosses should strive to be that one person.

One person can make a difference in the culture of an entire department. Never doubt the *power of one* to make a difference in a department's culture.

THREE TEXTS ON CHANGE

The field of organizational change is replete with volumes of literature. Some are better than others. After absorbing this short chapter, a new leader should become familiar with at least three. One is a classic. The second may well become a classic. The third is highly quoted, but also represents the *dark side* of change. It attempts to undermine the virtues of honesty, freedom, and liberty in a capitalist society.

Leading Change[87]

Among the true classics of change literature is John Kotter's *Leading Change*. Published in 1996, Dr. Kotter of the Harvard Business School promotes an eight-step process to effect change. These are:

1. Establish a sense of urgency. Without a burning platform, motivation to change is difficult.
2. Create a guiding coalition. This is similar to the second skill of leadership in figure 1 in chapter 1, *Build a Small Team*.
3. Develop a vision and strategy, as discussed in chapter 4.
4. Communicate the change vision, as discussed in chapter 13.
5. Empower broad-based action. This includes changing management systems as described above.
6. Generate short-term wins.
7. Consolidate gains and produce more change.
8. Anchor new approaches in the culture.

Kotter clearly asserts the order is vitally important. None of the eight steps should be attempted until the prior steps are successfully implemented.

Influencer: The Power to Change Anything[88]

If *Leading Change* represents a classic in change literature, *Influencer*, published in 2008, is destined to become a classic. Written by five principals from the consulting firm, *Vital Smarts*, the book's authors, Patterson, Grenny, Maxfield, McMillian, and Switzler, have captured a powerful model to influence and change any process or outcome from large companies, nations, industries, and individual personal life.

Their four-step behavior-based approach is simple. First, identify the behaviors that lead to the current *un*desired outcomes. Second, from this list of behaviors, determine the few behaviors that, when changed, really drive improved outcomes. Third, identify and train recovery behaviors for people to use when they make mistakes. Finally, test results, and move forward or modify your change strategy accordingly.

Influencer describes five diverse case studies to illustrate the power of the approach. From personal weight loss to solving a national crisis, these examples should convince the new leader that it is a useful tool for change in the workplace.

Rules for Radicals[89]

New students of change must be careful about some sources of knowledge. Some writers on change venture into or even focus on social and political change, not change to improve organizational effectiveness. Some of these authors are trying to promote antisocial values that may be cleverly camouflaged within its pages. One famous read on change with dubious moral implications is Saul Alinsky's *Rules for Radicals*. Alinsky is worshiped by some and vilified by others.

Alinsky was an irreverent, socialist community organizer in the middle decades of the twentieth century. Much of his work was about gaining power from the *haves* and giving it to the *have-nots* through social upheaval. *Rules for Radicals* is the owner's manual for those promoting radical social change. His philosophy was adopted by the radicals of the 1960s. Some still promote Alinsky's agenda.

His ideology was based on the end justifies the means. It is okay in Alinsky's world to lie to get one's way. Most of us reject that notion. Compare Alinsky to Gandhi who advocated that evil means degrade both the end purpose and the people who use them.[90]

As noted in chapter 6 and again in chapter 17, capitalism is only really effective when people have a basic sense of honesty in dealing with one another. Alinsky's ideology is an anathema to honest behavior. Nonetheless, many powerful social and political figures have risen to prominence having been cultured and educated in Alinsky's methods. It is interesting to read his tenets and see how some powerful people have used his teachings. It should be read with an understanding that the values therein are contrary to those of most honest and successful people. Thus, new leaders must know their values to avoid being tossed to and fro by every wind of opinion.

THE SHEPHERD AND THE COLLEGE STUDENT—PART 2

After pondering the older man's comment about not finding leadership in a management book, the student spoke, "Why do you think my text book won't teach me how to get people to follow me?"

"Well, young man, it's much like the difference between management and leadership. Some bosses push and some pull. Some keep things together, maintaining the status quo. Some lead their team to higher ground, leaving the status quo. The title of your book says management. It sounds like the former approach."

"With such understanding, I think you must have done more than herd sheep, er, I mean, shepherd sheep."

"Did I say I shepherded sheep? I said several hundred *heads*. Actually, I was founder and CEO of Applied Magnetronics. In May each year, we would begin communicating our strategic direction with employees, which eventually topped three thousand. My direct reports and I had studied the marketplace, our core competencies, and our competitors and formulated a change in direction for the next year or so. We constantly needed to inspire our frontline employees, their immediate supervision, and middle management.

"We challenged them to find ways to make our goals a reality. Some years, the higher ground was not too far away. Other years, it was a march up Mt. Everest. But we always had a strategy. And we always had a perspective on where we needed to go and how fast. Then, all I needed to do was get out of the way. The way to implement our vision came from all corners of the organization."

"This is really intriguing. I wish we could talk more."

"Oh, we probably will," the older man said, showing a wry grin. "It looks like I'm your new MGMT 401 professor."

Realizing his curiosity had led into this embarrassing moment; all the student could do was laugh. Then it hit him. "Hey, I don't get somethin'. From what you said, why are you using this *management* book anyway and not a book on *leadership?*"

A look of disgust came over the professor's face. "The department chair wrote it! So much for office politics."

QUESTIONS FOR CURRENT LEADERS

1. Do the current processes or management tools in your department advance or hinder progress toward department goals?

2. Does any individual in your area need to change, as in improve skills, modify an attitude, or be supportive of your direction? How will you help them with this change?
3. What emotional support do you provide for your people when implementing a change?

TECHNICAL ANALOG ON LIFE AND LEADERSHIP: THE PRIME MOVER

A prime mover is a common phrase in mechanical engineering. It refers to an engine or a turbine that transfers mechanical energy to another component, such as an electric generator or an airplane wing. As stated earlier, projects are the prime movers of change in an organization.

This term, however, is also used in medicine to describe a certain muscle within a muscle group. The prime mover initiates the coordinated action of the entire muscle group. In this sense, project managers are prime movers. The ability to coordinate employees, vendors of equipment, suppliers of services, internal and external customers, even regulators, other project managers, and top management is a valued skill set. It is no wonder why successful project managers often move onto other leadership positions. They have learned to be the muscle that initiates change among the organization's broad muscle groups.

PART IV

WILL I LAST?

CHAPTER 17

LEADERSHIP LAND MINES

THE LEADERSHIP BOLL WEEVIL

In Enterprise, Alabama, in 1915, a tragic event took place. The cotton crop, which was the mainstay of economic stability for many in the area, failed. An infestation of boll weevils destroyed the livelihood of the community. This led one entrepreneur farmer to plant a new crop—peanuts. The peanut crop was a success, and soon the entire county's income was more diversified. The economic well being of the area was vastly improved.

In 1919, the citizens of Enterprise erected a beautiful statue in the town square. A lovely Greek goddess, draped in a flowing gown, held up an ornate plate on which was a very large boll weevil. The historical marker reads, "In profound appreciation to the Boll Weevil and what it has done as [our] herald of prosperity." The statue remains the only such monument dedicated to an agricultural pest. Without the boll weevil, the town would not have prospered.[91]

Sometimes talented leaders run into career boll weevils. The existence of really bad bosses is not funny, particularly if you are reporting to one.

Most of the truly bad bosses have some deep-rooted psychological hang-up. One mean-spirited boss was finally decoded by his new administrative assistant. Her Caesar-esque boss could not read…yes, he was illiterate! He made up for it by being a tyrant to keep everybody off guard. What a revelation it was to understand the *why* behind the *what*.

Regardless of their underlying motives, sometimes, these psyche cases win. They can exhibit enormous power because of their position. Some very talented leaders can find their successful career in leadership scuttled by a bad boss. As we tell our children as they grow up, "Sometimes, bad things happen to good people."

If this happens to you, just remember, you will land on your feet. You are the one with the ability. You will someday look back and see that your boll weevil did you a favor although it did not seem like it at the time. If you don't let such an all-too-common scenario knock you down, someday you will see your career boll weevil was your herald of prosperity.

The Biz Bucks Guy knows this firsthand. He is grateful for a boll weevil that temporarily ruined his career many years ago. The past fifteen years of creative, meaningful, difference-making, exciting professional life is the result of being awoken by a boll weevil.

LAND MINES OF LEADERSHIP

Those considering leadership should not be overwhelmed with this chapter. It considers the dark side of careers in leadership. The next chapter will focus on a more optimistic side of leadership. Sometimes things just don't work out. You can be right and ready for leadership, as discussed in chapter 1, but careers are long. There is ample time to accidentally step on a career land mine. The higher your leadership visibility goes, the more opportunity there is for career-fatal mistakes. This chapter summarizes several ways careers in leadership get scuttled.

In addition to running into a boll weevil, a leader may have their title changed to former leader for a variety of reasons. These include issues of the following:

- performance
- culture
- unimpressive moments
- ineffectively managing up
- sabotage
- bad luck
- lack of technical growth
- poor health
- discrimination
- reverse discrimination
- personal preference
- ethics.

Some of these land mines can be avoided. Some are just part of life. Let's examine each more closely.

PERFORMANCE POTHOLES

The most logical reason for a leader to be *de-leadered* is lack of results. The organization promoted the individual, agreed to clear expectations, provided scarce resources, and injected ample time and training to succeed. Unfortunately, the results did not materialize. This can happen to leaders who manage simple routine processes. This can also happen to those who manage complex, difficult-to-change processes. The chapters of this book are intended to help minimize this possibility.

If this happens, so what? The person gave it their all and hopefully can return to their frontline position. We should respect them for having the fortitude to step up to the plate, regardless of whether they hit a home run or struck out.

CULTURE CHANGES

Every boss is influenced by their prior bosses. Most people pick up on subtle things in people's style. This is leadership-style eclecticism; that is, borrowing from a variety of sources. These observations coupled with their own personality form their own natural way of leading. Sometimes that natural leadership style is contrary to the stated direction (or more likely the new direction) of an organization.

Consider a person who worked for a series of dictators and adopted much the same blustery, forceful, dominant style when a leadership opportunity came. Then, the organization realized it was a *dictator farm* and performance will improve if the leadership culture is changed to a more participative style throughout the company. It may be nearly impossible for a known dictator to get with the program and change styles. It is heavy baggage, and *baggage is tough to lose unless you are an airline.*

Consider the example of one talented leader who was not a dictator with his people but was with his peers. He was unable to work cooperatively with certain other bosses. He saw one particular staff department as a rival infiltrating *his* domain. The leader often said, "I've tried everything to nail the doors shut to keep them out of my work. But no matter how many nails I use, they eventually squeeze under the door like a green ooze." Widely known for such comments, he didn't stand a chance when the company began to transform its culture by blowing up silos and fiefdoms and removing dictators. It was a shame. He really was a talented manager and eventually did well in a new company. He was unable to change his personal leadership brand in time to match the newly desired culture.

A new leader should evaluate the examples they have had from their prior bosses and consciously determine if emulating their styles is what an organization needs in the future.

UNIMPRESSIVE MOMENTS

Sometimes a person will inadvertently walk into a tough situation where many are watching and things don't go well. For example, you might give a bad presentation to a large group, and your leadership stock falls like 1929. Perhaps, you discuss the good points of another manager in public and you find out later your boss despises this person and wants him gone. You may be next!

Usually, an occasional unimpressive moment alone will not cause you to lose your leadership position. The late Stephen R. Covey discussed the notion of an emotional bank account.[92] Hopefully the relationship with your boss has enough in the bank account to allow a few withdrawals for such unimpressive moments.

INEFFECTIVELY MANAGING UP

Every boss needs to manage not only their direct reports (managing down) but also relationships with those above them on the organization chart (managing up). This is a constant effort. Many wonderful bosses, loved by their subordinates, are removed because of confidence problems from above. The subordinates are amazed. They had a good thing going, and suddenly, it is gone.

To avoid this, every boss should be asking for regular feedback on her performance.

One Mr. Big was notorious for promoting a person, making him his pet for a period, losing confidence, and then busting him out of leadership or sending him to organizational Siberia with no explanation. As the saying went, "Did you hear what happened to Sam? His picture fell off Mr. Big's piano!" A good leader was not nurtured properly. He did not keep score on the expectations of his immediate boss and others up the chain.

SABOTAGE

Another common way a boss's career is destroyed is by outright sabotage. Some people are just plain Judas Iscariots.

An upper level boss may see you as a threat. Consider a midlevel leader who was known to have a strong relationship with a top executive from a prior assignment. Now in a new role, some saw him as a spy for that executive. Some years later, a new friend admitted there was a covert plan fostered by another leader to reduce cooperation, avoid openness, and generally help this spy fail.

Another leader who was assigned the difficult job of transforming a large organization's leadership skills took on a well-respected peer who simply did not exemplify the values of new leadership culture. This war was between just two people. But at the opportune time, the *old school* boss went to top management and made a *creative* complaint about the transformational leader. Top management did not check out the trumped up charges but bought the whole notion—hook, line, and sinker. The support for the transformational leader waned slowly. After more than a year, the transformational leader found out what had happened. One top manager's jaw dropped as he realized he had been *had*. But the damage was done. The transformational leader's career was already on the rocks.

JUST PLAIN BAD LUCK

Sometimes, leaders need to take frontline jobs because of things that are totally out of their control. This is usually some type of organizational change. In the nineties, corporate America was on a new fad—*delayering*. For several decades, good employees were rewarded by receiving promotions. As globalization forced greater competition, many American companies realized they were top heavy with bosses. Through an often not-too-smooth process, many midlevel managers were moved down to first-line supervision. Some first-line supervisors were moved down to the frontline employee level. Those that were demoted were simply in the wrong place at the wrong time. Bad luck.

LACK OF TECHNICAL GROWTH

Sometimes, a new organization develops quickly. New tools are invented. New processes are implemented and streamlined. Top management delegates additional duties and has increasingly higher expectations. New employees with expanded skills or new talents are brought in to fill key frontline positions.

In this evolution of the new organization, the technical skills of current bosses, particularly first-line supervisors, may have been sufficient in the beginning but may now be insufficient to handle the new environment. This is tough. Eventually the old guard has to step aside to let the organization continue to grow.

POOR HEALTH

Obviously, some people need to step down from leadership due to health issues, either physical or psychological. This might particularly happen to those who cannot handle the constant stress of being boss.

DISCRIMINATION AND REVERSE DISCRIMINATION

In the United States, it is illegal to discriminate against certain minority groups, including race, color, sex, religion, or national origin. (See Appendix C, "Labor Law Overview".) However, it is possible such discrimination might still happen to you. If the boss who promoted you moves on and the new boss has some ingrained, irrational, bigoted problem with you, your leadership success may be thwarted.

Additionally, beginning in the 1990s, companies have subtly engaged in a form of reverse discrimination. This was the effect of many companies' desire to become more diverse ethnically in their management ranks. Affirmative action laws and the general desire to right the discriminatory practices of the past can drive this phenomenon. In some functions in many companies, white males were no longer considered for leadership or were allowed to stagnate as others were moved up. This is tough duty if this happens to you. There is not much you can do short of leaving your firm.

PERSONAL PREFERENCE

In chapter 3, we discussed the Career Concept framework of linear, expert, spiral, and transitory. When a nonlinear gets promoted, their leadership half-life may be shorter than expected by others.

An expert, once they realize they are losing expertise (and that leadership is truly a new career), may opt to return to frontline work.

A spiral will eventually see leadership as just another stop on a route of personal growth. Eventually, with that notch on their gun, they may look for more creative ways to contribute.

A transitory will probably enjoy the ride for a couple of years, then start looking for some other avenue of fulfillment.

Those who leave leadership for these reasons are actually not stepping on a land mine at all. They are being true to their personal motives and values. But the realization and awakening of these personal traits may be shocking if one has spent considerable time in a leadership position.

ETHICAL LAPSES

The final leadership land mine is ethical lapses. This topic demands more focus than any of the others, so fasten your seat belt. The Biz Bucks Guy calls this section *business Sunday school*.

This section is intended to be helpful to two groups:

1. Those who attempt to be ethical in their personal and professional lives. They will understand that ethical behavior is not always easy. Situations occasionally arise in leadership where the right direction is not clear.
2. Those who attempt to navigate on the edge or even across the edge of ethical behavior. Perhaps these people have been suckered into believing Hollywood, which always portrays business people as the villains. They should learn that it is easy for their low ethical standards to be discovered. If you are in this group, it is time to seriously review your *modus operandi*.

Dr. Alan Shapiro, professor of economics at the Marshall School of Business at the University of Southern California, says that two ingredients are necessary for capitalism to work. One is a properly functioning accounting and legal system. The other is honest people.

Regarding the latter ingredient, among the most disappointing events in one's career is developing a working relationship with a colleague, only to find out that she was on the take, got caught, and was let go immediately.

A close second to such a catastrophic event is discovering that a previously trusted ally in the workplace has proved untrustworthy. When someone can't be trusted, relations are severed quickly. Commerce stops between them and any other person or entity who is aware of this trust issue. As Thomas Jefferson said, "Honesty is the first chapter in the book of wisdom."[93]

Ethical behavior is simply defined as doing what is right, not what is wrong. Humankind has an inner voice that guides people in determining what is right and wrong. That inner voice goes by many names, such as conscience, moral compass, and Holy Ghost.

Honesty, or one of its synonyms, is often the first item of any list of virtues. For example, the Boy Scout law starts with *trustworthy*.

During his MBA program, The Biz Bucks Guy was one of sixty classmates. Before the end of the first year, the few who were less than ethical were pretty much identified. These were the ones who cut ethical corners on assignments, who argued that business was about shafting others before they shaft you, who bragged about his bad, even criminal, behavior in their past. No one wanted to be on their team when team projects evolved the second year.

For most, unethical behavior will be discovered eventually.

We often hear (and may have used ourselves) certain phrases that usually indicate a decision is at least on the edge of ethics. These are clues to deciding what is the right and wrong way and resolving ethical dilemmas:

1. Everybody else does it.
2. If we don't do it, someone else will.
3. That's the way we always have done it.
4. We'll wait until the lawyers tell us it's wrong.
5. It really doesn't hurt anybody.
6. The system is unfair.
7. I was just following orders.[94]

New leaders should understand that these phrases are code words for rationalization and unethical behavior.

Ethical Dilemmas

What may not be obvious to a quantoid moving into his first leadership assignment is that right and wrong is not always clear in every business situation. When there is no clear ethical way, the situation is called an *ethical dilemma*. Take these examples:

- A pharmaceutical drug is saving many lives from a disease, but you find it has a statistical link as a cause of another disease.
- A proposed manufacturing facility in a third world country will help the local starving population. The noise level in the facility will cause hearing loss in a decade, even with earplugs. The market price of the product does not allow sound-attenuating baffles to be constructed.
- Your company is replacing safety equipment because of the need to comply with latest codes. Another company that can't afford the latest version wants to buy the used, out-of-code equipment for its aging facility. You have used the older equipment with no problems. The employees of the other company will be safer with the older equipment.

If there is truly no clear path that is right, Ken Blanchard and Norman Vincent Peale developed three questions that may help.

Is it legal? Is it balanced? How does it make me feel?

By honestly assessing an ethical dilemma with these three questions, one may be able to know the best direction.

Group Think

Group think is a psychological phenomenon identified by social psychologist Irving Janus in 1972. Group think occurs when a cohesive team reaches consensus on a decision without critical thinking, analysis, and evaluation of other alternatives. Often the decision is the wrong one. Sometimes it is fatal.

It is imperative that teams know of and avoid group think. Dr. Janus provides seven tips to stop group think:

1. Leaders should assign each member the role of critical evaluator. This allows each member to freely air objections and doubts.

2. Higher-ups should not express an opinion when assigning a task to a group.
3. The organization should set up several independent groups working on the same problem.
4. All effective alternatives should be examined.
5. Each member should discuss the group's ideas with trusted people outside of the group.
6. The group should invite outside experts into meetings. Group members should be allowed to discuss with and question the outside experts.
7. At least one group member should be assigned the role of devil's advocate. This should be a different person for each meeting.[95]

In essence, the principle antidote for group think is someone speaking up boldly. This causes others to rethink their position. This is an example of the emboldening principle discussed in the prior chapter.

A well known example of group think is the Challenger disaster. The problem with o-rings was discovered before the launch. The subcontractor was bullied into approving the launch. Several people went along with the decision in the final and fateful meeting. One person speaking up in that meeting would have made the difference.

LAST WORDS ON LAND MINES

Of all the ways your leadership career may get scuttled, unethical behavior is the most pathetic. In the final analysis, your integrity is one of the few things in life that you can completely control.[96] It is up to you and no one else. Learn to lean to the right and avoid the wrong.

Yes, life in leadership is not always fair, and it is never easy. You will be challenged by many of these land mines. It is a rite of passage. As the sailors say,

> Calm seas don't make great mariners.

Leadership difficulties will season you.

However, if circumstances conspire to shorten your tenure in leadership, you join a long list of successful people who pulled themselves up by their bootstraps and continued to make a difference in other ways or other organizations. Remember the famous quote of Confucius:

> Our greatest glory is not in never failing but in rising every time we fail.

We now turn to a brighter side of leadership; some tips to help you avoid many of these leadership-ending events.

QUESTIONS FOR CURRENT LEADERS

1. Could you be a boll weevil for someone in your organization? How would you know? If so, what can you do to change?
2. Are you sharpening your saw? Have you taken the time to advance your skills for your current and perhaps future assignment?
3. Have you kept proper focus on your personal health and family well being? Is it time to lose a few pounds or get some stress-reducing exercise?

TECHNICAL ANALOG FOR LIFE AND LEADERSHIP: BEN FRANKLIN BLEW IT!

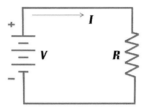

Figure 32 – Simple Electric Circuit

Figure 32 shows a typical simple electric circuit. The battery (V) has a plus sign (+) and a minus sign (-). This, in turn, shows the current flow (I) in a clockwise direction. As most quantoids and techies know, this is actually an incorrect representation of the true physical environment. What is flowing are electrons in the conductor, and they are flowing counter-clockwise. Why is this mixed up? Because Ben Franklin blew it!

Ben, one of the most beloved figures in American history, did much of the early work on electricity. He could not see an electron. It was evident that something was flowing around the circuit. He guessed the direction…and guessed wrong. Ben established a standard and it stuck. Later, the error was discovered, but the standard had been established.

Now students of electrical engineering are taught the flow is *hole flow*, not electron flow. Think of a set of boxcars on a north-south train track. The first car on the south is decoupled and pushed a few feet south. It flowed south. This creates a space or *hole* between it and the second car. If the second car is pushed south, the hole moves north. Thus, cars flow south, and the hole flows north. The clockwise orientation is often called Ben Franklin current, as opposed to electron current.

Leaders will make mistakes too. If Ben can make a famous mistake, then each of us are certainly talented enough to do the same. The key is to understand when you are taking a risk, understand the ramifications if you are wrong, and know that those ramifications will not ruin your organization or company. This is called *knowing when you bet the farm*. It would be wise to avoid that kind of risk. Ben made a great contribution to science, in spite of his bad guess. You will make a great contribution to your organization even though you will probably hose up a few decisions along the way.

CHAPTER 18

TIPS FOR NEW BOSSES: RESULTS OF RESEARCH

FROM LAND MINES TO STEPPING STONES

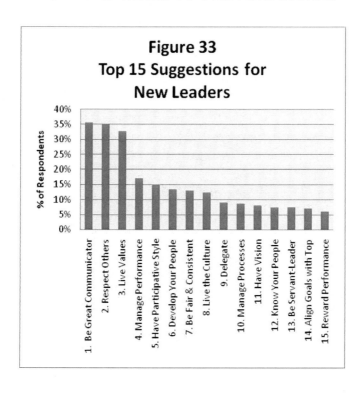

Figure 33
Top 15 Suggestions for
New Leaders

The prior chapter was, by necessity, the dark side of leadership. However, in discussing the question of "Will I last?" we can now mercifully leave land mines and focus on stepping stones. This chapter deals with pithy, practical principles to help any new supervisor succeed.

For six years, in preparation for this book, The Biz Bucks Guy collected responses to an online survey on his website. In addition to the demographics, the survey contained only a single question:

What advice would you give to a new supervisor?

The Biz Bucks Guy received 340 responses. Each respondent was able to provide more than one piece of advice. Many provided three or more particular suggestions to the new supervisor. The suggestions totaled 1,035.

Each item was analyzed using the powerful Llewellyn advanced personal qualitative analysis (LAPQA) technique (also known as plain ol' gut feel). These 1,035 suggestions grouped into ninety-six discrete suggestions. The following should prove helpful to most new and many seasoned bosses as well as those contemplating leadership careers.

Figure 33 shows the most highly mentioned fifteen suggestions of the ninety-six. The actual percent of respondents suggesting each item is included in the discussion below. The top three clearly stand out.

Each of these three tips was suggested by more than thirty percent of the respondents. While each has been mentioned in other parts of this book, they deserve some amplification here.

1. **Be a Great Communicator**

    As emphasized in chapter 13, having outstanding communication skills was a key recommendation of the survey respondents. There was particular interest in listening skills. Some advocated an open-door policy. Others suggested always tell *why* when making assignments or announcing decisions. Another important communication skill was mastering the art of asking questions, particularly open-ended questions, those that can't be answered by yes or no. Open-ended questions begin with *who, what, where, when, how,* and *why.*

2. **Respect Others**

In a variety of ways, the respondents' advice was clear that a successful supervisor respects others, particularly their subordinates. Many respondents promoted the golden rule, as discussed in chapter 2. Some said, "Never forget your roots." Others emphasized "Trust your people" and "Avoid elitism." The high response rate of *respect others* supports the first of the eight qualities of leadership rightness, *love people,* discussed in chapter 2.

3. **Live Your Values**

Many respondents were emphatic about a newly minted supervisor being in touch with their inner moral compass. This includes both knowing what you stand for—your values—and then never compromising them. Among the most mentioned values were, first, honesty, which has been woven throughout this volume, second, ethical behavior (covered in chapter 17), third, integrity, and fourth, trustworthiness. All four are mutually supportive.

THE NEXT DOZEN

The research identified twelve more frequently mentioned tips. Most relate to prior chapters.

4. *Performance Management* — See chapter 10.
5. *Participative Style* — See chapter 1
6. *Develop Your People* — See chapter 11
7. *Be Fair and Consistent*

8. *Live the Culture*
9. *Delegate* — See chapter 14.
10. *Business Process Management* — See chapter 8.
11. *Strategic Visioning* — See chapter 1.
12. *Know Your People* — See chapter 3.
13. *Be a Servant-Leader* — See chapter 1.
14. *Align Goals with Top Management* — See chapters 4 and 7.
15. *Reward Performance* — See chapter 10.

THE INFREQUENT, BUT IMPORTANT

The Biz Bucks Guy received several suggestions that were profound enough to be included in this chapter, even though they may have been mentioned infrequently or only once. Unlike the prior fifteen, most of these were unique and are not covered elsewhere in this book. New bosses should consider the following items of advice:

a. Continue your education.
b. Be positive. Have Fun. Be Happy.
c. Network and build good relationships with peers.
d. Don't fear mistakes. Learn from them.
e. Blame the process, not the people.
f. Do management by walking around (MBWA).
g. Praise in public; criticize in private.
h. Ask the *seven whys,* drill down into issues to find root causes.
i. Study real leaders.
j. Get a sponsor or a mentor for yourself.
k. Learn labor laws.[97]
l. Hire up (hire better people than yourself).
m. Hire diverse skills that complement your own.
n. Avoid being friends with subordinates.
0. Be decisive.
p. Manage up, meaning know your bosses' needs and meet them.

q. Leave frontline work to frontline people.

r. Be honest with each customer.

BE OPTIMISTIC

Will you last in your leadership assignment? Probably. Your innate skills, coupled with a lifetime of improving the twelve skills of leadership readiness will pay off.

You will have ups and downs.

Spirals and transitories relish that. Linears, however, are mortified by anything but a constant chug up the corporate organization chart. Careers are long. Be creative. Make a difference.

QUESTIONS FOR CURRENT LEADERS

1. What communication channels do you use most naturally? What other channels could you begin to use to improve your communication abilities?

2. Do your employees respect one another's differences? If not, what can you do to improve their attitude?

3. Has your company or organization caused you to do anything that was contrary to your personal values? How would you handle it if you were confronted with such a situation?

TECHNICAL ANALOG FOR LIFE AND LEADERSHIP: OHM'S LAW, ADVERSITY, AND LEADERSHIP POTENTIAL

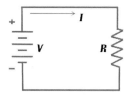

Figure 34 – Simple Electric Circuit

Ohm's Law is $V = IR$, voltage (V) in a simple circuit is equal to the current (I) times the resistance (R). As represented by the elements in figure 34, this is the famous equation learned by freshmen engineering students. On first thought, it seems like resistance is a negative thing, impeding the flow of electrons (current). Actually, resistance usually represents the usefulness of the circuit, a lightbulb, a toaster-heating element, or a dimmer switch. Without a resistance, the circuit accomplishes nothing. It is considered a *short* with the electrons racing around the conducting wire, dissipating energy needlessly, eventually heating the wire up to its melting point, and even causing a fire unless the circuit is protected with a fuse or circuit breaker.

The resistance determines the usefulness. The voltage, given adequate conducting wire, determines the circuit's capacity to perform.

Such are our lives. A life without some resistance is a short-circuited life. Adversity and challenge provide the means for growth and character building.

As Shakespeare wrote in *As You Like It*, "Sweet are the uses of adversity" (Act 2, Scene 1).

As the popular phrase suggests, "That which does not kill us makes us stronger." Leadership will provide many challenges. Few will kill you or your career. These challenges help you grow and increase your life's voltage, which is your capacity for future accomplishment or performance. Challenges increase your leadership potential or your leadership possibilities.

Isn't it interesting that voltage is sometimes called electrical *potential?*

EPILOGUE

THE PARABLE OF THE POOLS

The Biz Bucks Guy once heard an old Welsh fable, or more accurately a parable, about two shimmering pools of water on the top of Mount Snowdon in North Wales. Mount Snowdon is a beautiful range of *granite and green* that juts up over three thousand feet, overlooking the Irish Sea.

On a warm summer's day, two pools lay contented in the sun, near the top of Mount Snowdon. It was a wonderful day, and life seemed perfect for these two crystal clear pools.

But one became restless. He proposed that they each turn themselves into a little streamlet and wiggle down the hill in front of them.

"Let's see what it is like down the hill," he said to the other pool of water.

"No," said the second pool. "Life is wonderful here. Why should we leave it?"

"Okay, you can choose for yourself, friend," responded the first, "but I am going for a little ride."

So with a little exertion, the first pool squirmed out of his comfortable spot and began to flow down the hill. Faster and faster, he went. It was thrilling, but the ride was rough. He bumped into a big rock and then curved around a few trees. He fell over a small drop-off. Soon he began to wonder about his decision. Some of his droplets stayed in the soil. He was getting smaller.

But in a few minutes, he met up with another adventurous little streamlet, just like himself. They joined together to become a larger stream. Again and again, the stream was joined by other streams as the ride down Snowdon continued. Eventually, as a mighty river, the adventuresome little pool, together with his friends, rushed out into the Irish Sea.

The sun beamed bright, and soon our little pool evaporated into a beautiful fleecy cloud. A south wind blew him over Snowdon. He was awestruck by the view. Then suddenly he became a soothing rain, and before he knew what had happened, once again he was a crystal clear pool, right next to his friend at the top of the mountain.

"Wow, that was fun…I'm going again!" said the first pool. But as he squirmed and started down, he glanced back. His friend was no longer crystal clear. A little moss was growing around his edges. His pure shimmering beauty was now replaced with a faint tint of green.

As he began his second journey, the first little pool noticed many new flowers were growing along the way. They had not been there during his first ride. He suddenly realized they were *his* flowers.

As he flowed by them, they whispered, "Thank you for helping us grow."

GO FOR IT, AND ENJOY THE FLOWERS

Those quantoids contemplating leadership have much in common with the first little pool. They have a choice and may have some trepidation about the change. As Abraham Maslow wrote, "You will either step forward into growth or you will step back into safety."[98]

Sometimes we must leave a comfortable position to grow and to purify our existence. Such change can often provide the means of making a bigger difference. While there are risks, the rewards—particularly the intangible rewards—are many.

Change can come in a variety of ways. For the expert, it may mean drilling into your field deeper through advanced education. For the spiral or transitory, it may mean a change of assignment, laterally or even up the organization chart. For the linear, it may be that long-awaited opportunity for leadership.

If such an opportunity comes your way, like our adventurous pool of water, enjoy the flowers who say, "Thank you for helping us grow." They are your flowers. There will be many.

> What you leave behind is not what is engraved in stone monuments, but what is woven into the lives of others.[99]

APPENDIX A

THE RIGHT AND READY SELF-ASSESSMENT TOOL

This tool is designed to help those contemplating a leadership assignment gain some insights into their personal rightness and readiness for being a boss.

This tool consists of two lists based on the eight qualities of leadership rightness (figure 2) and the twelve skills of leadership readiness (figure 3). For items in both lists, the individual should read and ponder a group of statements called *reflection items*. These may evoke other statements or thoughts for reflection on that respective topic. The individual should make an honest self-assessment of their personal rightness or readiness depending on the list. It may be helpful to score the results on a ten scale (with ten being highest). If a quantoid will ponder each item thoughtfully while doing some honest self-talk, this list should provide a gut check on one's leadership rightness and readiness.

The scores for each item are not totaled, so the total can be compared to some standard to indicate a decision. This tool is designed simply to elicit honest thinking of one's own ability. If the reader strongly desires a scoring method to turn this leadership decision into a quantitative exercise, see quality 2 of leadership rightness (dealing with ambiguity)! In the vernacular, the decision to pursue leadership ain't no numbers game.

Before considering these two lists, one should recall and be convinced he or she has the *givens* mentioned in chapter 2. These are:

being honest, being results oriented, having the ability to organize, desiring to innovate, having basic technical/functional skills, seeking root causes of problems, being loyal to the organization and its direction, bringing sufficient IQ horsepower to navigate successfully with people, and finally, having a balanced strength in the physical, mental, emotional, and spiritual facets of life.

EIGHT QUALITIES OF LEADERSHIP RIGHTNESS

If you feel you are less than strong in any one of these eight qualities, you may want to postpone pursuing a leadership assignment. Please note people can and do develop in certain of these areas over a lengthy time.

Some reflection items represent the quality or skill. Some represent the opposite.

Quality	Reflection Item	Points (1 to 10)
Love people	a. I appreciate a person for whom they are and am not concerned for what they are not. b. I truly value diverse thinking. c. I can work with people of all religions and creeds. d. I think loving people is not important in leadership.	
Be able to deal with ambiguity	a. If things don't fit together perfectly, I am okay as long as progress is made. b. Figuratively, I can walk into a dark room. c. When I read item b above (which was purposely written ambiguously), it bothered me.	
Enjoy coaching	a. I enjoy helping others succeed. b. I have served a youth sports team or a Boy Scout/Girl Scout troop. c. I am a parent. d. When I was coached, I knew it was something I wanted to do.	
Apply judgment and take risk	a. I always shoot for perfection. b. I can see shades of gray in most decisions. c. I know when I am betting the farm. d. I can balance financial gain and intangible benefits against potential problems. e. I understand bad luck happens.	

Be able to work long hours	a. I feel exploited if I am asked to work more than straight time with no additional pay. b. I have sufficient health to work more hours than straight time. c. I am able to manage my stress. d. I am constantly seeking to keep my life balanced.	
Desire to make a bigger difference	a. I feel I have a legacy to leave. b. I am destined to make a large contribution. c. I want more power because of the financial rewards it will bring.	
Be willing to leave prior expertise	a. I spent four years getting a degree (or becoming a journeyman) and I don't want to waste it. b. My skills represent security to me. I don't want to lose them. c. I value gaining additional experience. d. I want to broaden myself. e. I need variety in my career.	
Have charisma	a. People generally listen when I say something. b. I think people naturally follow me. c. I have been told I carry myself well. d. I know people who fill up the room when they enter, and I think I have some of that.	

TWELVE SKILLS OF LEADERSHIP READINESS

After scoring each of the following twelve skills, focus on one or two of the lowest scores to help prepare you for a leadership assignment (should one develop). You should start by rereading the relevant chapter. Appendix D, "Additional Reading," will provide additional resources for your personal development.

Skill (Chapter)	Reflection Item	Points (1 to 10)
Strategy (4)	a. I understand the *future first* strategic perspective. b. I can dovetail my department into a higher-up's strategy. c. I appreciate my employees will crave a boss with vision.	

Knowing Your Customer (5)	a. I understand everyone has at least one customer at work. b. I recognize that no organization can meet all the needs of a customer without exceeding available resources. c. I know how to negotiate fairly and look for win-win situations.	
Quantoidal Business Smarts (6)	a. I have had formal education in: • Statistics • Accounting • Finance • Economics b. I understand my company's budget processes.	
Organizational Business Smarts (7)	a. I understand what a management system is. b. I understand that all management systems should fit together. c. I know the importance of both vertical and horizontal alignment.	
Managing Work: Processes and Projects (8 & 9)	a. I have drawn a process flowchart. b. In flowcharts, I can differentiate value-added steps from administrative steps. c. I have developed a work breakdown structure for a project.	
Managing Individual Performance (10)	a. I recognize the importance of planning individual performance. b. I know the difference between formal and informal coaching. c. I can conduct a 360-degree evaluation. d. I understand that good performance management takes time.	
Developing People (11)	a. I know my role of boss is to help release the full potential of my direct reports. b. I know a development plan will differ by the Career Concept of the individual. c. I understand being a people developer is the best part of being a boss.	
Decision-Making (12)	a. I understand the four types of decision-making. b. I know which of the four types the high-performing organizations use. c. I have constructed a decision tree. d. I understand intangibles can be the basis for decisions.	

Communicating (13)	a. I have strong interpersonal skills. b. I can speak to large groups well. c. I am a strong writer. d. I remember to communicate times ten. e. I know how to design and implement aggressive communications.	
Delegating (14)	a. I know the shades of delegation. b. I understand delegating is a key to life balance for me. c. I recognize delegation is a prime way to develop my people.	
Using Teams (15)	a. I have been on successful cross-functional teams. b. I know small teams can make a big difference. c. I understand Tuckman's stages of teaming. d. I can fit one of the seven types of special teams to the appropriate setting.	

Leading Change (16)	a. I can define *culture* in an organization.
	b. I know the importance of supporting
	   people emotionally during a change.
	c. I recognize the key to change is to change
	   management systems and processes.
	d. I understand my attitude can evoke
	   change in a small organization.	

APPENDIX B

PRINCIPLES OF *SAFE* SUBJECTS

Chapter 6 refers to statistics, accounting, finance and economics as *SAFE* subjects, the quantoidal business smarts. These principles are not easily learned. Mastery takes more than merely passively reading and rotely memorizing this appendix. Most leaders will gain basic competence by listening to experienced lecturers, working problems, and immersing in academic case studies. Yep, it is learned the old fashioned way, a deep dive in a classroom. However, The Biz Bucks Guy has developed a list of principles that, at least, can be read and contemplated.

As noted in the chapter, this list also is a self test to determine if one needs additional study to be an effective leader.

STATISTICS

S1. An important skill in business is process management, which is discussed in chapter 8. Advanced process management requires statistical process control (SPC), including the use of Ishikawa (or fishbone) diagrams, Pareto charts, and control charts. For a given business process, it is easy to become carried away with the SPC tools when a more basic approach to analyzing problems and finding improvements may be sufficient.

S2. Standard deviation (SD) is a measure of the *spread outed-ness* of a data distribution. If a bell curve is wide, it has a large SD. If the bell curve is sharp and thin, it has a small SD. Although the actual calculation of SD is much more rigorous, one SD includes about 68 percent of the bell curve, that is, 34 percent on each side of the mean. Two SD includes about 95.5 percent of the distribution. Six SDs are 99.9999998027 percent of the distribution.

The Greek letter sigma (σ) is often used to designate standard deviation. Six sigma is a process management philosophy invented by Motorola and repopularized by GE. For a manufacturing process, Six Sigma means one defect in over five hundred million occurrences. In other words, no defects allowed!

S3. Statistical Correlation—Given a set of data that can be regressed (approximated) into a straight line, the closeness of the fit of the line to predict outcomes is called correlation. Statisticians use a term R^2, called the coefficient of determination, to indicate how closely correlated the data is to the line, and thus its predictability. For $R^2 = 1.0$, there is complete correlation. Power plant electrical output is almost completely correlated to fuel burned.

For $R^2 = 0.0$, there is no correlation. Rain in Boston is not correlated to how many meteorologists graduate from MIT.

For $R^2 = -1.0$, there is complete but negative correlation. Gold prices often have been negatively correlated to GDP growth (perhaps not completely).

For $R^2 = 0.7$, it is said that the line predicts 70 percent of the forecast. The heating capability of a solar hot-water heater varies by three factors: (1) ambient temperature, (2) the angle of the solar collectors relative to the sun, and (3) the amount of cloud cover. Ambient temperature has the lowest R^2.

S4. Correlation does not mean causation. There is a strong R^2 correlation between those who have driver's licenses and those who run out of gas while driving. But it would be wrong to conclude that driver's licenses cause people to run out of gas.

S5. Linear Programming—Sometimes called the *mathematics of mixes*, linear programming is a sophisticated statistical tool to optimize an output given that multiple mixes of inputs are possible. For example, how does a refinery manager maximize daily profit when she could produce multiple products, like gasoline and heating oil, when the refining process requires at least two gallons of gasoline for every gallon of oil? Those new to linear programming should know it has nothing to do with programming a computer.

S6. Data envelop analysis (DEA) is another statistical technique to discover which of several manufacturing plants are operating the best in spite of natural differences that limit one versus another.

S7. A decision tree is a graphical tool to help make decisions when the inputs are uncertain…which is all the time. This tool is so powerful that it is a major portion of chapter 12, "Decision-Making." In that chapter, the decision tree methodology will be framed as a group facilitation tool.

S8. Understanding probability and statistics leads to an understanding of risk. Understanding risk is the essence of business.[100]

S9. About 87.3 percent of the population uses too many statistics.

ACCOUNTING

A1. There are four general types of accounting: financial, tax, regulatory, and managerial. Managerial includes cost accounting, such as activity-based accounting. Governmental regulators of business require businesses to use the first three. Firms do managerial accounting for themselves to help them manage the business. Unfortunately, many budget systems and accounting reports are designed to meet the needs of the first three types, not the managerial needs of the leaders of small groups or departments.

A2. If your company's stock is publicly traded, your company's financial information is regulated by the Securities and Exchange Commission (SEC).

A3. The SEC requires certain annual and quarterly reports including, among others, 10Ks, 8Ks, and annual reports to shareholders.

A4. The SEC dictates financial accounting and requires your books to be kept according to generally accepted accounting principles (GAAP). The body of GAAP has never actually been entered into law.

A5. The SEC accepts the Financial Accounting Standards Board (FASB), a seven-member independent board, as the owner of GAAP. Periodically, FASB amends GAAP by issuing statements of financial accounting standards (SFAS).

A6. The SEC requires a publicly traded company to issue a certain set of financial statements be produced quarterly and annually. The main three statements, among many others, are known by various names. The most common names are: the income statement, the balance sheet, and the statement of cash flows. [101]

Figure 35
Income Statement
Bobby's Bakery
For Year Ending December 31, 2011
($000)

Revenues from Sales	$135.0
Expenses:	
Variable (COGS)	(33.0)
Gross Margin	102.0
Salaries & Benefits	(68.0)
Supplies	(4.0)
Depreciation	(2.0)
EBIT	28.0
Interest	(1.6)
Pre-Tax Margin	26.4
Income Taxes @ 40%	(10.6)
Net Income	15.8
Dividends	(1.8)
Adder to Retained Earnings	14.0

A7. The income statement is based on the well-known formula:

$$\text{Revenue} - \text{Expenses} = \text{Profit}$$

The expenses are broken down in many ways, depending on the business. See figure 35 that shows a fictional income statement for Bobby's Bakery. This is purely a training example, not fully in accordance with GAAP.

Note that expenses—salaries and benefits, supplies, and depreciation—are variable (COGS or *cost of goods sold*). When these are subtracted from revenue, the subtotal is called EBIT, earnings before interest and taxes. Subtracting interest from EBIT leaves pretax margin. The bakery paid $10,600 in income taxes, leaving a net income of $15,400. This is the bottom line. Note, however, the bottom line is not the bottom line of the statement. FASB doesn't want to make this easy on newbies. According to GAAP, additional information concerning dividends and shares of stock must be included at the bottom of the statement, in effect, below the bottom line.

A8. *The PT/AT Principle*: There are many important things to pick up from the income statement. For example, our budgets and department expenses are based on pretax dollars in most companies. Assuming the tax rate is 40 percent, a dollar of expenses (pretax) flows to the bottom line at (1—tax rate) or $0.60. This is important in financial decision-making. The Biz Bucks Guy calls this the PT/AT principle (pretax/after-tax). If you have a pretax labor savings of $10,000 from purchasing a new tool, the actual savings is only $6,000 after taxes are paid on the labor saved. This means you can justify fewer purchases of this kind.

A9. *The Matching Principle*: Accountants are required to book expenses that help create revenue in the same period that the revenue is booked. How would the monthly income statement look if you booked $100,000 in April and the $75,000 of expenses used to earn the April revenue in May? April's profit would be erroneously inflated. May's would look like a disaster. The matching principle keeps this from happening.

A10. Depreciation is an effect of the matching principle. If Bobby buys a delivery truck that will last five years for $100,000, GAAP does *not* let the entire truck be expensed in the year it was purchased. It must be amortized (or spread) over the five-year life. Assuming straight-line amortization, the accountant for the bakery would book $20,000 of expense each year for five years. Otherwise, the profit would be distorted low in the first year and inflated for the next four. This means depreciation is *not* cash. It is a noncash entry.

A11. *The Depreciation Tax Shield (DTS) Principle*: Depreciation is noncash, but there is a cash component to consider regarding it. Depreciation, like other expenses, is tax deductible. The PT/AT principle comes into play. The cash savings from booking the noncash depreciation expense is the depreciation expense times the tax rate. If Bobby books $20,000 of noncash depreciation for the new delivery truck in a particular year, he saves $8,000 in cash when he pays his income tax. This is called the depreciation tax shield or DTS. DTS helps justify more such expenditures.

A12. There are many synonyms for *profit*, among them are: *bottom line, gain, margin, return, earnings, and net income. Net income* is the term for most income statements for after-tax profit. The Biz Bucks Guy's favorite is earnings. It shows you earned it.

A13. The net income on the income statement is not a true representation of how much cash a business made. There are many noncash entries in the expenses area, like depreciation. Net income, therefore, is a garbled representation of how much cash was earned.[102] This will be important to decision-making in the finance section below.

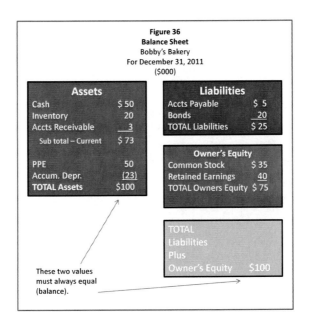

Figure 36
Balance Sheet
Bobby's Bakery
For December 31, 2011
($000)

Assets		Liabilities	
Cash	$ 50	Accts Payable	$ 5
Inventory	20	Bonds	20
Accts Receivable	3	TOTAL Liabilities	$ 25
Sub total – Current	$ 73		
		Owner's Equity	
PPE	50	Common Stock	$ 35
Accum. Depr.	(23)	Retained Earnings	40
TOTAL Assets	$100	TOTAL Owners Equity	$ 75

TOTAL Liabilities Plus Owner's Equity $100

These two values must always equal (balance).

A14. The balance sheet is based on a less well-known formula than the income statement:

Assets = Liabilities + Owner's Equity

Assets are things you control that help you make revenues.

Liabilities are claims on the assets by other entities (creditors from whom the business has borrowed money). Owner's equity is the claim on the assets by the owners of the business. Thus, the balance sheet shows your assets (left side) and who has claim on them (right side). Figure 36 is the fictitious balance sheet for Bobby's Bakery and, like the income statement, is not fully reflective of all GAAP principles.

A15. It is not a business's goal to maximize the cash account on the balance sheet. The goal is to invest that cash in property, plant, and equipment (PPE), which in turn, makes revenue and profit as noted on the income statement. This profit is largely cash, which flows back to the cash account on the balance sheet, and the process recycles.

A16. Accounts payable represents short-term liabilities, such as purchases bought on credit to be paid in thirty days. Bonds are long-term liabilities, which represent loans to buy PPE.

A17. Owner's Equity includes two accounts. First is the amount of funds received originally from the sale of common stock. This has nothing to do with the price of stock currently. It is the original contribution when the firm began.

A18. Second is retained earnings, which is *not* cash. Being on the right side of the balance sheet, it represents an increase *claim* on the assets by the owners. Retained earnings is all the profit—minus all dividends paid to owners—since the beginning of the business. The assets that retained earnings claim may be partly in cash, but most of it is buried in PPE and other assets.

A19. The ratio between the long-term liabilities (bonds) and the total of long-term liabilities plus owner's equity is the debt ratio. This is a measure of how the company has financed its assets. Higher debt ratios are more risky. This is also called leverage. For Bobby's Bakery, the debt ratio is 21 percent, being 20 divided by 95.

A20. Leverage is wonderful *if* the business does well. It maximizes profit. Leverage can be fatal if the business does not do well. It can lead to bankruptcy.

A21. Concerning leverage, two quips are useful:

Interest never sleeps.

Those who understand interest, get it. Those who don't, pay it.

That is not to say that some leverage is not appropriate for a business. A modest amount of leverage is appropriate. Knowing what is modest and what is not is tricky. Financial consultants often disagree.

A22. Adding the weighted cost of debt (after-tax) and the weighted cost of equity (a calculated number) yields the weighted average cost of capital (WACC). WACC is useful in making financial decisions. The weighting factors the debt and equity ratios mentioned above.

A23. The PPE minus the accumulated depreciation on the balance sheet represents the book value of those assets. PPE, itself, is the original price of the long-term assets. Book value should not be confused with the market value of the asset in a free market.

A24. By using various numbers from the income statement and the balance sheet, useful accounting ratios are obtained. One important ratio is return on equity (ROE). *Return* is a synonym for *profit* or *net income*. *Equity* means *owner's equity.* The ROE for Bobby's Bakery is 15.8 divided by 75 or 21 percent. This is the measure of profitability for a given period.

A25. Raw numbers usually provide poor information on a company. If a large company makes $100 million in profit, it sounds like a lot, but so what? If they have equity of $10 billion, the ROE is 1 percent. A bank pays better than that. Why be in business? Newspapers and politicians are skilled at using raw numbers to incite emotions in their constituencies.

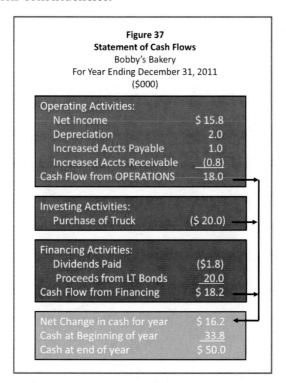

Figure 37
Statement of Cash Flows
Bobby's Bakery
For Year Ending December 31, 2011
($000)

Operating Activities:	
Net Income	$ 15.8
Depreciation	2.0
Increased Accts Payable	1.0
Increased Accts Receivable	(0.8)
Cash Flow from OPERATIONS	18.0

Investing Activities:	
Purchase of Truck	($ 20.0)

Financing Activities:	
Dividends Paid	($1.8)
Proceeds from LT Bonds	20.0
Cash Flow from Financing	$ 18.2

Net Change in cash for year	$ 16.2
Cash at Beginning of year	33.8
Cash at end of year	$ 50.0

A26. The statement of cash flow takes the garbled profit (a.k.a. net income) on the income statement and adjusts it to reflect a summary of real cash transactions for a period. It is summarized into three subtotals: cash flows from operations (how much cash the business actually made), cash flows from investing, and cash flows from financing. The cash at the end of the year matches the cash account on the balance sheet (see figure 37).

A27. There are four pairs of numbers that represent useful concepts:

a. Operation and Maintenance (O&M) versus Capital – O&M is written off (entered into the income statement) in the period it is booked. Capital is written off over its lifetime via depreciation. If it lasts more than a year, it is capital. Both are effects of the matching principle.

b. Marginal versus Average – Marginal implies the cost of the next (or last) item. Average is the cost of all items divided by the number of items. Most good decisions should deal with marginal costs, not averages.

c. Variable versus Fixed – Variable costs are those that vary in proportion to the revenue booked, such as soybean cost for a tofu factory. Fixed costs do *not* vary by revenue. Fixed, however, is a misnomer. Fixed costs can change, just not proportionally to revenues. For example, labor costs are considered fixed, but they change when a union contract is renegotiated.

d. Relevant versus Nonrelevant – This pair of terms relates to decision-making. Relevant costs (or cash flows) vary between two alternatives being considered, nonrelevant costs do not. Only use relevant costs in deciding between the two alternatives.

A28. If an accountant's wife has insomnia, what does she say?

"Darling, could you tell me about your work?"

FINANCE

F1. The finance department has three primary roles: (1) to raise capital for the operations of the firm, (2) to forecast long-term capital needs, and (3) to consult with management on financial decisions.

F2. Financial (spending) decisions can be grouped into two types: operating decisions (short-term, relatively smaller dollars) and investment decisions (long-term, typically larger dollars).

F3. In making spending decisions, separate the financial data from the intangibles. Use the financial data to "number out" a financial decision; then and only then, weigh the financial decision against the intangibles. Let your common sense determine if the intangibles outweigh the numbers.

F4. Cash flows, not earnings, are the first order of consideration when making financial decisions. Diagramming the relevant cash flows helps to understand the decision, particularly investment decisions. Figure 38 is a format that is useful. The up arrows are cash outflows (think of cash flowing out of the firm's checkbook). Down arrows are cash inflows (into the checkbook). I = investment, S = savings. These cash flow diagrams are based on,

Future, after-tax cash flows which vary between two alternatives.

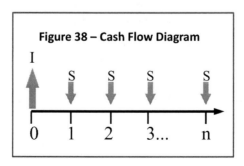

Figure 38 – Cash Flow Diagram

F5. In financial decision-making, each cash flow arrow is converted into its *present value equivalent*. This is done by using a discount rate. Formulae exist for doing this. Electronic spreadsheets also have *present value* and *net present value* formulae, which makes this very easy. By subtracting the present value of the outflows from the present value of the inflows, a net present value (NPV) is obtained. If the NPV is positive, the investment creates value for the investor and should be accepted. If the NPV is negative, the investment destroys value and should be rejected.

F6. The theory of how to determine the discount rate is complex. In many cases, the weighted average cost of capital (WACC) described earlier is a good surrogate for the discount rate.

F7. Any revenues and expenses used in a cash flow NPV analysis should be after-tax. Recall PT/AT principle above.

F8. An important cash flow to include is the depreciation tax shield (DTS) when a capital purchase is being considered. The DTS may be the cash flow that turns a project's NPV to positive. Recall the DTS principle above.

F9. Capital dollars and O&M dollars are the same for financial valuations of projects. They only represent cash flows on the diagram. You cannot mix them in accounting, but you can in finance.

F10. Intangibles, such as safety, customer satisfaction, improved communications, and community image, should also be used to make financial decisions.

F11. Wall Street financial analysts use NPV to value stocks. They also include intangibles. Studies vary, but 30–50 percent of stock price can be attributed to intangibles.

F12. Top ten nonfinancial variables considered by financial analysts in doing stock valuations:[103]

1. Execution of corporate strategy
2. Management credibility
3. Quality of corporate strategy
4. Innovation
5. Ability to attract and retain talented people
6. Market share
7. Management expertise
8. Alignment of compensation with shareholders' interests
9. Research leadership
10. Quality of major business processes

F13. When determining a capital budget, NPV does not ration capital as well as its cousin, profitability index (PI). PI is the ratio of the cash inflows to the cash outflows (Remember, NPV subtracts the same two numbers.). A PI above 1.0 is the same as an NPV greater than zero. To ration capital, the projects are ranked by PI. The cutoff line is drawn after the available capital is committed.

F14. Financial decisions should be based on what is best for the total firm, not a division within the firm otherwise the firm is suboptimizing.

F15. Two mutually exclusive projects are those in which you will do one or the other but not both. Consider the engineer who needs to purchase and install a lime slaker for a manufacturing process. He can buy a cheap one with higher maintenance cost or a heavy-duty one with lower maintenance cost. He will not buy both.

For mutually exclusive projects, the cash flows for each must be analyzed over the same time frame otherwise NPV yields illogical conclusions.

F16. Disregard *sunk cost* in financial valuations. Sunk costs are prior costs. They cannot affect a future decision. If you are building a store on an empty lot, the original purchase price of the lot is sunk.

F17. Include *opportunity costs* in financial valuations. Opportunity costs are cost of lost opportunities. If you build a store on an empty lot, the current market price of the lot is a lost opportunity. You cannot sell it if you build and operate a store on it. The current market price of the lot must be included in the cash outflows on the cash flow diagram.

F18. A financial derivative is a security that is *derived* from some underlying security or financial package. Derivatives include forwards, futures, options (puts and calls), and swaps. The derivative market provides an important financial vehicle to reduce risk. Reduced risk lowers the discount rate. A lower discount rate improves the NPV for projects. More projects improves our economy and, hence, our well-being. Beware of politicians who think they know how to improve our well-being by limiting derivative markets or snuffing out speculators.

F19. Never deal in derivatives without underlying natural positions. *Naked* derivatives, particularly writing call options, are a sure trip to bankruptcy court for the uninitiated.

F20. My broker made me a millionaire! I started out as a billionaire.

ECONOMICS

E1. Economics is the study of scarcity.[104]

E2. The two branches of economics are micro- and macroeconomics. Micro deals with price and quantity for individual products and services. There is almost complete unanimity between economists on the fundamentals of microeconomics.

Macroeconomics deals with the ramifications of economic policy on large entities, typically national economies. There is almost no consensus between economists on macroeconomics. Macro is fraught with political opinion.

E3. Many macroeconomic schools of thought exist. Among others, they include monetarists, neo-Keynesians, neo-classicists, supply siders, and rational expectationists. On important decisions to our national well-being, macroeconomists can disagree vehemently. John Maynard Keynes, the father of Keynesian economics, encouraged government spending to fix recessions. Fredrick Hayek, the father of market-based macroeconomics, believes recessions will end more quickly with lower taxes and reduced spending.

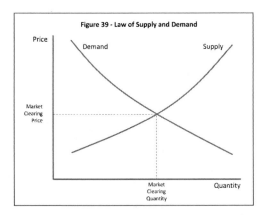

E4. Figure 39 shows a simplified but useful depiction of the laws of supply and demand. Suppliers will produce a product anywhere on the upward sloping curve. Demanders will consume that product on the downward sloping curve. The point at which both suppliers and demander agree is called the market clearing price. There is also a corresponding market clearing quantity.

E5. If a government entity forces a price on any product or service below the natural market clearing price, a shortage occurs for that product or service all the time not just once in awhile (see figure 40).

The principle is easily stated:

All shortages are caused by government intervention into a market.

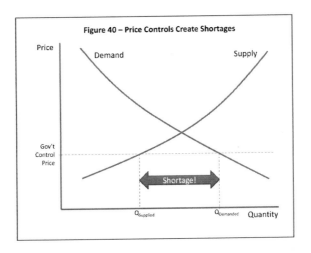

Figure 40 – Price Controls Create Shortages

Consider the gas shortage in 1974. OPEC cut its supplies. The gas prices went high, but gas was available to everyone at a price. The presidential administration felt Americans could not afford to pay that much. They imposed a lower price than the market clearing price. In a short time, long lines appeared at the pump. This principle is so esoteric that The Biz Bucks Guy has included a personal example to help cement this shortages issue. See "The Barstow Bargain" at the end of chapter 6.

E6. The opposite is also true. When a governmental entity sets prices above the market clearing price, a surplus occurs.

Consider price supports in agriculture that provides a surplus for aid to underdeveloped countries.

E7. Price gouging is a political term not an economic term. Prices always adjust when supply or demand changes.

E8. Prices are wonderful signals to direct our behavior.

E9. A commodity in business is a product or service that is differentiated in the market only by price. Market differentiation is how we make our buying decisions. An example of a commodity is wholesale electricity. The only thing that matters in that market is price. All megawatt hours are the same to those buyers. A car is an example of a noncommodity. We buy cars using many considerations besides price.

E10. Free market capitalism is the best economic system known on the planet to help the common person. All other economic systems are called command economies in which governmental entities set quantities and prices for goods and services.

The late eminent economist, Milton Friedman, in a TV debate with Phil Donahue (now available on YouTube) said, "So the record of history is absolutely crystal clear: That there is no alternative way...so far discovered...of improving the lot of the ordinary people that can hold a candle to the productive activities that are unleashed by a free enterprise system."[105]

E11. Capitalism requires a basic sense of honesty for it to work. Willi Schlaff, a German academic who turned from socialism to capitalism, wrote a profound statement in the 1930s.

> The problem with socialism is socialism. The problem with capitalism is capitalists.

This means socialism is a broken economics system. It doesn't work. Capitalism, the best economic system,

needs honest people to work. Gandhi listed seven traits most perilous to humanity, one was "Commerce without Morality."[106]
Winston Churchill said,

> The inherent vice of capitalism is the unequal sharing of blessings; the inherent virtue of socialism is the equal sharing of miseries.[107]

E12. Some people go into economics because they just don't have the personality to be an accountant.

E13. A man walks into a meat market. He notices brains for sale: $2 per pound for normal brains and $100 per pound for economist's brains. He says to the butcher, "Wow, there must be a real demand for economist's brains."

"Nope," said the butcher. "Do you know how many economists it takes to get a pound of brains?" A supply-side joke.

For more insights into macroeconomics, search on that word at the Biz Bucks Blog at www.BizBucksGuy.com.

APPENDIX C

EMPLOYMENT AND
LABOR LAW OVERVIEW

When The Biz Bucks Guy read the 1,035 responses to the survey discussed in chapter 18, one comment had a particular impact and led to this appendix. A new leader should have some sense of employment and labor law.

First, from the business word swamp, *employment law* generally refers to the body of law about any employee/employer relationship. *Labor law* refers typically to union/employer relations.

This appendix will use a historical perspective on labor/ employment law. The following sixteen federal acts were significant in shaping employment law in the United States. State and local laws provide added structure to the body of law under which your organization must operate.

The Railway Labor Act of 1926, as amended, promotes bargaining, mediation, or arbitration as a substitute for strikes. This act covers both railroads and airlines.

The Norris-LaGuardia Act of 1932 prevented yellow-dog contracts in which employers made it a condition of employees not to join a union. It also forbids courts from issuing injunctions to stop strikes and required noninterference of employers toward workers who joined trade unions.

The National Labor Relations (Wagner) Act of 1935 further limited the means by which employers can react to workers who join unions, engage in collective bargaining, and strike. It established the National Labor Relations Board (NLRB) to administer its principles. It moves the principles of the Railway Act to other industries.

The Fair Labor Standards Act of 1938 established time and a half for overtime, a national minimum wage, and prohibited child labor. It constructed standards to determine what jobs must be paid overtime.

The Labor-Management Relations (Taft-Hartley) Act of 1947 defined and prohibited unfair labor practices by unions. The NRLA previously only dealt with employers. It also allowed the states to pass right-to-work laws. At present, twenty-two states, mostly in the South and West, have done so.

The Employment Act of 1948 was a major shift in policy wherein the Federal government took a major responsibility in the national economy-at-large, not merely the trade and monetary control. Based on Keynesian economics of demand side spending, the act established the Council of Economic Advisors to the president of the United States.

The Labor Management Reporting and Disclosure (Landrum-Griffin) Act of 1959 establishes regulations to monitor internal fiduciary affairs within unions. It was a result of intense congressional scrutiny due to corruption and racketeering within unions during the fifties.

The Equal Pay Act of 1963 abolished discrimination of pay on the basis of gender.

The Civil Rights Act of 1964 (Title VII) abolished discrimination by employers based on race, color, sex, religion, or national origin. It also established the Equal Employment Opportunity Commission (EEOC) that eventually was given additional jurisdiction from other discrimination acts noted below.

The Age Discrimination in Employment Act of 1967 forbids employment discrimination for those over forty years of age, including promotions, wages, hiring, layoffs or terminations.

The Occupational Safety and Health Act of 1970 ensures that employers provide a work environment that is safe from hazards, including toxic chemicals, harmful noise levels, equipment dangers, heat or cold extremes, and unsanitary conditions.

The Employee Retirement Income Security Act of 1974 (ERISA) establishes standards for pension plans in the private sector protecting those with pensions from malfeasance by fiduciaries that manage the pension funds.

Federal Labor Relations Act of 1978 establishes the rights of federal employees to bargain collectively with managers of government functions.

The Worker Adjustment and Retraining Notification Act of 1988 (WARN Act) requires employers with more than one hundred employees to warn employees sixty days in advance of plant closings or significant layoffs.

The Americans with Disabilities Act (ADA) of 1990, amended in 2008, forbids, under certain circumstances, discrimination of those with mental or physical disabilities. For example, physical facilities of businesses must provide reasonable access accommodations to those in wheelchairs.

The Family and Medical Leave Act of 1993 provides in businesses with fifty or more employees a twelve-week unpaid, job-protected leave in the event of certain health situations of the employee's relatives, including the birth of a baby. The act provides for employers to restore the employee's position or equivalent position upon return.

For added information on employment law, a new leader might read the Department of Labor's Employment Law Guide at www.dol.gov/compliance/guide.

APPENDIX D

ADDITIONAL READING

Those wanting to deepen their understanding of various topics may find the following list useful.

- Accounting

  - *Essentials of Accounting* by Anthony and Perlman is a self-taught workbook that introduces the basics of accounting.
- Economics

  - Anything written by Stanford's Thomas Sowell such as *Basic Economics*

- Leadership and Organizational Theory

  - Anything by USC's Ed Lawler such as *Rewarding Excellence*, and anything by The Center for Effective Organizations at USC, which Dr. Lawler leads.
  - Anything by Michigan's Dave Ulrich such as *Results Based Leadership and the Leadership Code*
  - Anything by USC's Warren Bennis such as *On Becoming a Leader.*
  - Anything by Harvard's John Kotter such as *Leading Change.*

- Change, Communications, and Human Relations

  o *How to Present Like a Pro: Getting People to See Things Your Way* by Lani Arredondo
  o *Leadership and Self Deception* By The Arbinger Institute

- Life Balance

  o *Golf's Sacred Journey: Seven Days at the Links of Utopia by David L. Cook*

APPENDIX E

THE FINAL TECHNICAL ANALOG FOR LIFE AND LEADERSHIP: THE SECOND LAW OF THERMODYNAMICS

WE QUANTOIDS CAN THINK CRITICALLY ABOUT BIG QUESTIONS

This technical analog requires a lengthy discussion, and thus, it is not a conclusion to a chapter but a final appendix.

This final analog provides a review of two principles discussed in chapter 2—the need for leaders to have a spiritual strength, which, in turn, increases their love of people.

The Biz Bucks Guy has also included it to demonstrate to his fellow quantoids that philosophical musings on the essence of life are not limited to the liberal arts majors. We quantoids have much to contribute to the critical thinking about big questions, which is a good working definition of philosophy.

In the preface, The Biz Bucks Guy related the advice of his English professor who asserted that "You will never learn anything about life from engineering." This appendix refutes his myopic view.

THE SECOND LAW AND ENTROPY

The topic is the second law of thermodynamics. For many, it has deep implications. Some very smart people use it to justify atheism. Some other very smart people believe it is an indicator of a supreme creator. How could two groups of smart people be so diametrically opposite in their view of a scientific law? Read on.

The first law of thermodynamics expresses the conservation of energy, that is, energy can be transformed from one type to another, but it is never created or destroyed. Philosophically, that is not too earthshaking. The second law is, however, quite provocative for critical thinkers. For the record, there is also a zeroth law and a third law, not discussed here.

The second law expresses the universal principle of decay observed in nature. It explains the natural tendency of systems to decay from a state of high energy to low, or from a state of organization to disorganization, from order to disorder. It is fundamental in science. It is a law, not a theory.

The second law establishes a property called entropy. In the broadest sense, entropy is the measure of disorder of a system. Simply put, the second law states:

In a *closed* system, entropy increases.

This means that, given no outside influences, disorder or waste energy of a system always increases. An example is ice in a room. It melts. Its entropy increases. A sand castle on the beach will eventually be a flat bed of sand as the tide comes in. A house always needs maintenance. It doesn't paint itself. Entropy is increasing for the ice, the sand castle, and our houses.

THE BOX AND THE LEPRECHAUN

A simple example of the second law is a box with a partition down the middle. On one side of the partition are fifty red balls. On the other side are fifty blue balls. The partition has a hole just the size for one ball to sneak through. Assume something is agitating the box. Eventually one red ball with go into the blue zone and vice versa. In time, there will be no blue or red zone. There will be an approximately even distribution of both colors on either side of the partition. Statistically, you can shake the box forever and the original design, with two zones, will never reappear. The balls will not reorder themselves. The system has gone from organization to disorganization. Once again, the second law has been fulfilled. Entropy of the box has increased.

However, the orderliness of the original organized box can, indeed, be recreated. Simply arrange for the services of a local leprechaun with his shovel. Put the leprechaun on the partition with these instructions. Every time the leprechaun sees a red ball coming through the hole from one side, he puts his shovel down and keeps it on one side. He allows blue balls to go through that direction. In a short time, the red balls are all on one side and the blue balls on another. The second law is still valid, even though the entropy of the box decreased. Why is it still valid? Because the main premise was not held. We have violated the closed system by adding the leprechaun.

In essence, the leprechaun represents intelligence. The only thing that can reverse the second law is intelligence.

Electricity from a generator designed by intelligent people can power a freezer, and the melted ice can return to its original icy state. A little child can run onto the beach and recreate the sand castle. A homeowner can repaint their home. Intelligence reverses entropy.

So how is this analogous to principles of leadership? Let's answer that on three planes: the individual, the organization, and the universe.

THE ENTROPIC PROFESSIONAL

An old aphorism says,

> You have to grow a little each day to stay the same size.

Applying the second law to our skills as professionals and, for some, as leaders, we need to redo our education, our skill set, and our professional knowledge. Otherwise, we will be yet another example of entropy. We will decay in our abilities to perform. We will become, at minimum, dated and, most likely, stagnant, ineffective, and irrelevant. Every professional, from construction crafts to computer science, from microbiology to marketing, should devote a significant time to keep their saw sharp, as the late Dr. Stephen R. Covey[108] would say. This includes knowing our products and customers, improving our quantoidal and organizational business smarts, and keeping fresh our ability to develop people, manage work, make decisions, communicate, and delegate. All are very important topics of this comprehensive leadership text.

THE ENTROPIC ORGANIZATION

Likewise, organizations decay. Left alone, without the intelligence and enormous effort of top leaders, midlevel leaders, and first-line supervisors, an organization will quickly stagnate. The best way to keep an organization fresh is through the ardent implementation of strategy. Leaders of organizations must constantly inspect the health of the organization. Has the strategic direction been developed, communicated, assessed, and fine-tuned? Are the people within the organization being developed to support the strategy? Have the work processes and projects been aligned with the objectives? Are rewards focused on goals that cascade down from the total organization's goals?

With this intelligent application of organizational smarts, a decaying organization can revive itself, and an already thriving organization can maintain its high level of performance.

THE UNENTROPIC UNIVERSE

Unfortunately, the second law is occasionally used in college courses to teach atheistic principles. The Biz Bucks Guy had firsthand experience with this in his initial thermodynamics class in undergrad engineering (taken shortly after the earth cooled). The argument seems simple and compelling on the surface.

As his thermo professor said, "The world is decaying. It will eventually grow cold. The sun, also. The entire universe will slow down, then stop. We are all eventually doomed. For you who are still believing in a God…sorry. The second law proves there is no God. We are all doomed."

This is extremely shortsighted. A leprechaun can recreate and maintain an orderly box of balls.

And a supreme creator can create and maintain an orderly universe and apparently has.

In fact, a supreme intelligence is the only thing that can reverse the universe's decay. Clearly, some intelligent being has done a great job of it for the past half of eternity. What a beautiful, orderly, well-designed universe we live in. The second law is supportive of the existence of a supreme creator, not contrary to it.

WHAT DO SCIENTISTS THINK?

Even Charles Darwin knew of the need for a supreme creator, as divulged in a conversation between himself and Lord Alfred Tennyson. Tennyson was the poet laureate of England and a man of faith. Darwin, the author of natural selection and a high priest of atheism, admitted that there must have been some sort of a supreme creator behind evolutionary forces.[109]

After Tennyson asked if there was a higher power behind evolution, Darwin responded, "Certainly, I admit it…because evolution has always gone onward and upward, from lower to higher forms of life. That could not be chance. It is unscientific to postulate such a hypothesis because chance never moves in one direction."

Darwin did clarify that he felt this higher power was an impersonal being, not a God worthy of our worship. Fair enough.

Among those scientists with a belief in some type of creator is Albert Einstein. A famous saying of his was, "Science without religion is lame, religion without science is blind."[110]

Consider Sir Isaac Newton. In *Principia,* which some consider the greatest book ever written, he stated, "The most beautiful system of the sun, planets, and comets, could only proceed from the counsel and dominion on an intelligent and powerful Being."

Johannes Kepler, the German mathematician and astronomer, discovered and described the elliptical motion of the planets. Kepler said, "I was merely thinking God's thoughts after him."[111]

In fact, those with quantoid backgrounds who support the idea of a supreme creator need not feel alone. About one-third of scientists maintain some belief in God. This is according to sociological researcher Elaine Howard Ecklund of Rice University.[112]

Of course, there are many scientists who ignore this reasoning. The mainstream media seems wont to promote a few rock star atheist scientists. This leaves the impression that a godless science is *right*, and theology is for some past century. Currently, the Stephen Hawkings and Richard Dawkinses enjoy this notoriety. While they are certainly honest thinkers, they clearly don't represent many of their scientific peers. To delve further into the discussion of the group think regarding science and religion, The Biz Bucks Guy suggests obtaining a copy of the DVD *Expelled: No Intelligence Allowed* hosted by Ben Stein.[113]

ARE WE A CELESTIAL ANT FARM?

Of course, some of the religiously faithful may proffer the notion that the second law *proves* the existence of God. That is as shortsighted as my thermo professor's atheist assertion. The second law carries us only so far. A supreme being may not necessarily be God, in the traditional sense.

A real God, one worthy of our worship, has at least one other attribute beyond supreme power. God also loves us.

For quantoids, the following equation may assist:

$$\text{Supreme Creator} + \text{Love} = \text{God}$$

The second law only establishes the existence of the first term of this equation.

Those of us who buy into the notion of a loving God have an optimistic advantage over agnostics or atheists. Our faithful perspective negates the possibility that the universe is merely some celestial high school student's ant farm. Our supreme creator will not get rid of us at the end of the semester.

SPIRITUAL STRENGTH AND LEADERSHIP

Each of us needs to determine for ourself the veracity of a loving God. That decision will not be based solely on the second law or any other principle of science,

Epistemology is the branch of philosophy that deals with how we gain knowledge. Simply put, we gain knowledge in five ways: by reason, experimentation, the scientific method, trusted authority, and revelation. All five sources should be used to approach this most fundamental philosophical question about the existence of deity.

No matter how one finds it, all good bosses need some type of spiritual or humane foundation to excel in the important principles of leadership. Some outstanding bosses get such a foundation or inner moral compass from principles of secular humanism, an atheistic but benevolent philosophy. Others glean their spiritual strength from a belief in a loving God. Regardless of which you are, each prospective leader should understand that real leaders embrace *the power of love over the love of power.*

The notion of love of fellow mankind undergirds the application of the twelve leadership skills. For example, great leaders develop their people because they know, according to their moral compass, it is the right thing to do.

So this discussion of the philosophical implications of the second law of thermodynamics is a final coda for this text on leadership for quantitative and technical people. The second lawleads us to end with a recapitulation of the first of the eight qualities of leadership rightness:

> Bosses must truly love people to be effective.

It is a supernal and primary quality for your journey into leadership.

AFTERWORD

TECHNICAL ANALOGS FOR LIFE AND LEADERSHIP: AN INVITATION TO CONTRIBUTE

The Biz Bucks Guy hopes you have enjoyed the technical analogs that have ended each chapter in *Leadership for the Recovering Quantoid*. The Biz Bucks Guy invites you to provide a short synopsis of a technical analog that you have found that applies to an important principle of life or leadership. Submit your analog to BizBucksGuy@cox.net. If your submittal is used commercially, you will be given proper attribution. The Biz Bucks Guy anticipates publishing a volume of these analogs.

INDEX

ENDNOTES

Preface

1   See *HR Magazine: Guide to Managing People*, Society of Human Resource Management (2006).

Chapter 1

2   John P. Kotter, *Leading Change* (Boston, MA: Harvard Business School Press, 1996).

3   For a concise discussion of Taylor, see http://www.netmba.com/mgmt/scientific/

4   Leslie Pockell and Adrienne Avila, *The 100 Greatest Leadership Principles of All Time* (New York, NY: Business Plus, 2007), page 62.

5   Kotter, *x*.

6   Ibid., 25.

7   David Hunt, IT Professional and world-class reunion organizer

8   Stephen R. Covey, *Seven Habits of Highly Effective People*, as quoted in Pockell, 16.

9   Pockell, v. The time of Sun Tzu's life is in dispute. A traditional birthday is 544 BC. Various translations of his work *The Art of War* have been rendered.

10 Proverbs 29:18

11 Kotter, 9.

12 Low and Siesfield, *Measures That Matter* (Boston: Ernst & Young, 1998), as quoted in Becker, Huselid, and Ulrich,

The HR Scorecard (Boston, MA: Harvard Business School Press, 2001), 9.

13 For example, see Big Dog and Little Dog at http://www. nwlink.com/~donclark/leader/leadcon. html#back4

14 K. Lewin, R. Lippitt, R.K. White, "Patterns of Aggressive Behavior in Experimentally Created Social Climates," *Journal of Social Psychology* 10 (1939): 271–301.

15 From The Biz Bucks Guy's memory bank. Reference unobtained.

16 From personal knowledge and online searches such as Answers.com and Wikipedia.

17 Pockell, 5.

18 Ibid, 88.

19 Ibid, 44.

20 David Gergen, "Does Leadership Matter?" *US News and World Report*, October 31, 2005. See http://www.usnews. com/usnews/news/articles/ 051031/31gergen.htm

21 http://www.nwlink.com/~donclark/leader/leadcon.html

Chapter 2

22 See Matthew 7:12 for the actual quote. Also, see "Golden Rule" in Wikipedia for an interesting discussion of this principle which is common to many cultures, philosophies, and religions.

23 www.alessandra.com.

24 Included in a letter from Warren Bennis to USC Marshall School Alumni, January 2010.

25 Abraham Maslow, *Motivation and Personality* (New York: Harper, 1954).

26 Wikipedia, "Maslow's Hierarchy of Needs"

27 Dr. Deming, the father of the quality movement, was careful not to take credit for this cycle. He preferred calling it the Shewhart Cycle, after his professor who taught it

to him. See W. Edwards Deming, *Out of the Crisis* (MIT Center for Advanced Engineering Study, 1986).

28   The Biz Bucks training courses from Llewellyn Consulting provide an affordable and effective option to the college experience needed. Please excuse this rare moment of shameless marketing.

29   The Biz Bucks Guy uses *manage*, as opposed to *lead* here because that is the term used in HR theory and literature. Clearly, performance management is a tool of both management and leadership skills.

Chapter 3

30   http://www.brainyquote.com/quotes/authors/s/sun_tzu_2.html

31   Many other scholars have expanded Dr. Driver's work. Among them are Ken Brousseau, Michael Coombs, Tom Olson, Bruce Prince, Dianne Sundby, Bob Morrison, and Meryl Louis. See Rikard Larsson et al., "Building Motivational Capital through Career Concept and Culture Fit," *Career Development International* 12 (2007): 4.

32   CareerView is a trademark of Decision Dynamics LLC.

33   To access this online assessment, which uses content-derived titles for the four Career Concepts, contact Dr. Dianne Sundby, psychologist and head of Career Counseling and Assessment Associates in Los Angeles at www.DSCounseling.com. Dr. Sundby, the widow of Dr. Driver, has worked extensively with this questionnaire since its inception.

34   M. Coombs, "Measuring Career Concepts: An Examination of the Concepts, Constructs, and Validity of the Career Concept Questionnaire" (dissertation, University of Southern California, Los Angeles, CA, 1989).

35 M. Driver and D. Sundby, "The Construct Validity of the CCQ" (paper presented at the Academy of Management Conference, Dallas, TX, 1983).

Chapter 4

36 For example, see http://www.bain.com/bainweb/PDFs/cms/Public/Management%20Tools%202007%20BB.pdf.

37 See the entire list of ten intangibles in chapter 6.

38 Erica Olsen, *Strategic Planning for Dummies* (Indianapolis: Wiley, 2007), 11.

39 Thanks to Wayne Widdis of Focused Change International for this insightful principle.

40 Developed by Rensis Likert (1903–1981) of University of Michigan.

41 See www.balancedscorecard.org.

42 Gerald A. Michaelson, *Sun Tzu, the Art of War for Managers* (Avon, MA: Adams Media, 2001), 131.

43 Michael E. Porter, *Competitive Advantage* (New York: Free Press, 1985).

44 http://www.savetrees.org/redwood2520primer.htm

Chapter 5

45 Ron Zemke and Chip R. Bell, *Knock Your Socks Off Service Recovery* (New York, NY: AMACOM, 2000).

46 Dave Ulrich, Steve Kerr, and Ron Ashkenas, *GE Work-Out* (New York, NY: McGraw-Hill, 2002).

47 James T. Summerhays, "Twisted Thoughts and Elastic Molcules, " www.meridianmagazine.com/article/3945-twisted-thoughts-and-elastic molecules. Summerhays quotes several psychologists including the bestseller *Feeling Good: The New Mood Therapy* by Dr. David D. Burns.

Chapter 6

48 Thomas Sowell, *Basic Economics: A Citizens' Guide to the Economy* (New York, NY: Basic Books, 2004). This is written in English for noneconomists. Sowell is a national treasure of insights into our economic system.

Chapter 7

49 Bill Perry of GFF Inc purveyors of award-winning Girard's salad dressings. Bill was a colleague at USC's EMBA program and provided The Biz Bucks Guy with his first gig in consulting after graduation.

50 Edward E. Lawler III, *Rewarding Excellence* (San Francisco, CA: Jossey-Bass, 2000), 35. Ed and Center for Effective Organizations (CEO) are a national treasure of scholarship on organizational effectiveness. All leaders should read everything they can from CEO.

51 Marvin R. Weisbord, *Organizational Diagnosis: A Workbook of Theory and Practice* (Reading, MA: Addison-Wesley, 1978), 9.

52 http://www.mindtools.com/pages/article/newSTR_91.htm

53 Larry is the architect of USC's executive MBA program and taught The Biz Bucks Guy the principles of fit using this eleven-point model of which I nicknamed a *road map*.

54 A real such survey would contain many more questions tied to the cultural behaviors identified in the organization and people strategy of the corporate strategic plan.

55 http://www.devtopics.com/40-years-of-cubicles/

56 See Wikipedia for *Gibbs Free Energy*, *Entropy*, and *Enthalpy*.

Chapter 8

57 One top independent consultant in this field is Dennis Sowards of Quality Support Services, www.YourQSS.com.

58 H. James Harrington, *Business Process Improvement* (New York, NY: McGraw-Hill, 1991).

59 Adapted from NV Energy's Generation Capital Projects Process. Used with permission.

60 Consider the Memory Jogger series at www.GOALQPC.com as a good starting point.

Chapter 9

61 Contact the Project Management Institute at www.pmi.org for additional references and resources.

62 For example, compare Joseph W. Weiss and Robert K. Wysocki, *.5-Phase Project Management: A Practical Planning and Implementation Guide* (Reading, MA: Addison Wesley, 1992) with *Managing Projects Large and Small: The Fundamental Skills for Delivering on Budget and on Time*, The Harvard Business Essentials Series Boston (MA: Harvard Business School Press, 2004). The later uses a four-phase process.

Chapter 10

63 Visit www.worldatwork.org for a more comprehensive discussion of total rewards, including direct compensation, benefits, and nonmonetary rewards.

64 Hewitt Associates LLC, "The Impact of Performance Management on Organizational Success" (July 1994) (in-house paper).

65 Scott Cohen and Nidhi Verma, *Rethinking Performance Management as a Business Tool to Spark a High-Performance Culture* (Hewitt Associates LLC, 2008) (in-house paper).

Chapter 11

66 Jack Welch, *Jack—Straight From the Gut* (New York: Warner Business Books, 2001), 184.

67 Guangrong Dai, King Yii Tang, and Kenneth P. De Meuse, "The Leadership Architect 2009 Global Norms, A Technical Paper" (Korn/Ferry International, Powered by Lominger, 2009).

68 Michael M. Lombardo and Robert W. Eichinger, *The Leadership Machine* (Minneapolis: Lominger Limited Inc., 2002), 33, www.lominger.com.

69 Warren Bennis, *On Becoming a Leader* (Addison-Wesley, Reading, 1989), 87. Italics added.

70 "California: Mister San Quentin," *Time*, Jan. 7, 1952, http://www.time.com/time/magazine/article/0,9171,815769-1,00.html.

71 Thomas S. Monson, "To the Rescue," *Ensign* (May 2001), 49.

72 Ibid., Cohen and Verma.

Chapter 12

73 The Enigma Decisions, http://www.weeklystandard.com/Content/Public/Articles/000/000/005/894mnyyl.asp?page=7.

74 Arizona State University's outstanding engineering school and History Channel 8/23/10. The issue of the possibility of the earth disintegrating was also confirmed with an archivist at the Truman Library in Independence, MO.

75 http://thinkexist.com/quotation/when_your_values_are_clear_to_you-making/253570.html

Chapter 13

76 See chapter 15 that references a book on change entitled *Influence*. This book provides a more in-depth treatise on the importance of storytelling.

77 Lani Arredondo, *How to Present Like a Pro: Getting People To See Things Your Way* (New York: McGraw-Hill, 1991).
78 James Heskett, W. Earl Sasser, and Leonard A. Schlesinger, *The Service-Profit Chain* (New York: The Free Press, 1997).
79 Lamb & McKee of the Hay Group (2004) as quoted in http://www.nwlink.com/~donclark/leader/leadcon.html

Chapter 14

80 I have used *soldier* in this quotation. Patton used a more color term. See "Patton Speech" on YouTube.

Chapter 15

81 http://www.brainyquote.com/quotes/authors/m/margaret_mead.html
82 From Warren Bennis, the leadership guru, in a USC fund-raising letter to alumni, December 2009.
83 His story is told in *A Sacred Duty* by Ester Rasband and Richard Wilkins (Bookcraft: West Valley City, Utah, 1999).
84 United Families International

Chapter 16

85 John Kotter and Heskett James, *Corporate Culture and Performance* (New York: The Free Press, 1992).
86 Many thanks to clinical psychologist and friend, Dr. Ed Lauritsen, for information on this research study.
87 John P. Kotter, *Leading Change* (Boston: Harvard Business School Press, 1996).
88 Kerry Patterson et al., *Influencer: The Power to Change Anything* (New York: McGraw-Hill, 2007).
89 Saul D. Alinsky, *Rules for Radicals: A Pragmatic Primer for Realistic Radicals* (New York: Random House, 1971).
90 Sissela Bok, foreword to *Gandhi: An Autobiography* (Boston: Beacon Press, 1993), xvii.

Chapter 17

91 See Wikipedia "Boll Weevil Monument" for a picture.
92 Stephen R. Covey, *Seven Habit of Highly Effective People* (New York: Simon and Schuster, 1989), 188.
93 http://www.virtuescience.com/honesty.html
94 Marianne M. Jennings, *Business: Its Legal, Ethical, and Global Environment*.
95 http://en.wikipedia.org/wiki/Groupthink
96 Thanks for Tim Laughlin of Sargent and Lundy Engineers for this insight.

Chapter 18

97 See appendix B for a brief discussion of key labor laws.

Epilogue

98 http://www.woopidoo.com/business_quotes/decision-quotes.htm
99 Pericles, *Ancient Greek Politician and General* (495 Bc–429 Bc).

Appendix B

100 Peter L. Bernstein, *Against the Gods: The Remarkable Story of Risk* (New York, NY: John Wiley and Sons, 1998). This is a fascinating deep dive into risk and probability.
101 For a self-taught workbook on financial accounting, see Robert N. Anthony and Leslie K. Pearlman *Essentials of Accounting*, 3rd ed. (Reading, MA: Addison-Wesley).
102 Many thanks to Jeff Coles of the WP Carey School of Business at Arizona State University for "garbled." It is an apt descriptor of net income not being true cash.
103 Low and Siesfield, *Measures that Matter* (Boston, MA: Ernst and Young, 1998). As quoted in Huselid, Becker

and Ulrich, *The HR Scorecard* (Boston: Harvard Business School Press, 2001), 9.

104 Thomas Sowell, *Basic Economics: A Citizens' Guide to the Economy* (New York, NY: Basic Books, 2004). This is written in English for noneconomists. Sowell is a wealth of insights into our economic system.

105 Search *YouTube.com* for "Friedman and Donohue" to view this interesting discussion of free markets.

106 www.sfheart.com/Gandhi.html.

107 http://jpetrie.myweb.uga.edu/bulldog.html

Appendix E

108 Stephen R. Covey, *The Seven Habits of Highly Effective People* (New York: Simon and Schuster, 1989).

109 Arthur M. Abell, *Talks with Great Composers* (New York: Citadel Press, 1994), 32.

110 http://www.godandscience.org/apologetics/sciencefaith.html

111 http://www.newworldencyclopedia.org/entry/Johannes_Kepler

112 Elaine Howard Ecklund, *Science and Religion: What Scientists Really Think* (Oxford: Oxford University Press, 2010)

113 *Expelled, No Intelligence Allowed* (DVD) Directed by Nathan Frankowski (2008).